Sport in the Global Society

General Editor: J.A. Mangan

SPORT AND MEMORY IN NORTH AMERICA

SPORT IN THE GLOBAL SOCIETY
General Editor: J.A. Mangan

The interest in sports studies around the world is growing and will continue to do so. This unique series combines aspects of the expanding study of *sport in the global society*, providing comprehensiveness and comparison under one editorial umbrella. It is particularly timely, with studies in the cultural, economic, ethnographic, geographical, political, social, anthropological, sociological and aesthetic elements of sport proliferating in institutions of higher education.

Eric Hobsbawm once called sport one of the most significant practices of the late nineteenth century. Its significance was even more marked in the late twentieth century and will continue to grow in importance into the new millennium as the world develops into a 'global village' sharing the English language, technology and sport.

SPORT AND MEMORY
IN NORTH AMERICA

Editor

STEPHEN G. WIETING
University of Iowa

FRANK CASS
LONDON • PORTLAND, OR

First published in 2001 in Great Britain by
FRANK CASS PUBLISHERS
Crown House, 47 Chase Side, Southgate, London N14 5BP

and in the United States of America by
FRANK CASS PUBLISHERS
c/o ISBS, 5824 N.E. Hassalo Street
Portland, Oregon 97213-3644

Website: www.frankcass.com

British Library Cataloguing in Publication Data

Sport and memory in North America. – (Sport in the global
society; no. 32)
1. Sports – Social aspects – North America 2. Memory
(Philosophy)
I. Wieting, Stephen G.
306. 4'83'097

ISBN 0-7146-5219-9 (cloth)
ISBN 0-7146-8205-5 (paper)
ISSN 1368-9789

Library of Congress Cataloging-in-Publication Data

Sport and memory in North America / editor, Stephen G. Wieting.
    p.cm. – (Sport in the global society, ISSN 1368-9789; no. 32)
"This group of studies first appeared as a special issue of
Culture, sport, society ... vol. 4, no. 2" – T.p. verso.
    Includes bibliographical references and index.
    ISBN 0-7146-5219-9 – ISBN 0-7146-8205-5
    1. Sports – Social aspects – United States. 2. Sports –
Social aspects – Canada. 3. Sports – Psychological aspects –
United States. 4. Sports – Psychological aspects – Canada.
I. Wieting, Stephen G. II. Culture, sport, society. Vol. 4, no. 2.
III. Cass series – sport in the global society; 32.

GV706.5 .S6942 2001
306.4'83'097–dc21   2001028808

This group of studies first appeared as a special issue of *Culture, Sport, Society*
(ISSN 1461-0981), Vol.4, No.2, Summer 2001, published by Frank Cass

Printed in Great Britain by
Antony Rowe Ltd., Chippenham, Wilts

Contents

List of Illustrations

Acknowledgments

Support for parts of the work in this book came from several institutional units of the University of Iowa. These include the Iowa Arts and Humanities Initiative (administered by the Office of the Vice President for Research at the University of Iowa), the Office of the Vice President for Research for supplemental funds for the preparation of the manuscript, the Obermann Center for Advanced Studies, the Center for Asian and Pacific Studies, and the Departments of Sociology and Journalism and Mass Communication.

A number of people over a two-year period graciously provided technical assistance on separate chapters and the design of the whole. These include: Jean Allgood, Joyce Craig, Raul Curto, Ben Earnhardt, Jill Fishbaugh, James Harris, Jae-on Kim, Martine Kintziger, Gudmundur Magnusson, John Njue, Lorna Olson, Tina Parratt, Liz Pearce, Phyllis Rosenwinkel, Eric Rothenbuhler, Micaela Schuneman, Jay Semel, David Skorton, Mary Smith, and Karla Tonella. Sincere and deep thanks are given to these agencies and friends.

All of the authors have been diligent in putting their diverse disciplinary, sport, and regional interests in the service of the volume's themes and intentions. Steven Jackson, Pam Ponic, Sean Hayes, and Danny Lamoureux worked under especially stringent scheduling demands in the preparation of their material. The grace and vigor of all the contributors is much appreciated. J.A. Mangan and Jonathan Manley of Frank Cass gave essential advice on the work's development. Judy Polumbaum has been a superb colleague over many years during which a great deal of the preparatory work on ideas in the volume occurred and was a formidable force in organizing interdisciplinary symposia at the University of Iowa on the themes being addressed.

SGW
Iowa
May 2001

Series Editor's Foreword

In his *The Long Revolution*, Raymond Williams argued that:

> The evolution of the human brain, and then the particular interpretations carried by particular cultures, give us certain 'rules' or 'models', without which no human being can 'see' in the ordinary sense ... In each individual, the learning of these rules, through inheritance and culture, is a kind of creation, in that ... the ordinary 'reality' that his culture defines, forms only as the rules are learned.[1]

'Culture', Williams defined as a particular way of life, which expressed certain meanings and values not only in art and learning but also in institutions and behavior.[2]

Particular cultures then create, and consist of, particular realities. Those who absorb these particularities can alter and extend them and, of course, communicate these changes. With the result that 'The man makes the shape and the shape remakes the man.'[3] Realities are seldom static but they are often shared.

Human communication, of course, is of a high order:

> ... in man, the process of learning and relearning, which is made possible by social organisation and tradition, has led to a number of communication-systems of great complexity and power. Gesture, language, music, mathematics are all systems of this kind.[4]

Williams suggests that the arts comprise especially sophisticated and powerful rhythmic means of communicating experience: 'The dance of the body, the movement of the voice, the sounds of instruments are, like colours, forms, patterns, means of transmitting his experience in so powerful a way that the experience can be literally lived by others ... it is a physical experience as real as any other.'[5]

Now what is more physical than sport? Is it too fanciful to add sport to the arts as a potent transmitter of communal experience? Is the 'poetry of motion' a meaningless platitude? Alive in the memory it too makes the past the future.

> The human bodies which carry the meanings die, but either the lasting monument, or the inherited and traditional artistic skills, embodied in the making of certain images, patterns, rhythms, survive to continue the process of ... a continual recreation of meaning, by the society as a whole and by every individual in it.[6]

Past transmission becomes present transmission. The value is permanence. Change is complex. Shared meanings simplify the process. Receiving meanings assist adjustment to emerging meanings. And memory is the catalyst.

> Memory [is] like a film of sharply focused images, the set arranged and brightly lit, the character is formally disposed, the dialogue learnt and unchangeable. ...[7]

Sharply focused memories of sporting moments – played or watched – are among the most frequently recalled and infrequently forgotten. Such 'poetic' images enjoyed in pensive mood are rooted in particular places and perhaps, above all, in particular things: 'images which are the life of poetry, cannot be raised in any perfection but by introducing particular objects':[8] fresh mown grass on an early summer cricket outfield, the smooth new ball – round or oval – of the new season, the first flashing puck sizzling into the winter netting. As Stephen Wieting and Judy Polumbaum remark in their Prologue, such memories offer a 'certification of uniqueness' proclaiming a cultural security – source of a sense of belonging.

Sport is thus a 'common archive for collective, as well as individual, memory'(p.4) – an archive replete with opportunities for pleasure:

> Praising what is lost
> Makes remembrance dear.[9]

Stored memories provide a future for the past. Special moments common to friends, parents, siblings, lovers, whole towns and whole nations offer escape from anomie. Such memories are mediated, *in part*, not so much through the culture of sport as the cultures of sport. The global 'collective memory' in sport remains stubbornly fractured and on occasion, even confrontational. Memory transactions are far from being universal transactions. Sport still shapes 'local' identities. This is the convincing thrust of *Sport and Memory in North America*. The past is not quite the foreign country famously claimed; it is more often the source of the present country! Shared moments in sport played their part in linking past and future.

There is no need to be unduly modest in making such claims for sport:

> ... there are three reasons [at least] for this serviceability: the fact that sport for many is a common coin of public discourse; that the physical and emotional interests accompanying sports participation and spectatorship brings sport's significance in particularly vivid ways; and that sports' formal properties draw moral boundaries relatively starkly. (p.13)

It may be a moot point as to whether or not, in an age of powerful media globalization, 'local' cultural distinctiveness is being blurred at the edges but reassuringly as yet soccer mostly bores the citizens of the United States, baseball is received mostly indifferently in the United Kingdom and while Rugby League may fuel passion in Northern England, it certainly fails to raise the pulse in Northern Canada. The Olympics furnish a profound illustration 'of the intricate interplay between global and local dynamics ... of sport' (p.14). Simply stated: they unite and they divide nations.

A final point: it is surely time to recognize the merging of memory, capitalism, consumerism and sport has produced its own 'long cultural revolution' increasingly, inexorably and unrelentingly impacting on more and more millions as modern decades slip by. The human memory, stimulated in specific cultural circumstances feeds the appetite for sensations and much else. For this reason, capitalism through consumerism has been able to utilize sport successfully in the pursuit of profit. 'The vulgarity of the intruding masses' has been welcomed; the media mass spectacle has triumphed; moments made into memories are marvellously marketable and mostly because memory holds open the door to active and passive pleasures.

J.A. MANGAN
International Research Centre for Sport, Socialisation, Society
University of Strathclyde

May 2001

NOTES

1. Raymond Williams, *The Long Revolution* (London: Chatto and Windus, 1961), p.18.
2. Ibid., p.41. This was his 'social' definition of culture.
3. Ibid., p.27.
4. Ibid., p.22.
5. Ibid., p.25.
6. Ibid., p.31.
7. P.D. James, *A Certain Justice* (Harmondsworth: Penguin, 1998), p.42.
8. Henry Home, Lord Kames, *The Oxford Dictionary of Quotations* (Oxford: OUP, 1996), p.385, 3.
9. William Shakespeare, *All's Well That Ends Well*, Act 5, Scene 3, line 19.

Prologue

STEPHEN G. WIETING and JUDY POLUMBAUM

'To see a World in a Grain of Sand...'
William Blake, 'Auguries of Innocence'

This collection is about sport in North America. It has been prepared
with three main objectives in mind: to draw on sports phenomena in
documenting generic processes of collective memory; to highlight the
potency of sport within the tightly woven fabric of national cultures; and
to explore how the sport–memory association and the sport–public
cultural interaction may serve as portals into current debates on
globalization. Although the cases laid out here derive from Canada and
the United States, the intent is to illustrate the broad, evocative
attraction of athletics for fans and participants among successively
encompassing groups of people – from schoolyard and neighborhood to
city, state, and nation, and eventually among representatives of many and
diverse nations – and sport's consequent social utility as a vehicle of
remembrance, certification of uniqueness, and method of proclaiming
and broadcasting special cultural features.

We start from the recognition that, for good or ill, sport is a widely
distributed and commonly invoked metaphor in public discourse, locally
and at the national level as well as among nation states. Debates continue
as to exactly why sport is so generally serviceable as a common coin of
cultural expression and exchange. One might say the reason is that a
sport is just a game, a time-out from 'real life', and hence not sufficiently
serious to be divisive. This volume considers the reason to be quite the
contrary. The capacity of sport to capture cultural distinctiveness – to
embody, refract, and sometimes reframe or refashion a society's
fundamental patterns – is the impetus for our work.

By way of introduction we offer the example of the 1999 Hollywood
film *The Hurricane*, a distinctively American product with concurrent
Canadian elements that supplies an intricate and potent amalgam of

sport, popular culture, and memory. Albeit with considerable license, the film recounts actual occurrences: the conviction and imprisonment of an African-American boxer, Rubin 'Hurricane' Carter, for three grisly murders in 1966, and the ultimately successful attempts over a 22-years period to free Carter and his purported accomplices as wrongly charged.

The movie is at once a remembrance of specific events and a depiction of the agonized history of race and crime in the United States leading up to the 1966 killings. It was a time when black professional baseball players traveling with their teams were denied access to hotels and restaurants. Anti-miscegenation laws had yet to be struck down as unconstitutional in the 1967 Supreme Court case *Loving* v. *Virginia* (the same year as the film *Guess Who's Coming to Dinner?* played the race theme when Katherine Hepburn and Spencer Tracy struggled with the prospect of Sidney Poitier marrying their daughter). The Supreme Court's Miranda ruling assuring arrested persons of access to legal advice and discretion in offering self-incriminating confessions preceded by just days the killings of which Carter was accused, and there was contention throughout the appeal process over whether the suspects had been accorded these rights. From the vantage point of the late twentieth century, the film indicts the racism of the 1960s and the continued inertia of the U.S. courts into the late 1980s. But the intimation is that by the end of the century this grievous cultural blight has been substantially altered, with American society now redemptively improved in its posture toward blacks.

Key social indicators will show how exorbitantly oversimplified this picture of current U.S. race relations is. In 1979, a pivotal moment in the movie, one in four young black men were incarcerated or otherwise under the supervision of the U.S. criminal justice system. The figure now is one in three. Between 1975 and 1995 the disparity in fundamental life chances of blacks relative to whites as defined by infant mortality and life expectancy has increased. *The Hurricane* version of collective memory would suggest the opposite. The film's selective retelling, while maintaining a degree of fidelity to the socio-legal backdrop, ultimately distorts in the service of the perspective of remembrance.

Canadian culture also plays an important role in the film representation of the troubled progression of events from 1968 to 1988. A group of friends from a commune near Toronto becomes aware of the Carter case, and, in fact, this group did work long and assiduously for Carter's release. Two of the three friends featured prominently in the movie, Sam Chaiton and Terry Swinton, wrote the book on which it was based. The third movie principal from the commune was Lisa Peters, who married Carter after his release. In Hollywood style, the commune members are extraordinarily altruistic, selling cherished real estate holdings and moving to New Jersey to expedite their work for Carter.[1] Another biography by James S. Hirsch provides a considerably more complex picture of this commune and of the unusual and tension-filled relationships between Chaiton, Swinton, and Peters, and eventually between Carter and Peters.[2] Yet there is also considerable plausibility in the movie characterization of a special Canadian flavor to the motivation and style of the communards. The expenditures and sacrifices of the whole group, and especially of the three highlighted (along with a fourth supporter, the young African American man Lesra Martin), conform to the prevalent view of Canadian culture – not only an impassioned insistence that Canadians are 'nice'[3] but also more substantive and institutional analysis[4] informing us that, in comparison with the United States, Canada has a superior historical appreciation of cultural richness and diversity and a more humane legal and political history regarding the treatment of minorities.[5]

The Hurricane drives home this distinction in a scene when Carter is finally free to travel out of the United States in 1988 and does so with his commune friends, destined for Toronto. Their car is stopped at the border, where Carter is sequestered and questioned by immigration officials. To the dreaded question about earlier criminal convictions, he replies in the affirmative and is told that he cannot enter Canada. The exchange continues, with Carter acknowledging his imprisonment for triple homicide and explaining how he won his freedom through procedural successes in New Jersey, the appeals court in Pennsylvania, and the U.S. Supreme Court. In Hirsch's recounting:

> The official looked at him for a long moment, then raised his eyebrows. 'Hey Joe!', he yelled across the room. 'This is the guy I was telling you about, the guy on TV who spent twenty years in prison for something he didn't do.' He reached across the desk and extended his hand. 'Welcome to Canada, Mr Carter.'[6]

While sport provides part of the backdrop as opposed to the foreground in *The Hurricane*, Carter's experience and persona as a boxer have become indispensable elements of the mythologized story. The incorporation of sport even peripherally sharpens the sorts of element that make for stirring narrative and moral declaration: qualities of physicality and emotionality, purity of purpose, delineation of action, clarity of rules. Sporting events and sports personages, while far from unique in feeding the collective imagination, yield particularly vivid, compelling, accessible material to be memorialized and ascribed contemporary meaning in the retelling.

The three sections of this collection exploit this capacity along three dimensions. First, we seek to show how sport in its many manifestations serves as an efficient common archive for collective as well as individual memory. Secondly, through illustrations from two contemporary societies, we wish to show how sport connects with a country's most definitive and visible public culture, sometimes laying excruciatingly bare and at times concealing and distorting features agreed by its members to be most distinctive. Thirdly, we want to begin a strategic examination of how cross–national exchanges may occur through sports phenomena, in this case, across the U.S.–Canada divide.

The pairing of Canada and the United States, while not necessarily representative in substance, suggests a great deal about processes of globalization – that perhaps overused term, given an inexorable and warm cast by some writers[7] and seen as destructive by others,[8] referring to the ease with which images, capital, and labor flow across national boundaries. The two countries, the world's second and third largest in land mass, afford by virtue of their 8,893-km common border transactions high in visibility, variety, and volume; and, at the same time, with Canada's population being one-tenth of that of the U.S. and 80 per cent of Canadians living within 160 km of that perceived cultural behemoth, the relationship reveals much about the most acrimonious issues in discussions of globalization, related to unbalanced exchange, economic advantage and cultural intrusion. Canadian cultural distinctiveness is often framed defensively *vis-à-vis* the United States. As one commentator put it, in reference to the negotiations that eventually led to the North American Free Trade Agreement, 'Only by standing up to the Yanks can we survive.'[9] Sport provides a convenient focal point for statements of this collective consciousness, and sometimes assertions of higher conscience. An Act of Parliament names hockey and lacrosse as the country's official 'national sports',[10] a recent government report declares sports to be 'everybody's business', and a national sports website maintains that 'Nothing unites Canadians like sport...More than anything else, sport reflects what Canadians value most: the pursuit of excellence, fairness and ethics, inclusion, and participation.'[11]

THE IMPORTANCE OF SPORT FOR COLLECTIVE MEMORY

Memory is a conscious sensation in the present that captures select features of a past experience. It may be expressed as a singular moment or a group conviction, but, either way, memory joins individual and collective experience. Peter Novick says: 'When we speak of collective memory, we often forget that we're employing a metaphor – an organic metaphor that makes an analogy between the memory of an individual and that of a community.'[12]

Individual memory as the vital link in cultural transmission and collective memory as the very embodiment of a culture's persistence, long core assumptions of anthropology, have come to assume high priority across an array of other social science disciplines. A recent history of the concept of memory locates its present meaning within the formative period of modern psychology in late-nineteenth century France (1874–86). Memory, in this account, replaced the notion of the soul as the essence of the human mind. Thus emerged the modern secularized version of this science of the person, supplanting the earlier, metaphysical, if not theological, core of psychology's object.[13] Maurice Halbwachs's seminal studies on how societies remember contributed to the foundation of modern sociology.[14] Strategic efforts by groups to mold and enliven their collective histories have been studied in contexts ranging from the Holocaust to artistic communities.[15] Collective memory even enters prominently as a theme in the eclectic field of cognitive science.[16]

The varied disciplines converge on the discovery that collective memory elects special means for its purposes. These include material technologies for recording and dissemination, and also strategic genres that lend themselves to memory retention in the absence of the material aids. Riddles, puns, aphorisms, special poetic meters, and formulaic stories all have been used efficiently to encode fundamental cultural knowledge in special linguistic structures.[17] Additionally, domains of human conduct that are salient to the adaptive life of the culture and potentially evocative of its most intense feelings are singled out as aids in remembering and passing on valued and essential knowledge. Sport as performed, watched, and recorded is one such sphere of human conduct.

Consider, for example, an evocation of sport framed as private recollection in a memoir by Bill Bradley, former basketball star, U.S. senator, and presidential candidate:

> When you win a Senate seat, it is not supposed to be a thrill. You have won the right to serve the people of your state and nation. If you are conscientious, that means you work fourteen hours every day, year around; and if you are lucky, you make a small, positive difference in the lives of millions of Americans. It is an honor, but it is not a thrill. It is nothing at all like standing on the floor of the Garden as world champion, with your fists raised, with the chills coursing up and down your spine, with your face aching from smiling, secure in the knowledge that all the work for all the years was worth it, and that on this night and for this season you are the best in the world. *That* is a thrill.[18]

And consider an account from a different context, framed as public knowledge and addressed to a purported audience presumed to appreciate the emotions and sensations involved. In this historicized passage about American-style football, retrieved sport also is the preferred vehicle for cultural observation:

> One of the strangest tribal rites in American society is the Harvard–Yale football weekend. The most traditional of rivals, Harvard and Yale have been playing one another in football since 1875…Victorious Yale students established the custom of tearing down the loser's goalposts, and Tad Jones, a Yale coach, once told his players, 'Gentlemen, you are about to play football for Yale against Harvard. Never in your lives will you do anything so important.' According to dark legend, a Harvard coach once deeply inspired his players without saying a word. As they watched in mounting fascination, he slowly and silently choked a bulldog [the Yale mascot] to death, then tossed the carcass at their feet. Perhaps the most rabid Harvard cheerleader of all time was John Reed '10, the Bolshevik sympathizer buried in the walls of the Kremlin. Nothing aroused Reed like the Yale game, and he wrote a song proposing to 'twist the bull-dog's tail' and 'call up the hearse for dear old Yale'.[19]

The first passage channels cultural values and expectations through a singular private moment, while the second subsumes individuals in a ritualistic public occasion. Both illustrate the serviceability of sports memories in constituting and reconstituting culture, whether by invoking sensory processes, such as the sensibilities of athletes, coaches or spectators, or by use of narrative and expository conventions, from popular legend to academic history.

Turning to the Canadian context, we might consider news accounts reflecting and contributing to the hagiography surrounding the ice hockey star Maurice 'Rocket' Richard, who died at the age of 78 in May 2000. At his state funeral, televised live from Montreal's Notre Dame Basilica and attended by the Canadian Premier Jean Chrétien, fans in red Montreal Canadiens sweaters sat in the upper pews. One Canadian reporter set the scene as follows:

> It is late at night, 12 hours before The Rocket will make his last journey through the streets of Montreal, and I push open a side door of the Notre Dame Basilica, and enter.
>
> The pews are empty, but standing at the altar before a microphone is a woman in a black and white polka-dot dress. She is singing a song in French, and I sit in one of the pews and listen to her wonderful voice soaring up into the highest reaches of the cathedral.
>
> 'That was beautiful', I tell her when she finishes.
>
> 'Thank you', she says ... 'It is about a very much loved man, a man loved by all the people, who died and goes to paradise. I will be singing it here tomorrow for Maurice Richard. He was everything to us.'
>
> Ginette Reno is Quebec's most famous chanteuse, a much beloved legend in her own right, but The Rocket is dead and she has come to sing his soul to heaven.[20]

Another Canadian journalist noted the irony of the television saturation, since Richard's 'greatest feats' were performed in the 1940s and the 1950s, before televised sports loomed large; but he observed that memories from those times 'have been no doubt passed along to today's TV generation', especially in Montreal and Quebec, where the reverence for Richard is almost unfathomable...' And in tribute to Canada's proud posture of bilingualism as well as to the hockey star, this English-language journalist ended his column with 'Adieu, Maurice. Et merci.'[21]

The U.S. examples suggest that everything from electoral politics to revolution pales beside the fervor of partaking of or watching sport. In the Canadian case, sport itself seems infused with particular Canadian takes on politics, religion, language, and ethnicity. In all these settings, however, we encounter the social uses of sport for purposes of cultural remembrance.[22]

MECHANISMS OF COLLECTIVE MEMORY:
TEXT, BODY, RITUAL

Provocative scholarship integrating ethnography and social history concludes that collective memory is inscribed and enacted in three main arenas: public texts, actors' bodies, and public celebrations.[23] The rich traditions in sport, from perspectives of both participation and documentation, provide excellent materials in all three fields.

Memory and Texts

A persuasive interpretation of the *Iliad* and the *Odyssey*, in which certain narratives with ingredients known and compelling to contemporaries of the accounts are seen to capture the normative essence of Greek culture, also shows how sport has long been an object of vivid storytelling.[24] Some of the earliest Norse literature occurs in the Icelandic sagas where a special kind of swimming sport is recounted, pitting contestants in battles to stay beneath the water the longest.[25] Sports pages of modern newspapers, beyond recounting the facts of contests, embody sports events in telling narratives, often with persuasive lessons for readers; and sports stories in mass-circulation magazines do the same, generally with more explicit intent. The publishing world further emphasizes the enduring value to be retrieved from these sorts of account in series such as the annual *Best Sports Stories*, which Dutton Publishers produced from 1944 until 1990, and *Best American Sports Writing*, appearing yearly since 1991. We even have a millennial monument to U.S. (as well as some Canadian) sports writing in a collection celebrating works from the last century.[26]

The Body in Sport

Although the work of Michel Foucault is frequently cited as marking a watershed in studies of the body,[27] Marcel Mauss offered important precursors.[28] Ways of theorizing the body have been adopted variously by analysts of sport, with Frank and later Maguire providing especially good overviews of developments in this area.[29] Maguire's refinement of

Frank's fourfold organization of themes is a useful classification. His first category, 'biomedical bodies', acknowledges the enormous infusion of biological research into the social sciences over the past ten years and also opens needed space for debates about the increased use of technologically-aided training methods as well as both legal and banned drugs in elite sport practises. The second category, 'disciplined bodies', builds direct on Foucault's observations on the cultural encapsulation of bodies through regimens of discipline. The third category, 'symbolic bodies', employs concepts of performance, agency and figuration through which actors embody cultural dictates. Finally, 'commodified bodies', reflecting cultural studies and feminist scholarship on processes of commercialized sport, refers to stereotypical images in advertising, journalism, and other mass-mediated representations driven by prevailing cultural ideals.

Sport and Ritual

Allen Guttmann provides a highly serviceable framework for understanding modern sport relative to forms and practises in ancient and primitive societies.[30] Tracing a trajectory 'from ritual to record', he emphasizes the rise of the secular, preference for equality, specialization, rationalization, bureaucratic organization, quantification, and the quest for records characteristic of modern sport. His observations are roundly confirmed by the weight of research on sport within modern industrial societies. At the same time, scholarship has greatly enriched our views of the persistence and recasting of ritual in modern sporting contexts. Research on the huge public displays, mediated by commercial interests, of modern sport suggests a formidable investment in veneration surrounding these 'secular' pursuits. Sporting productions in collegiate, professional, and certainly international arenas have been imbued with ultimate meanings for spectators and participants (and in turn for the constituencies represented, for example, the campus, the community, the nation) that approach religious intensity.[31]

Within any given nation one can identify ceremonial dimensions of sport that take on outsized significance beyond the mere facts of the athletic activities themselves. For instance, France's victory in the 1998 World Cup, on French soil, became a memorial celebration of the history of France; in the words of the Prime Minister Jacques Chirac, who spoke from the stands, the triumph displayed what distinguishes the Republic – its epic failures and defeats, but also its epic successes.[32] Similarly, the drug crises surrounding the 1998 and the 1999 Tour de France were interpreted as fraught with implications for French civilization, threatening not merely the legitimacy of the riders and teams involved, but the moral fabric of the nation.[33]

Social Factors Influencing Collective Memory

Key factors affecting the substance, integrity, and forms of collective memory include the degree of homogeneity of the collective, the presence of competing interests in the production of collective meaning, and the surrounding context, particularly prevailing estimates of collective priorities and fears of crises and external threats. Considerable dynamism exists among these three variables. This is certainly the case whenever sport is appropriated as a vehicle for fostering desired images and memories within a group.

Relative homogeneity is a baseline variable, necessary if not sufficient. Memory attempts to extract pasts with selective criteria and strategic frames that are considered suitable to those doing the remembering in the present, as well as with an eye toward future uses. But to do this requires resources of time and material goods, along with sufficient agreement to invest in the activity. Thus memory work is likely to be most potent within a fairly homogeneous group in a relatively stable state.

Regardless of stability and relative agreement over the value of memorializing, however, participants in a group effort who agree on the import of the effort may differ sharply over substance and modes of dissemination. Which icons, relics, and events are selected from the past for retrieval, how they are packaged to serve present collective ends, and what use the elements and the package will have in the future are all contested ground. The processes of selectivity and framing involved in the recovery and assignation of meaning to past relics and events are largely determined by present circumstances. Further, because recovery also anticipates future evaluations, competing bets about which memorializing choices will best benefit the collective vie for eminence.

The third factor in the mix concerns the changing cultural context. Certainly decisions about recollection and commemoration must be seen to be based on collective needs to maintain coherence and preserve desired values. Circumstances of felt threats to internal integrity or incursions from outside in the form of other institutions, other localities, or other nations drive the pace and choices of what and how to remember.

Several notable efforts in the last quarter-century to generate a faithful and effective collective memory display these components. Work chronicling the stages in Holocaust memory provides clear evidence of the need for a sufficient group homogeneity and common intent.[34] Preparations for the bicentennial commemoration of the French Revolution stirred a storm of debate among highly disparate interest groups and scholars, with intense disagreement over the substance and forms the commemoration should take.[35] Evolving U.S. government plans to mark the 500th anniversary of Columbus's exploration of the 'New World' with unalloyed celebration encountered a political and scholarly context in the early 1990s starkly different than official organizers had envisioned. A range of loyalties that included 'diversity', 'multiculturalism', and identity group visibility of Hispanics and native Americans, among others, posed stern opposition to a memorial that did not reflect the grave negative consequences of the exploration.[36]

In the sports realm these components readily come to light in cases of the retirement or death of an athletic icon; moral crises embroiling an athlete or team; achievement of media-hyped predictions in sports performance; and, in the United States perhaps most abundantly, any of an unending stream of commercially-exploitable historic anniversaries. Baseball's 1997 season evoked historic memory with a focus on Jackie Robinson's breaking the color bar in Major League Baseball 50 years earlier, with the present purposes combining self-congratulation on purported progress in integration with modern marketing techniques – up to $50 million in anniversary merchandise available, the African American player's face appearing on everything from coins to T-shirts to cereal boxes.[37]

LOCAL AND GLOBAL RECOLLECTIONS:
DIFFERENCES THAT MAKE A DIFFERENCE

Cultures are inventive, prodigious, and at times desperate in their creative endeavors to memorialize themselves, with the preferred vehicles ranging from literature, journalism, and historiography to the fine and the performing arts to sports. What disparate methods for cultural remembrance and commemoration have in common is their inevitable illustration of the acknowledgement underlying much cultural anthropology that 'A culture is its stories'.[38] Stories must be told, but they also must be listened to, and both obligations require compelling narrative with appropriate degrees of accuracy or verisimilitude in scene and character. Jane Miller's observation that novels, a relatively modern form of story, must answer the reader's 'So what?' is applicable across forms.[39] And stories require the assent 'That's right' from purported audiences. These are transactions of memory which take place at the local level.

Indeed, those Canadian and U.S. fiction writers who can be identified as distinctively 'Canadian' or 'American' are consummate cultural archivists. Two examples are Canada's Alice Munro and the American author John Updike.

Munro, whose genre is densely-woven short stories that can approach the illusion of the novel in their evocation of a complete tapestry of life, deftly illuminates intricacies of Canadian society through a prolific stream of work produced over more than three decades.[40] The psychic as well as the geographic setting is rural Ontario, where Munro grew up – a flat, mundane landscape where the unbelievable happens believably. Munro herself has said, 'I love the landscape [of rural Ontario], not as "scenery" but as something intimately known. Also the weather, the villages, and towns, not in their picturesque aspects but in all phases.' And she acknowledges the power of memory in her work and her conscious effort to explore how individuals deal with shared experiences. 'Memory is the way we keep telling ourselves our stories – and telling other people a somewhat different version of our stories. We can hardly manage our lives without a powerful on-going narrative.'[41]

Updike marks cultural and political points in American life across five decades through his novels about the ordinary existence of Harry 'Rabbit' Angstrom.[42] In the first book of this series the protagonist struggles to assert a meaningful individual identity amid the conformity, complacency and stagnation of 1950s post-war America. By the fourth, which evokes the alienating post-modern climate of the 1980s, the non-hero contemplates a country and a world corroded by uncertainty, terror, destruction, and death.

These are two authors of very different sensibilities – certainly, the gendered qualities of their writing contrast markedly. But they are alike in their recording the finest of cultural detail from their respective societies, so that in reading both it is difficult not to be struck by national differences that are consequential.

Historians also may be implicit or explicit memorializers of culture. Their primary obligation is to tell the local facts, and in the process to assure that the sources are authentic, the recounting of events reliable, and the manner of reconstitution credible. But some go further, widening the vision to place the local account within broader social and political currents. It is here that historians' role in discerning definitive cultural differences can be formidable. In U.S. historiography, for instance, Linda Gordon situates the detailed investigation of apparently marginal local events within a larger national context, thus illuminating distinctive elements of gender, race, law, and social class in U.S. culture.[43]

Sometimes global events impinge on national self-identity, and historical writing may be burdened with a certain clarifying or even apologetic task. Kenneth McNaught's elegant, brilliantly informative history of Canada represents this approach, requiring successive revisions and additions as the global surroundings of that nation altered over a quarter of a century.[44] Saul identifies Canada's uniqueness in its innovative experiment to blend three cultural streams – native, francophone, and anglophone – and provides a passionate argument for the accurate memory of the past in understanding and conducting current political efforts.[45] Ferguson provides a more popular articulation of Canada's national essence, clarified for the benefit of both Canadian and non-Canadian readers.[46]

We single out the arena of sports, not to claim its superior value as a vehicle for memorializing cultural distinctiveness in national and global contexts, but rather for its extreme analytic utility. As we have written elsewhere, there are three reasons for this serviceability: the fact that sport for many is a common coin of public discourse; that the physical and emotional intensity accompanying sports participation and spectatorship brings out its significance in particularly vivid ways; and that sport's formal properties draw moral boundaries relatively starkly.[47] The sport studies included here give deference to writing, images, and rituals of sport to document central human preoccupations and unique national priorities, following what we consider the finest traditions of the investigation of sport within Canadian and U.S. societies as well as those studies which focus on the sports-related exchanges of labor, capital, and images across the common border.[48]

GLOBALIZATION AND THE MANAGEMENT OF
NATIONAL CULTURE

America's 'newspaper of record', the *New York Times*, helped to bring coverage of the 2000 Olympic Games in Sydney to a close with an editorial observing that the Olympics evoke disparate meanings for different nations while also providing 'moments awe-inspiring enough to transcend parochialism and pull in all the separate narratives'.[49] This is an intriguing sort of post-modern restatement of the Olympic ideal – acknowledging that different vantage points make for sharply variant experiences, and also granting that there is no going back on the taints of bureaucratism, corruption, drug scandals, and moronic broadcasting, yet ultimately confident in the comforting commonalities that restore all nations and peoples to the same zone.

This certitude that passion and commemoration refracted through so many lenses ultimately will converge in the utopian vision of Olympian internationalism should remind us of the extraordinary potency of sport as a vehicle of collective meaning across many levels. That heartfelt assertions of camaraderie, unity, equity, and purity can persist despite the well-recognized realities of combativeness, exceptionalism, striving for relative advantage, and spoiling for commercial gain should remind us that facts are only the starting point for what societies wish to make of them.

The Olympics themselves, along with the enveloping commentary, remind us, of course, of the intricate interplay between global and local dynamics in athletic performance, perceptions and readings of sporting endeavors, and psychic as well as financial pay-offs of sport. The realities and meanings of globalization have moved to the center of much sports scholarship, and this compilation likewise is concerned with how flows of capital, labor, and images among states, between states and transnational organizations, and among actors and entities operating across national borders emerge through sport.

In sport as in all other social institutions, the world's increasing systemic complexity along with the persistence of local agency demands our attention to both the phenomenal aggregations of resources at the global level and the ways in which local players find avenues for insertion into large streams of global exchange.[50] Sport studies have addressed matters of globalization for about ten years, attending to movements of labor and images, which are rather more thoroughly covered, and capital, which is somewhat harder to trace, and achieving considerable development in talking about both general hegemonic patterns of the global system and local responses. The picture being drawn and gradually filled in is that, along with trends toward colonization and increasing similarity across nations, there is considerable retention of local and national sport styles and great variability in degrees of assimilation.[51]

The essays here draw together material from the dimensions of capital, labor, and images to illuminate dominance by larger powers while also detailing the persistence of local patterns. Globalization in the cultural realm, as described by John Tomlinson, may be seen as the most invasive of national identity, for instance, in its corrosion of language and images. Yet we and our collaborators, too, find that groups continue to manifest resistance, resilience, and selectivity when faced with potentially invasive, global forces and products.[52] Because of the centrality of sport for memory and its close association with public culture, we believe this work further demonstrates the substantial utility of sport to capture variations and contribute to a more richly textured understanding of globalization processes. Even as the colossus of sport as a global phenomenon becomes increasingly obvious, sport as a repository of cultural memory at the local level continues to show vivid and consequential differences.

CONTEXT AND OUR MEMORY

Our community, Iowa City, sits at a crossroads of both national and global highways. It is located along U.S. Interstate 80, an east–west thoroughfare bisecting the top portion of the United States, about one-third of the way from Manhattan on the east coast to Hollywood on the west. A journey of some 1,600 km east will take you across the Hudson River and into New York City, where a right turn begins a traverse of the western edge of the boroughs and the road and what starts as the Henry Hudson Parkway becomes Joe DiMaggio Highway, a memorial to a cherished baseball icon. Going west from Iowa City, with a southerly adjustment on to I-15 at Salt Lake City, site of the 2002 Winter Olympics, a trip of 3,200 km will get you to Los Angeles. Or one may leave I-80 much earlier to take the shortest route to Canada or Mexico – turning right to trace I-35 North with a slow arc around Lake Superior and entering Ontario just below Thunder Bay; or turning left at the same junction on to I-35 South, eventually crossing from Laredo, Texas, into Nuevo Laredo.

These physical co-ordinates are emblematic of the linkages stressed by chroniclers of globalization. We are connected, East and West on these thoroughfares, to two Meccas of sport and popular culture, and North and South to the geographic delimiters of our focus. The ubiquitous electronic conduits of modern mass media expand the physical linkages exponentially. With a starting point in Iowa City – the location of an international conference in the spring of 1999 from which many of these chapters originated – we begin with local nodes and work outward.

Our sequence begins with a pivotal moment in U.S. legal and cultural history: the passage of national legislation known as Title IX, designed to advance parity in sport for American men and women. Christine Grant, former player and coach of the Canadian national field hockey team and long-time director of a separate department of women's athletics at the University of Iowa, was a major figure in the passage of this bill. She has just retired, and the independent women's athletic department she headed and which impressively represented the implications of that bill, will now be reunited with the department of men's athletics. This reunion is a locus for considerable dispute over the record of progress for sexual equity in sport: to wit, is this an acknowledgement of symmetry or restitution of a formerly unequal arrangement? In ways that are especially significant to us personally, Dr Grant's biography, her work in international and collegiate sport, the separation and now the reconciliation of two university departments, define a small entryway to a world of sport, national images, and memory.

Stressing the encapsulation of the large within the small, the national and the global within the local, the story competing for U.S. sports media space for the first two weeks in September 2000 was the firing of Bobby Knight as coach of the Indiana University men's basketball team. A comparatively parochial event in the world scheme of things – certainly so in contrast to the Olympics, whose claims on media allocation were remarkably invaded by the Knight episode – the matter acquired astounding reach in the United States. A flaming red-and-black cover of *Sports Illustrated* with the legend 'Fired: the Downfall of Bob Knight' endeavored to capture the hysteria which ensued.[53] The university president who fired the coach had to go into hiding in response to death threats and the vandalism of his home.[54] Here in Iowa City, the number one story following the event was obsessive speculation over the likelihood that Steve Alford, the University of Iowa men's basketball coach and a former Knight protégé, might go for the Indiana job – a story Alford's repeated denial of interest could not put to rest for some time.

Canada and the considerable number of sport participants and observers may gaze with incredulity at the drastically warped proportionality of the response of students, fans, and monetary contributors to the firing of a coach. Indeed, the proportions seemed freakish not only to cultural outsiders but to many Americans. Is this what U.S. higher education has nurtured through its robust, if not maniacal, romance with athletics?[55] The Knight episode seems foreign, as does the odd history of Title IX in our country.

We should not forget, however, that sport anywhere provides access to manifestations of cultural distinctiveness that may amaze outsiders and sometimes even insiders. In this volume studies providing cultural and historical context for some of the grotesqueries of U.S. sport are complemented by studies of national crises ensconced in sport in Canada. The collection, we hope, will affirm our central theme of the special place of sport in the distillation of collective memory.

NOTES

1. Carter's own biography appeared as R. Carter, *The Sixteenth Round* (New York, NY: Viking, 1974. The book which served as material for the movie is S. Chaiton and T. Swinton, *Lazarus and the Hurricane: the Freeing of Rubin 'Hurricane' Carter* (New York, NY: St. Martin's Griffin, 1991 and 2000).
2. J.S. Hirsch, *Hurrricane* (Boston, MA: Houghton Mifflin, 2000) appeared after the movie's release.
3. For instance, W. Ferguson, *Why I Hate Canadians* (Vancouver: Douglas & McIntyre, 1997).
4. Such as J.R. Saul, *Reflections of a Siamese Twin: Canada at the End of the Twentieth Century* (Toronto: Viking, 1997).
5. See, for instance, Canadian Consultative Council on Multiculturalism report to the Canadian Radio-Television and Telecommunications Commission on the Review of Canadian Content Regulations (1980).
6. Hirsch, *Hurricane*, p.311.
7. T.L. Friedman *The Lexus and the Olive Tree: Understanding Globalization* (New York, NY: Farrar, Straus & Giroux, 1999).
8. S. Sassen, *Globalization and Its Discontents* (New York, NY: New Press, 1998); M. Chossudovsky, *The Globalization of Poverty* (Penang, Malaysia: Third World Network, 1997); J. Gray, *False Dawn* (New York, NY: New Press, 1998).
9. P.C. Newman, 'Defending the Canadian Dream', *Macleans* (8 July 1991), 50.
10. The National Sports of Canada Act, Chapter N-16.7 (1994, c. 16), proclaims hockey the national winter sport and lacrosse the national summer sport.
11. 'Sport in Canada: Everybody's Business', Report of the Leadership, Partnership and

Accountability Standing Committee on Canadian Heritage, Sub-Committee on the Study of Sport in Canada (December 1998); http://www.ualberta.ca/~bleeck/canada/canadasport. htm

12. P. Novick, *The Holocaust in American Life* (Boston, MA: Houghton Mifflin, 1999).

13. I. Hacking, *Rewriting the Soul: Multiple Personality and the Sciences of Memory* (Princeton, NJ: Princeton University Press, 1995).

14. M. Halbwachs, *Les Cadres sociaux de la mémoire*, Les Travaux De L'Année Sociologique (Paris: Alcan, 1995); edited English version as *On Collective Memory* (introduced by Lewis Coser (Chicago, IL: University of Chicago, 1992.); *La Mémoire collective*, preface by J. Duvignaud, introduced by M. Alexandre (Paris: Presses Universitaires de France, 1950); English version as *The Collective Memory*, introduced by M. Douglas (New York, NY: Harper & Row, 1980).

15. Novick, *Holocaust in American Life*; G.L. Lang and K. Lang, *Etched in Memory: The Building of Artistic Reputation* (Chapel Hill, NC: University of North Carolina Press, 1990).

16. G. Lakoff, *Women, Fire, and Dangerous Things: What Categories Reveal about the Human Mind* (Chicago, IL: University of Chicago Press, 1987); *Moral Politics: What Conservatives Know that Liberals Don't* (Chicago, IL: University of Chicago Press, 1996); G. Lakoff and M. Johnson, *Philosophy in the Flesh: the Embodied Mind and Its Challenge to Western Thought* (New York, NY: Basic Books, 1999).

17. M. Finley, *The World of Odysseus* (London: Chatto and Windus, revised edn, 1977); E.A. Havelock, *The Greek Concept of Justice* (Cambridge, MA: Harvard University Press, 1977); S. Wieting and T. Thórlindsson, 'Divorce in the Old Icelandic Commonwealth: an Interactionist Approach to the Past', *Studies in Symbolic Interaction*, 11 (1990), 163–89.

18. B. Bradley, *Life on the Run* (New York, NY: Vintage, 1976 and 1995, pp.ix–x).

19. R.H. Boyle, *Sport – Mirror of American Life* (Boston, MA: Little, Brown, 1963), pp.215–16.

20. E. McRae, '"He was everything to us": Thousands pay tribute at funeral for Canadiens hockey legend', *Ottawa Sun* (1 June 2000).

21. R. Brodie, 'Forum for a true icon: Magical TV moment said it all about Rocket's legendary status', ibid. (3 June 2000).

22. A substantial body of scholarship specifically addresses remembrance and collective memory through sport, including: A. Baker, 'Sports Films, History, and Identity', *Journal of Sport History*, 25 (1998), 217–33; J. Bale, 'Capturing "The African Body?" Visual Images and Imaginative Sports', ibid., 25 (1998), 234–51; L. Blasdell, 'Legends as an Expression of Baseball Memory', ibid., 19 (1992), 227–43; J.F. Healey, 'An Exploration of the Relationship between Memory and Sport', *Sociology of Sport Journal*, 8 (1991), 213–27; J. Howell, 'A Revolution in Motion: Advertising and the Politics of Nostalgia', ibid., 8 (1991), 258–71; S.D. Mosher, 'Fielding Our Dreams: Rounding Third in Dyersville', ibid., 8 (1991), 272–80; R.L. Schmitt and W.M. Leonard, 'Immortalizing the Self through Sport', *American Journal of Sociology*, 91 (1986), 1088–111; S.S. Slowikowski, 'Burning Desire: Nostalgia, Ritual, and the Sport-Festival Flame Ceremony', *Sociology of Sport Journal*, 8 (1991), 239–57; E.E. Snyder, 'Sociology of Nostalgia: Sports Halls of Fame and Museums in America', ibid., 8 (1991), 228–38; W. Vamplew, 'Facts and Artifacts: Sports Historians and Sports Museums', *Journal of Sports History*, 25 (1998), 269–82.

23. P. Connerton, *How Societies Remember* (Cambridge: Cambridge University Press, 1989); A. Kleinman and J. Kleinman, 'How Bodies Remember: Social Memory and Bodily Experience of Criticism, Resistance, and Deligitimation Following China's Cultural Revolution', *New Literary History*, 25 (1994), 707–23.

24. M. Finley, *World of Odysseus*; the point on sport is especially evident in Book 13 of the *Iliad*.

25. *Laxdæla Saga*, *Íslendinga Sögur*, Vol.IV (Reykjavík: Íslendingasagnaútgáfan, 1981), 40: 117, 118.

26. D. Halberstam (ed.), *Best American Sports Writing of the Century* (Boston, MA: Houghton Mifflin, 1999). This collection, while self-consciously memorializing, is also remarkably unrepresentative in certain ways. Of 51 authors featured, two are women. Of the 'American' geographical claim, two of 59 entries are of Canadian events. Fewer than five of the story topics come from sport events beyond North America. Seeking to redress partiality in both authorship and gender topic, are recent collections such as J. Sandoz (ed.), *A Whole Other Ball Game: Women's Literature on Women's Sport* (New York, NY: Noonday Press, 1997) and J.

Sandoz and J. Winans (eds), *Whatever It Takes: Women on Women's Sport* (New York; Farrar, Straus & Giroux, 1999).

27. M. Foucault, *La volenté de savoir* (Paris: Gallimard, 1976); *L'usage des plaisirs* (Paris: Gallimard, 1984).

28. M. Mauss, 'Les techniques du corps', *Journal de psychologie*, 32 (1935), 271–93.

29. A. Frank, 'For a Sociology of the Body: an Analytical Review', in M. Featherstone, M. Hepworth, and B. Turner (eds), *The Body: Social Process and Cultural Theory* (London: Sage, 1991); J. Maguire, 'Bodies, Sportcultures and Societies: A Critical Review of Some Theories in the Sociology of the Body', *International Review for the Sociology of Sport*, 28 (1993), 33–52. A key work is K. Heineman, 'Sport and the Sociology of the Body', *International Review for the Sociology of Sport*, 15 (1980), 41–55; see also N. Theberge, 'Reflections on the Body in the Sociology of Sport', *Quest*, 43 (1991), 123–34.

30. A. Guttmann, *From Ritual to Record* (New York, NY: Columbia University Press, 1978).

31. J.J. MacAloon, *This Great Symbol* (Chicago, IL: University of Chicago Press, 1981); Slowikowski, 'Burning Desire'.

32. See also H. Dauncey and G. Hare (eds), *France and the 1998 World Cup: the National Impact of a World Sporting Event* (London and Portland, OR: Frank Cass, 1999).

33. S. Wieting, 'Twilight of the Hero in the Tour de France', *International Review for the Sociology of Sport*, 35 (2000), 369–84.

34. Novick, *Holocaust in American Life*; J. Young, *The Texture of Memory: Holocaust Memorials and Meaning* (New Haven, CT: Yale University Press, 1993).

35. S.L. Kaplan, *Farewell Revolution: Disputed Lagacies, France 1789/1989* (Ithaca, NY: Cornell University Press, 1995) and *Farewell, Revolution: The Historian Feud, France, 1789/1989* (Ithaca, NY: Cornell University Press, 1995).

36. K. Sale, *The Conquest of Paradise: Christopher Columbus and the Columbian Legacy* (New York, NY: Penguin, 1990) was one work that made a 'preemptory strike' on the unquestioned ceremony plans; see also D.E. Stannard, *American Holocaust* (New York, NY: Oxford, 1992).

37. B. Horovitz, 'Field of Items Commemorate Jackie Robinson Milestone', *USA Today* (13 February 1997), 2B.

38. The quotation comes from J. Miller, *Women Writing about Men* (New York, NY: Pantheon, 1980). The same conviction is evident in works of historically-oriented anthropologists, notably Clifford Geertz, as well as ethnographically-oriented historians such as Robert Darnton.

39. Miller, *Women Writing about Men*.

40. A. Munro's first collection of stories is *Dance of the Happy Shades* (Toronto: Ryerson, 1968). Her most recent collection, *Selected Stories* (New York, NY: Vintage, 1997) draws selectively from the eight previous ones.

41. 'A conversation with Alice Munro', Vintage Books Reading Group Center, http://www.randomhouse.com/vintage/read/secrets/munro.html.

42. J. Updike, *Rabbit, Run* (New York, NY: Knopf, 1960); *Rabbit Redux* (New York, NY: Ballantine, 1971); *Rabbit Is Rich* (New York, NY: Knopf, 1981); *Rabbit at Rest* (New York, NY: Knopf, 1990).

43. L. Gordon, *Heroes of Their Own Lives: The History and Politics of Family Violence* (New York, NY: Viking/Putnam, 1988) and *The Great Arizona Orphan Abduction* (Cambridge, MA: Harvard University Press, 1999.

44. K. McNaught, *The Penguin History of Canada* (London: Penguin, 1988).

45. Saul, *Reflections of a Siamese Twin*.

46. Ferguson, *Why I Hate Canadians*.

47. J. Polumbaum and S. Wieting, 'Stories of Sport and the Moral Order: Unraveling the Cultural Construction of Tiger Woods', *Journalism and Communication Monographs*, 1 (1999), 69–118.

48. Exemplary material concerned with these sporting relationships includes: B. Kidd, *The Struggle for Canadian Sport* (Toronto: University of Toronto Press, 1996); H. Hall, T. Slack, G. Smith, and D. Whitson, *Sport in Canadian Society* (Toronto: McClelland & Stewart, 1991); D. Cooper, 'Canadians Declare "It Isn't Cricket": a Century of Rejection of the Imperial Game, 1860–1960', *Journal of Sport History*, 26 (1999), 51–81; J. Harvey and H. Cantelon, *Not Just a Game: Essays in Canadian Sport Sociology* (Ottawa: University of Ottawa Press); T. Joyce, 'Canadian Sport and State Control: Toronto 1845–1886', *International Journal of the History of*

Sport, 16 (1999), 22–37; B. Kidd, 'The Culture Wars of the Montreal Olympics', *International Review for the Sociology of Sport*, 27 (1992), 151–61; B. Kidd, 'How Do We Find Our Own Voices in the "New World Order"? A Commentary on Americanization', *Sociology of Sport Journal*, 8 (1991), 178–84; S. Laberge, 'Sociology of Sport in Quebec: a Field Deeply Rooted in Society', ibid., 12 (1995), 213–23; V. Paraschak, 'Variations in Race Relations: Sporting Events for Native Peoples in Canada', ibid., 14 (1997), 1–21; P. White and B. Wilson, 'Distinctions in the Stands: an Investigation of Bourdieu's "Habitus", Socioeconomic Status and Sport Spectatorship in Canada', *International Review for the Sociology of Sport*, 34 (1999), 245–64; and N. Theberge, 'Gender, Sport, and the Construction of Community: a Case Study from Women's Ice Hockey', *Sociology of Sport Journal*, 12 (1995), 389–402.

49. 'Olympian Narratives', *New York Times* (1 October 2000), 14-WK.

50. Hence Friedman's imagery of the maximally standardized and systemically complex ('The Lexus') and the remnants of local agents ('The Olive Tree') as poles along a global to a local continuum; Friedman, *The Lexus and the Olive Tree*.

51. Useful integrative statements occur in the special issue on globalization of *Journal of Sport and Social Issues*, 23 (1996). Items in that issue we have followed with special profit in developing themes in this volume are: P. Donnelly, 'The Local and the Global: Globalization in the Sociology of Sport', pp.239–57 and J. Harvey, G. Rail, and L. Thibault, 'Globalization and Sport: Sketching a Theoretical Model for Empirical Analyses', pp.258–77. Illustrative materials close to the themes of this volume are in: J. Bale and J. Maguire (eds), *The Global Sports Arena: Athletic Talent Migration in an Interdependent World* (London and Portland, OR: Frank Cass, 1994); D. Andrews, B. Carrington, S. Jackson, and Z. Mazur, 'Jordanscapes: a Preliminary Analysis of the Global Popular', *Sociology of Sport Journal*, 13 (1996), 428–57; S. Jackson and D. Andrews, 'Between and Beyond the Global and the Local', *International Review for the Sociology of Sport*, 34 (1999), 31–42; J. Maguire, 'Blade Runners: Canadian Migrants, Ice Hockey and the Global Sports Process', *Journal of Sport and Social Issues*, 20 (1993), 335–60; and M. Silk, 'Local/Global Flows and Altered Production Practices', *International Review for the Sociology of Sport*, 34 (1999), 113–23.

52. J. Tomlinson, *Globalization and Culture* (Chicago, IL: University of Chicago Press, 1999).

53. *Sports Illustrated* (8 September 2000).

54. Similar threats toward a colleague and friend of many authors here, Murray Sperber, long a visible critic of the sports system Knight represents, had already prompted Sperber to spend a semester in his hometown of Montreal – the relatively more civilized ambiance of Canada where nobody knows who Knight is). See M. Sperber, 'My Life and Times with Bob Knight', *Chronicle of Higher Education*, 46 (26 May 2000), B7, B8; and C. Leatherman, 'Indiana U. Professors Seek a Strong Defense of Free Speech', ibid., 46 (28 July 2000), A18.

55. Not a new question for those familiar with the critiques, including M. Sperber, *College Sports Inc.: The Athletic Department vs. the University* (New York, NY: Henry Holt, 1990) and his new *Beer and Circus: How Big-time College Sports is Crippling Undergraduate Education* (New York, NY: Henry Holt, 2000); and A. Zimbalist, *Unpaid Professionals: Commercialism and Conflict in Big-time College Sports* (Princeton, NJ: Princeton University Press, 1999).

THE SOCIAL IMAGE IN MEMORY AND REPRESENTATION

1

Cultural Identity, Law, and Baseball

SARAH K. FIELDS

Baseball is integrally linked to the cultural identity of the United States. Because it is its game, the national pastime, baseball is part of what it means to be an American. Yet baseball was traditionally a game for men, for fathers and sons. When society changed, however, and daughters asked to play with their brothers, America was divided over whether or not girls should play baseball or whether their presence would somehow undermine the sport as it related to America's identity. Although the Title IX legislation and the Equal Protection Clause of the U.S. Constitution promised sexual equality, those who controlled youth baseball wanted to exclude girls, and so the girls went to court and sued for the right to try out for youth baseball leagues. The battle over baseball, symbolic of American culture more broadly, was contested fiercely in the courts and the courtroom of public opinion.

BASEBALL AND AMERICAN CULTURAL IDENTITY

For over a hundred years, until the 1950s, no other sport even came close to challenging baseball's supremacy in the American imagination. The game has inspired cultural critics to comment on baseball and its role in society. Walt Whitman said:

> it's our game: that's the chief fact in connection with it: America's game; it has the snap, go, fling of the American atmosphere; it belongs as much to our institutions, fits into them as significantly as our Constitution's laws; is just as important in the sum total of our historic life.[1]

Mark Twain had his Connecticut Yankee in King Arthur's court teach the game to the knights of England. Cynics such as George F. Will have become sentimental about baseball, while academics such as A. Bartlett Giamatti have left the solitude of their ivory towers for the ivy of

Wrigley Field. Baseball is as American as mom and apple pie, and both mom and the pie have been sent to the back burner during a pennant race. But if baseball is America's game, baseball is also a man's game.

Baseball's cultural significance arises in part because it reflects aspects of America's image. Many believe the myth that the game was invented in, by, and for Americans; that, like America itself, baseball was exceptional. A commission in 1907 led by the sporting goods magnate Albert Spalding officially concluded that Abner Doubleday had invented the game in Cooperstown, New York in 1839. This commission countered suggestions that baseball derived from the British game of rounders because, after all, an American power needed an All-American game.[2] Baseball also seemed reflective of a mythologized world, providing both heroes and tragedies. On the one hand, Babe Ruth was a larger than life hero who was molded into the American dream, a poor boy who through his own talent gained fame and fortune. Young boys throughout the country could dream of pulling themselves up by their bootstraps, of being the next Ruth. On the other hand, when heroes failed, when the mighty Casey struck out, when the Boston Red Sox sent Babe Ruth to the Yankees, the tragic side of baseball appealed to Americans' appreciation of struggle: one must overcome obstacles in order to succeed.

Women and girls were not formally banished from the game and the culture as a whole; on the contrary, the occasional female has always crossed the baseline and stepped on to the diamond. In 1866, just one year after the college's establishment, the women of Vassar had formed two teams.[3] In the early 1890s women interested in playing professionally could join Bloomer Girls, barnstormers who played any team willing to compete, and in the years between 1943 and 1954 women could play in the All American Girls Professional Baseball League.[4]

Generally, however, females have not been welcomed with open arms into the dugout. Girls were expected to play other games and not infringe on this aspect of US culture, and those females who tried were subsequently forbidden. For example, after five women joined in a game at the University of Pennsylvania in 1904 the university took swift action and ordered the men not to play on campus and the women not to play at all.[5] In 1928 Margaret Gisolo, aged 14, was a pitcher for Blanford, Indiana's American Legion Junior Baseball team. While playing in the tournament leading to the Junior World Series, Gisolo singled in the game winning run. The opposing and losing team subsequently challenged her eligibility because of her sex. After a lengthy debate among league officials in consultation with the Major League baseball's commissioner Kennesaw Mountain Landis,[6] Gisolo was allowed to play because nothing in the rules stated that the league was only for boys. The next year, however, the league amended the rules and prohibited girls from playing.[7] In 1931 Jackie Mitchell, aged 17, signed a minor league contact. After she struck out Babe Ruth and Lou Gehrig in an exhibition game, Landis voided her contract on the grounds that life in baseball was 'too strenuous' for women. Babe Ruth said that he had no idea what would happen if women were allowed in the game, because 'of course they will never make good. Why? Because they are too delicate. It would kill them to play ball every day.'[8] In 1952, after Eleanor Engle signed a minor league baseball contract, Commissioner Ford Frick issued a rule prohibiting women from playing professional baseball.[9] Generally the rules against women's participation in the game were unwritten – until women tried to play, at which point the rules became written and the American pastime remained a masculine one. 'Baseball is a serious business', wrote a sportswriter in 1974: 'It is also clearly understood to be a man's business.'[10]

As these women and girls struggled to gain access to baseball, the game was being formally propagated among American boys.[11] Little League Baseball began in 1939 as a summer program for boys in Pennsylvania and was intended to teach baseball, Americanism, and masculinity. The organization grew exponentially and by 1964 over 1.25 million boys played in approximately 6,000 leagues in the United States, Canada, Japan, and Australia. In 1964 Congress made the organization a federal corporation when President Lyndon B. Johnson signed the federal charter of incorporation which gave the group tax-exempt status and encouraged the league to 'promote Americanism'. Little League also promoted masculinity. According to the sociologists Lewis Yablonsky and Jonathan Brower, to learn to play baseball was to learn to be a man: 'softball is for girls, old people and those who do not have the skill or inclination to prepare for baseball', they quote an informant in Little League baseball as saying. Baseball requires toughness, dedication, and discipline, all attributes of a good man.[12] Robert Stirrat, a league vice-president in 1974, said that 'we've always assumed baseball was a boy's sport. We think most people have always felt that way. We assume they've accepted baseball as a male prerogative of some sort.'[13] Even the rhetoric of Little League reflected this subtext of masculinity. The official Little League motto stated 'From the ranks of boys who stand now on the morning side of the hill will come the leaders, the future strength and the character of the nation.'[14] In its statement of objectives and purposes, the charter stated their goals were: '(1) To promote ... the interest of boys who will participate in Little League Baseball. (2) To assist ... boys in developing qualities of citizenship, sportsmanship, and manhood.'[15] The language around Little League referred only to males and boys. In ten years Little League would be an American Institution, and the fact that the charter limited that institution to boys would be challenged.

BASEBALL AND THE LAW

Ironically, given the charter's sexist language, during the 1960s America had begun to change both politically and socially. Minority groups, often minorities in terms of power rather than actual numbers, began to demand and to receive recognition of their rights and privileges as citizens. Women in particular were vocal about being treated equally and their demands for access to all aspects of society carried over into the politically more conservative early 1970s. In 1972 President Richard Nixon signed into law Title IX of the United States Civil Code which guaranteed that no educational program or activity receiving federal funds could discriminate on the basis of sex.[16] At the time, Title IX seemed a natural evolution of the women's rights movement from the previous decade. According to records of the Congressional debate at the time, proponents of the law believed that it would force institutions to allow females equal access in the classroom.[17] The enactment of Title IX, however, changed the outline of the athletic landscape: the number of U.S. females playing sports skyrocketed after 1972.

Although Title IX's impact on female athletics was almost immediate, its legal power was undercut even before it was implemented. Congress instructed the Department of Health, Education, and Welfare (HEW) to promulgate regulations defining an enforcement structure for the new law. The regulations HEW created exempted contact sports from Title IX. The regulations stated that:

> where a recipient [of federal funding] operates or sponsors a team in a particular sport for members of one sex but operates or sponsors no such team for members of the other sex, and athletic

opportunities for members of that sex have previously been limited, members of the excluded sex must be allowed to try out for the team offered unless the sport involved is a contact sport.[18]

Nothing in the literal language of Title IX excluded females and contact sport from each other, but over the course of an extended comment period, HEW concluded that the two should be mutually exclusive, or, at the very least, girls should not participate with boys in contact sports. HEW failed, however, to define contact sports adequately, stating simply 'contact sports include boxing, wrestling, rugby, ice hockey, football, basketball and other sports the purpose or major activity of which involved bodily contact'.[19] Baseball was not included, but the list was not exhaustive. Whether baseball was a contact sport would be a matter of much debate when girls began to sue to play America's game.

Despite its legal limitations, Title IX was a crucial piece of legislation for female athletes because it created a clear distinction between contact and non-contact sports, and it carried a great deal of weight in the social imagination if not in any legal reality. Title IX created a clear line between contact and non-contact sport. While the regulations gave girls full access to non-contact sports, they continued to limit girls' opportunities in contact sports. The regulations underlined the old notions (the same reasons given by Babe Ruth and Kennesaw Mountain Landis to keep women out of baseball) that women and girls were not physically capable of playing sports, and particularly tough, contact sports.[20] More importantly, however, Title IX was a social catalyst in a way no legislator could have imagined. In fact, the mere enactment of the law seemed to change Americans' vision of sport because, soon afterward, girls began suing sporting organizations across the country trying to gain access to sports that historically were male-dominated: basketball, football, and, of course, baseball.

Ironically, girls could not usually rely on Title IX as a specific reason for playing baseball.[21] Instead, girls sued under the Equal Protection Clause of the Fourteenth Amendment of the Constitution or their own state constitution's equivalent clause. The Equal Protection Clause guarantees that that 'no state shall … deny to any person within its jurisdiction the equal protection of the laws'.[22] One of the two Amendments that Congress enacted after the Civil War, the Fourteenth Amendment was initially intended to prevent racial discrimination against newly freed slaves. The Amendment was ratified in 1868, yet only after Title IX was enacted was it used extensively in conjunction with female access to sport.

Perhaps contrary to the literal language of the Equal Protection Clause, courts have defined equal protection as treating similarly situated people similarly. If states want to distinguish between different groups of people, they may, but they must have at least what the courts believe to be a legitimate reason and the classification must bear a rational relation to that reasonable state objective.[23] When Title IX distinguished between contact and non-contact sports, the legislation implied that Congress was willing to differentiate on the basis of sex for various categories of sport, which meant that the courts could as well. The questions the courts would face was whether baseball was a contact sport and, if so, whether girls could be excluded solely because of their sex.

THE BASEBALL CASES

The legal floodgates opened in 1973 when the first of five pivotal baseball cases was decided.[24] Pamela Magill was ten years old and she wanted to play in the Avonworth Baseball Conference (ABC) in her western Pennsylvania hometown, but her application was rejected because the league did not allow girls to play. Her parents sued the ABC on her behalf, claiming that her equal protection rights had been violated.[25] In order to claim protection under the Fourteenth Amendment, a plaintiff must establish that the defendant, if not a direct branch of the state or local government, is acting as a representative of that government because private groups can discriminate on almost any grounds they choose. Without some evidence that the defendant is acting under the auspices of state law, the Fourteenth Amendment does not apply. The ABC claimed that they were not a state actor but rather a private organization, and the federal district court judge agreed.[26] Had the judge stopped there, the decision would have made sense. Determining state action is rather subjective, but the judge had ample legal precedents to justify the decision and, with a decision at this point, the case would not be terribly interesting.[27] Determining whether the court really believed its decision or whether it was merely an excuse to exclude girls from baseball would have been impossible.

But the district court did not stop there. The judge wrote over a page of dicta discussing how the case would turn out if the ABC were acting under color of law.[28] This language, especially the language considering Magill's Fourteenth Amendment claim, indicated that the judge personally believed that girls should not play baseball. The ABC had argued that they excluded girls for two reasons: (1) girls would get hurt playing, and (2) if girls played, boys would quit.[29] Although the court did not address the second justification, the very fact that the ABC suggested it as a rationale is significant. The ABC believed that it was more important for American boys to play baseball than for girls to. Thus the league believed that it was better to deliberately exclude one-half of the youth in the population than to risk having a few boys voluntarily leave the league. The court, however, focused on the league's first claim: girls would get hurt if they played because baseball was a contact sport.

The directors of the ABC believed that baseball was a contact sport, and the court agreed. The judge explained this conclusion, noting that 'there was no question that a runner who tried to beat a throw to the plate was frequently blocked by a catcher. The contact is severe if not violent. The directors spoke of their concern with wild pitchers and, of course, we know the consequences of trying to steal second or third.'[30]

The court never commented on medical evidence, relying instead on the testimony of the directors of the league being sued, trusting that its wise patriarchs would know what was best for their players. Further the court seemed unaware of the irony of claiming that 'of course, we know the consequences'. The judge could only be speaking to males who had played baseball because a person who had never tried to steal a base would not really know what the consequences would be. Because this decision would exclude girls, it would exclude girls and women from even understanding the language of the decision.[31]

The second major baseball decision arose after 11-years-old Maria Pepe won a position on her local Little League team. When the national organization, Little League Baseball, Inc. (LLB) learned of her success, they ordered her removed from the team or they claimed that they would revoke the team's charter (causing the team to lose insurance, funding, and access to other LLB teams).[32] When the team excluded Maria the local chapter of the National Organization for Women (NOW) sued LLB for violating her equal protection rights as guaranteed under the New Jersey constitution. After Examiner Sylvia B. Pressler ordered LLB to admit girls aged eight to 12 into the league, LLB appealed.[33] The verdict of the appellate court was anxiously awaited by Little League officials across the country, some of whom seemed to see a female conspiracy to take over the sport. One official in Houston, explaining why his league would wait for the appellate decision before changing their policy, said that 'it was a lady judge who ruled in favor of the girls. The case hasn't moved up to male judges yet.'[34]

The Superior Court of New Jersey upheld the lower court order, and in the decision the court took the time to describe and comment upon the LLB arguments against girls' participation.[35] LLB argued primarily that girls were too physically frail to play baseball. Unlike the defendant in Magill, however, LLB relied on medical evidence to prove their point. Unfortunately, that evidence was based on research into bone strength in Japanese cadavers of people between the ages of 18 and 80. NOW's medical expert countered with the argument that boys and girls between the ages of eight and 12 are physiologically very similar. LLB's expert claimed that girls who suffered contact with the chest or the breast would have breast cancer as an adult. NOW's expert completely disagreed. The court concluded that NOW's evidence that girls were physically capable of playing baseball was more compelling. LLB also argued that boys and girls needed 'islands of privateness' [*sic*] to engage in same-sex social activities or they would risk later psychological problems. NOW argued that sex-integrated baseball would, in fact, teach girls and boys to work together. The court thought both theories far-fetched but rejected LLB's suggestion that girls should not play for psychological reasons.[36]

LLB also made a series of arguments trying to justify segregation that the court thought particularly unpersuasive. LLB claimed that coed baseball would threaten the bodily privacy of the girls; for example, if a girl were injured, her presumably male coach would have to give first aid and hence perhaps touch her. The court called this claim 'frivolous'. LLB claimed that after puberty girls would lose interest in baseball and would, in fact, be unable to play well because of their physiological changes; therefore LLB thought it best not to waste time teaching the game to those who would not play for long. Further, if girls were squandering the coaches' efforts, the boys who could gain 'permanent baseball skills' would suffer. LLB generously encouraged girls to take up a sport they could enjoy for the rest of their lives. The court was no more persuaded by this argument than by any other. The court noted that the purpose of sex-discrimination legislation was to 'emancipate the female sex from stereotyped conceptions as to its limitations embedded in our mores but discordant with current rational views'. The court saw no reason not to teach girls to play and found no evidence that boys would suffer if girls did join the team.[37]

Finally, LLB pointed to its national charter as evidence. LLB suggested that the charter called for improving the qualities of 'citizenship, sportsmanship, and manhood', and they argued that the admission of females to the league would foil that effort. The court equated manhood with maturity of character and concluded that girls too should have these qualities developed. The court also rejected LLB's argument that no court should tamper with Congress's decree that LLB be for boys. The court noted that Congress could not create legal corporations, and thus the charter was more symbolic than significant, and that, although Congress seemed to deem LLB for boys, no evidence indicated an effort to exclude girls. Therefore the New Jersey court rejected LLB's arguments and ordered them to admit girls.[38]

After this decision many in American society were distraught. *Newsweek* reported that 'the battle has reached new levels of chauvinism and near hysteria' and, referring to LLB's safety concerns, added that the 'real "traumatic impact" in the case was on the adults'.[39] An official with the New Jersey chapter of NOW claimed, just two years after the emotional *Roe* v. *Wade* decision legalized abortion, that 'this particular issue is as fraught with emotional backlash as any I've ever seen'.[40] The importance of baseball as both a man's game and as America's game was highlighted by the violent reaction of the public to the court's decision. Many feared what would happen if girls were to intrude on a masculine preserve.[41] While LLB considered appealing to the New Jersey Supreme Court, most individual teams voted to suspend play rather than admit girls. Two thousand teams in New Jersey alone refused to play if they had to open the dugout to girls.[42] The New Jersey Assembly was presented with 50,000 signatures on a petition demanding a law to keep girls off the diamond. After an emotional debate the bill was lost by three votes.[43] The *New York Times Magazine* emphasized that the battle was about sex as much as baseball: 'the challenge [of girls' gaining access to baseball] is not merely to male supremacy but to an established institution in American life [Little League]'.[44] The sportswriter Frank Deford, trying to explain the emotional outcry, wrote that 'the real dispute is social'; girls were not just 'monkeying with men's baseball but with men's childhood'.[45]

Despite the legal precedent of the New Jersey decision, or perhaps because of the social reaction to it, the third major baseball decision which was released two months later disagreed with the New Jersey decision. The U.S. District Court of Rhode Island decided in 1974 that the Darlington Little League could exclude ten-years-old Allison 'Pookie' Fortin from the league because of her sex.[46] Allison had sued on equal protection grounds and the court reached a decision quickly. The league was a state actor, the court ruled, because the public fields were designed for the league and controlled by it. The court added, however, that the league was correct: baseball was a contact sport and girls would get hurt playing with boys. The court noted the Magill decision's dicta and cited it with approval; safety, the court said, was a legitimate reason for the gender-based classification.[47]

On appeal, however, the United States Court of Appeals First Circuit disagreed. Ironically, after the lower court decision in 1974, Congress had amended the Little League Baseball charter, striking out the words 'boys' and 'manhood' and inserting 'young people'. Little League Baseball had given up the fight and admitted girls.[48] The Darlington Little League, however, refused to surrender and also refused to assure the court that the league would admit girls, despite the shift in the national organization's position. Hence the First Circuit heard the appeal and ruled in favor of Pookie Fortin.

Unlike the lower court, the First Circuit dedicated much of the written decision to describing the trial's testimony and to explaining which evidence was the most compelling and why. The debate in this case was strikingly similar to that in the Magill case and the New Jersey NOW decision. Darlington argued in essence that baseball was too dangerous for girls. The court summarized the evidence from both sides. Pookie's father, a physician, testified that his daughter was physically fit and capable of playing the game. The plaintiff's expert, a pediatrician, testified that girls and boys from the age of eight to 12 were physically similar, with girls, in fact, often being bigger and stronger at that age. Another expert, a radiologist, presented evidence that girls' bones were no different from boys' and that structurally no skeletal reasons suggested that girls were more prone to injury. Darlington's expert witness, an orthopedist at Brown University who worked overwhelmingly with male athletes and who had never actually seen girls play baseball, testified to the contrary. He believed that girls could not throw overhand, that girls' bones were more likely to be damaged by exercise, and that the pelvis of girls made their gait unstable. The court condemned Darlington's expert, noting that the doctor's opinions 'rested mostly on the observation that girls, being more sedentary, were likely to be in poorer condition than boys'. The court also questioned whether the doctor's beliefs rested on scientific study or his personal views, which, he apparently admitted, included that 'it was the normal activity of a young lady to keep off baseball fields and play with dolls'. After examining Darlington's expert, the First Circuit questioned the lower court's decision to ignore the plaintiff's experts whom the First Circuit had found compelling. The First Circuit also noted that girls were playing baseball with the blessing of Congress and their parents – neither of whom would deliberately endanger American girls. Finally, because Darlington allowed physically-disabled boys to play in the league, the court determined the physical dangers of playing in it to be minimal.[49]

After dismissing the physical safety arguments, the court of appeals also dismissed Darlington's other justifications for excluding girls. Darlington claimed to be concerned that the presence of girls would detract from the quality of the game and from training boys with a baseball future. At the same time, Darlington feared that if girls played, boys would quit. Further, if girls did play (assuming that enough boys stayed to field a team), they would get hurt, and they and the male coaches would be embarrassed by the need for first aid. Finally, apparently believing that Pookie was a bizarre aberration from the typical American girl, Darlington suggested that girls really wanted to play with girls and not boys. The court, citing the New Jersey decision with approval, rejected all these arguments as being 'archaic and overbroad generalizations' and devoted less than a paragraph to dismissing them.[50]

The last major baseball decision came less than a year later in 1976. These earlier decisions opened Little League baseball to girls, but the final one opened the door for girls to play on their high school boys' teams. Jo Ann Carnes was a high school senior in Wartburg, Tennessee, who tried out for her school team and was selected. The Tennessee Secondary School Athletic Association (TSSAA), however, told the school that she could not play because the TSSAA regulations stated that baseball was a contact sport and hence coed teams were not allowed. Carnes, just as the girls before her, filed suit claiming that her equal protection rights were violated.[51]

The TSSAA argued that they had enacted the rule for two reasons: (1) to protect females from the physical dangers of contact, and (2) to protect female sport programs from male intrusion. The federal district court was unimpressed with the relationship between the rule and the rationale. The judge found the first justification to be overbroad, noting that some girls were likely to be physically capable of playing. The judge emphasized that even Carnes's coach believed that she was a competent player. The judge also questioned whether or not baseball really was a contact sport, given that collisions were infrequent and often incidental or accidental. With regard to the TSSAA's claim that they were protecting female teams, the judge dismissed that assertion by noting that no female baseball teams existed for males to take over. Carnes, the court asserted, either played baseball with the boys or not at all. Not playing, the court believed, was a violation of the Equal Protection Clause of the Constitution, and Carnes was back on the team.[52]

CULTURAL IDENTITY, BASEBALL, AND SEX

The battle over baseball was fought on multiple fronts in the courtroom and in the arena of public opinion. Regardless of the location of the skirmish though, the arguments were similar. No one who wanted to keep baseball as a masculine institution suggested that girls be excluded for any reason but their sex.

The underlying position of supporters of all-male baseball was that the game was a contact sport which that meant girls could be excluded because they would get hurt playing it. Although the legal definition of baseball as a contact sport was important in arguing their case in court, emphasizing that the leagues wanted only to protect frail young females from the risks of a physically dangerous game was important as well in trying to sway public opinion. To this end, the defendants argued that girls did not have the right bone structure to play safely and further that they would get breast cancer from any contact. For these arguments the defendants relied, although often unsuccessfully, on old medical myths and unsubstantiated medical opinions. Some in the public and the courts, however, accepted these views. The Little League manager and sociologist David Q. Voight wrote in 1974 that, although his teams never had any female players, he would accept them if they wanted to play; however, the league president worried that, if girls played, the league would 'get sued if they [females] get breast cancer from getting tagged out on the boobs'.[53] Further, the New Jersey State Assemblyman Christopher Jackman introduced the bill to keep girls off the baseball diamond so that they would not get 'hurt in their vital parts'.[54] Little League's contention that baseball was a dangerous contact sport was ironic, however, because of its own 1967 study which determined an injury rate of 1.96 per cent – injury defined as that sufficient enough to warrant medical attention. Dr Creighton Hale, the Little League executive who testified from 1973 onward that girls were too frail to play, had characterized the injury rate in 1967 as 'low'.[55]

Youth league officials, however, did not really seem as anxious about the collisions between players as about the potential contact between female players and their male coaches. A surprisingly major concern was how a female player should be congratulated for a good play. Apparently, patting a boy on the buttocks was the most traditional manner of letting him know that he had done well. Players and coaches worried about what to do with a female. One coach in New Jersey lamented to his star player – who happened to be a girl, 'I can't even pat you on the backside'.[56] A 12-years-old boy told of his conflicting feelings after his female teammate hit a home run. He wanted to pat her on the butt like a guy, but 'I didn't want her to think I was getting fresh', so he patted her shoulder instead.[57] Creighton Hale, the Little League executive and PhD in physical education, argued that the league must exclude girls because

> it just wouldn't be proper for coaches to pat girls on the rear end the way they naturally do boys. And suppose a girl gets hurt on the legs? Why that's not going to go over – some grown man rubbing a little girl's leg.[58]

If girls played, the league reasoned, they would get hurt, and everyone would be embarrassed if a man (because presumably only men would want to coach baseball) gave first aid to a girl. In fact, when Union, New Jersey's Little League program accepted girls, they did so with a caveat: if a girl was on the field, her parent or guardian must be in the stands so that if the girl were injured 'coaches will not have to suffer the "embarrassment" of unbuttoning a girl's uniform'.[59]

In case the physiological arguments failed to work, opponents of coed baseball often relied on psychological arguments. When Dr Joyce Brothers, a popular psychologist in the early 1970s, argued that boys and girls needed homosocial activity to develop islands of 'privateness' in order to become well-adjusted adults, Little League baseball cheered and quickly incorporated her theory into their arguments.[60]

In this same vein, that girls and boys needed separate play time, youth baseball suggested that, if girls were allowed to play on all-boy baseball squads, the entire system of girls' sports would collapse. Thus a few, particularly athletic girls would be able to play, but the average, presumably non-athletic girls, would have no outlet. Others, outside the leagues, agreed. For example, Dr Melvin L. Thornton argued that girls should participate in more endurance-building forms of exercise to improve their health. Baseball, he believed, did not provide enough exercise. He either did not care about boys' health since he never suggested the disbanding of youth baseball or he assumed that boys in baseball engaged in other, more strenuous activities. Further, Thornton feared that, if communities saw a few girls in youth baseball, they would claim that they had programs adequate to meet girls' physical needs. He suggested that 'there is no game for the other 230 girls in town who cannot swing a bat as smoothly as Dorothy Dombrowski or who, unlike Ellen Vetromile, don't care about being as good or better than the boys down the block.'[61]

Despite youth baseball's self-righteous assertions that they were protecting little girls from the rigors of the game and their contention that girls' sport generally would collapse if a few girls played youth baseball, the real concern with girls' entering youth baseball was about what that would do to the boys playing and to the manliness of the game itself. Many seemed concerned about somehow diminishing the experience for the male players. After 13-years-old Yvonne Burch was removed from a Babe Ruth League team in North Carolina because the national organization threatened to revoke the local league's charter, the league president said, 'it was a matter of depriving either Yvonne or 200 boys.'[62] The fact that Yvonne simply represented countless girls being deprived never occurred to him. On the other hand, a vice-president of a New Jersey Little League system said 'most of us didn't want the girls playing but we figured rather than penalize 500 or so boys by not having any baseball at all, we would let girls play.'[63] The leagues and many in the public believed that the girls on the team would diminish the quality of the coaching for the other male players who had a better chance of playing longer and, at least theoretically, professionally. One manager claimed that coaching girls was a 'waste of time' because when they got older they would stop playing, to do presumably 'girl-things'.[64] For leagues such as the Darlington Little League that allowed physically-handicapped boys to play, to argue that girls were too physically frail to play or that teaching them the game was pointless because they would never play professionally seemed particularly illogical.

Another concern of Little League Baseball officials reflected the fear of what admitting girls to the game would do to the male volunteers. Accounts in the *New York Times* from 1973 to 1978 repeatedly refer to Little League's fears that the volunteer coaches and administrators would quit because they did not want to work with girls. The volunteers themselves were quoted as saying they did not want the government nor the courts to tell them whom they could or could not coach. Many volunteers thought that their rights were being violated. A *New York Times* article suggested that after girls 'muscled their way' into Little League Baseball, 'a lot of middle-aged men in windbreakers caught a glimpse of their future and didn't like what they saw.'[65]

A major fear for youth baseball and for the men who ran the leagues was that the presence of girls would lower the masculinity of the game and the masculine ego of the boys who played. Robert Stirrat, a Little League Baseball vice-president, argued that 'baseball is traditionally a boy's game. To admit girls would certainly cripple the program.'[66] If girls played, boys might leave and that would be the end of America's pastime. A New Jersey Little League manager said:

> I want girls to play ball, and I would have been glad to take an all-girl team in a separate division. What I'm afraid of is that if you have a girl who is good and plays more than some of the boys, it's bad for the boys. The kid's friends may get on him and say, 'Hey, how come a girl is playing more than you?'[67]

Another manager said, 'I think in most instances men are afraid the girls are going to play better than their sons or compete better than boys in general.'[68] Rather than risk jarring their sons' egos, many New Jersey teams chose not to play at all.

As violent as the reaction was by many to the courts' decisions, many were shocked by the opposition to girls' playing America's game. Judge George Gelman, a former Little League manager, ordered Ridgefield (NJ) Boys Athletic Organization to allow an 11-years-old female short stop to play in 1974. Counsel for Ridgefield announced that the league would fold first, and Judge Gelman exclaimed from the bench, 'I don't understand. What's the big deal?'[69] Governor Brendan Thomas Byrne of New Jersey, whose state was at the center of much of the turmoil, voiced his support of 'qualified' girls in baseball, adding, 'I know very few boys

– including my own son – who would object to being beaten out by a better girl.'[70] The Martha Griffith Little League Bill was introduced in March 1974 in the U.S. Congress to open up the league to girls.[71] Frank Deford, a well-respected sportswriter, openly mocked youth baseball's arguments against girls on the diamond.[72]

CONCLUSION

Today, more than 25 years after the first case for girls to play was decided, change in the sex balance of baseball has been slow. When Little League opened the door for girls, they emphasized that the change simply meant girls could try out. 'The girls,' said a league official, 'would have to prove equal competency in baseball skills, physical endowments, and other attributes.'[73] This statement set the tone with the inference that only the exceptional girl could play with the boys, and, indeed, boys still vastly outnumber girls in youth baseball. As late as 1987 sociologists studied little league in order to 'describe and analyse how the sport makes men out of boys'.[74] Only a handful of women have played college ball and only one professional female team, the Silver Bullets, survived for any length of time or with any publicity.[75] Softball is more generally considered a girls' sport, and as Title IX and equal protection cases more clearly underline, in the prevailing philosophy of 'separate but equal' with regard to sporting programs softball is usually baseball's female counterpart.[76]

The struggle to get girls into baseball was hotly contested in numerous jurisdictions because Americans felt passionately about their national pastime. Some girls felt strongly about playing Babe Ruth's game, and other people felt just as strongly that the Babe should be the only babe in baseball. Little League teams in New Jersey rebelled against the court orders and the national organization mandate for years.[77] Baseball spawned more lawsuits in America about whether or not girls could play the game than any other sport. The lawsuits arose because America's identity was linked to baseball and to allow females access to America's game was to foreshadow female access to all aspects of American culture, and not all of America was ready to change without a fight.

NOTES

1. H. Trauble (ed.), *With Walt Whitman in Camden*, Vol. 4 (New York, NY: Mitchell Kennerley, 1915), p.508.
2. See B.G. Rader, *American Sports: From the Age of Folk Games to the Age of Televised Sports* (Englewood Cliffs, NJ: Prentice Hall, 2nd edn, 1990) and A. Guttmann, *A Whole New Ball Game* (Chapel Hill, NC: University of North Carolina Press, 1988).
3. B. Gregorich, *Women at Play: The Story of Women in Baseball* (New York, NY: Harcourt Brace, 1993).
4. S.E. Johnson, *When Women Played Hardball* (Seattle, WA: Seal Press, 1994) and W.C. Madden, *The Women of the All-American Girls Professional Baseball League: A Biographical Dictionary* (North Carolina: McFarland, 1997) describe the history of the league and its evolution from softball to baseball.
5. Gregorich, *Women at Play*, p.4.
6. Judge Kennesaw Mountain Landis was named baseball commissioner after the infamous 'Black Sox' scandal in 1919 when members of the Chicago White Sox were accused of throwing the World Series. Landis was charged with cleaning up major league baseball and its image: he was given almost absolute authority over the league.
7. Gregorich, *Women at Play*, pp.60–5.
8. Ibid., pp.66–71.
9. M.L. Anderson, 'A Legal History and Analysis of Sex Discrimination in Athletics: Mixed Gender Competition, 1970–1987' (PhD thesis, University of Minnesota, 1989).
10. J.B. Treaster, 'Town's Little League Reluctantly Signs Three Girls', *New York Times* (27 April 1974), 33.
11. Boys played baseball long before Little League; Little League was a national organization that provided even more structure to the youth game. See R. Pruter, 'Youth Baseball in Chicago, 1868–1890: Not Always Sandlot Ball', *Journal of Sport History*, 26 (1999), 1–28.
12. L. Yablonsky and J. Brower, *The Little League Game: How Kids, Coaches, and Parents Really Play It* (New York, NY: Times Books, 1979), p.35.
13. J.B. Treaster, 'Girls a Hit in Debut on Diamond', *New York Times* (25 March 1974), 67.
14. Yablonsky and Brower, *Little League*, pp.4–6.
15. Anderson, 'Legal History', pp.170–1.
16. Education Amendments of 1972, Publ. L. No. 92-318, §§ 901-09, 86 Stat. 235 (codified at 20 U.S.C. §§ 1681–1688 (1990)) [hereinafter Title IX]. Only after Congress enacted, over President George Bush's veto, the Civil Rights Restoration Act of 1987 (1988 Amendments) did Title IX clearly apply to all public institution sporting venues. Pub. L. 100-259, 102 Stat. 28 (codified at 20 U.S.C. § 1687 (1990)) [hereinafter Civil Rights Restoration Act]. Title IX's Canadian parallel, the 1982 Canadian Charter of Rights and Freedoms, was used by 13-year-old Justine Blaney for the opportunity to play boys' hockey in Ontario. 'Girl Wins Appeal to Play Boy's Hockey', *Calgary Herald* (5 December 1988), A7.
17. D. Heckman, 'Women and Athletics: A Twenty Year Retrospective on Title IX', *University of Miami Entertainment and Sports Law Review*, 9 (1992), 9, n.30. Title IX was adopted without a formal hearing or committee report. Its legislative history has been deciphered by scholars and courts from floor debate recorded in the *Congressional Record*.
18. 34 C.F.R. § 106.41(b) (1991).
19. Ibid.
20. See H. Lenskyj, *Out of Bounds: Women, Sport and Sexuality* (Toronto: Women's Press, 1986) for an analysis of medical evidence to exclude women from sport.
21. Only one suit used Title IX as a grounds to gain access to baseball. In *Croteau v. Fair*, 686 F. Supp.552 (E.D. Va. 1988) the court ruled that Title IX did not guarantee a spot on a team, merely the right to try out. Julie Croteau had been allowed to try out for her high school baseball team and had been excluded, the court concluded, because of her skill level and not because of her sex. Interestingly, Croteau and her parents went to court without legal representation which might explain why they alone relied on Title IX and why they neglected to file an equal protection claim as well.
22. U.S. Constitution, amend. 14, sec. 1 (1868).

23. The U.S. Supreme Court was slow to determine what level of scrutiny sexual classifications should receive. Some classifications, like race, are more strictly scrutinized, meaning that for a law based on racial classifications to survive the law must be necessary to attaining a compelling governmental interest. In 1976 the Court finally seemed to settle on an intermediate level of scrutiny for sexual classifications; a law must be substantially related to attaining an important governmental interest. *Craig v. Boren*, 429 U.S. 190 (1976). Most of the baseball cases, however, were decided before the Court made this decision and hence the baseball courts rely on the lowest level of scrutiny, a classification rationally related to a reasonable governmental objective.

24. Two branches of the U.S. court system exist, state and federal. State courts hear cases dealing with state law and federal courts with federal law; however, state courts often rely on the federal courts' interpretations of the federal constitution to interpret their own state constitution; thus to interpret the equal protection clause of their own state constitution, state courts rely on the Supreme Court's interpretation of the federal equal protection clause. In the federal courts a case is tried first in a district court, then appealed to the court of appeals, and then ultimately to the Supreme Court. Any higher court can affirm a lower court decision by refusing to hear the case. State courts have a parallel hierarchy, although the names sometimes differ.

25. *Magill v. Avonworth* Baseball Conference, 364 F. Supp.1212 (W.D. Pa., 1973).

26. *Magill*, 1213–16.

27. Other baseball cases were decided on the grounds that there was no state action involved, see, for instance, *King v. Little League Baseball*, 505 F.2d 264 (6th Cir. 1974) and *McDonald v. New Palestine Youth Baseball League, Inc.*, 561 F. Supp.1167 (S.D. Ind. 1983).

28. Dicta is language that is superfluous or unnecessary to discussing the legal question at hand. Judges are supposed to answer only the question asked; if they can make a legal determination (as opposed to deciding a factual issue) they should do so. This case was vacated and remanded without opinion by the Third Circuit Court of Appeals, 497 F.2d 921 (3rd Cir. 1974) and was later decided on the grounds that there was no state action. 516 F.2d 1328 (3rd Cir. 1975). The district court judge seemed to have learned a lesson about avoiding dicta.

29. *Magill*, 1216.

30. Ibid.

31. M.J. Yelnosky's 'If You Write it, (S)he Will Come: Judicial Decisions, Metaphors, Baseball, and "the Sex Stuff"', *Connecticut Law Review*, 28 (1996), 813–54 explores whether or not baseball metaphors in judicial opinions exclude female readers. Yelnosky concludes, in part because of girls' increased participation in baseball in recent years, that they do not.

32. Anderson, 'Legal History', p.170.

33. 'Cathy at the Bat?', *Newsweek* (1 April 1974), 53. The New Jersey court system required that the first hearing be in front of an examiner from the state's Division of Civil rights. The decision could then be appealed, as it was, in front of the Superior Court. The examiner's decision was binding as law until the appeal.

34. 'Cathy at the Bat?'.

35. On appeal, Little League Baseball chose to focus their argument on the idea that the baseball diamond was a place of public accommodation, which, according to New Jersey law, would have allowed discrimination on the basis of sex. The court rejected this argument. *National Organization for Women v. Little League Baseball, Inc.*, 318 A.2d. 33 (NJ Super. 1974).

36. Ibid., 35–6.

37. Ibid., 38–9. The dissenting judge, however, accepted this last argument that girls would waste the coaches' time and that boys who could have a baseball future would suffer. Ibid., 43.

38. Ibid., 39–41.

39. 'Cathy at the Bat?', 53.

40. F. Deford, 'Now Georgy-Porgy Runs Away', *Sports Illustrated* (22 April 1974), 26.

41. See Anderson, 'Legal History', pp.180–5.

42. L.C. Pogrebin, 'Baseball Diamonds Are a Girl's Best Friend', *Ms.* (September 1974), 80.

43. 'Say It Ain't So, Flo', *Newsweek* (24 June 1974), 75 and R.W. Peterson, '"You Really Hit That One, Man!", Said the Little League Boy to the Little League Girl', *New York Times Magazine* (19 May 1974), 36.

44. Peterson, '"You Really Hit That One, Man!"', 36.

45. Deford, 'Georgy-Porgy', 30.
46. *Fortin* v. *Darlington Little League, Inc. (American Division)*, 376 F. Supp.473 (D. R.I., 1974).
47. Ibid., 475–9.
48. *Fortin* v. *Darlington Little League, Inc. (American Division)*, 514 F. 2d 344, 346 (1st Cir. 1975) [hereinafter *Fortin II*]. LLB might have given up because of 22 class action suits against them throughout the country. After LLB admitted girls, most of these suits were dismissed as moot, see for example, *Rappaport* v. *Little League Baseball*, 65 F.R.D. 515 (D. Del., 1975).
49. *Fortin II*, 348–50.
50. Ibid., 351.
51. *Carnes* v. *Tennessee Secondary School Athletic Association*, 415 F. Supp.569 (E.D. Tenn. 1976). In 1973 the American Civil Liberties Union (ACLU) threatened to sue on behalf of a girl who wanted to play catcher on her New Jersey High School team but was banned because of New Jersey Interscholastic Athletic Association Rules. 'Girl Goes to Bat Against Ban in Sports', *New York Times* (11 April 1973), 99. After her local school board ordered the coach to give her a try-out, the player demurred, saying she did not want special treatment. R. Phalon, 'Girl Wins but Rejects the Right to Tryout for Baseball Team', *New York Times* (27 April 1973), 72.
52. *Carnes*, 572. By the time the order was granted, only one game remained in the regular season.
53. D.Q. Voight, *A Little League Journal* (Bowling Green, OH: Bowling Green University Popular Press, 1974), p.62.
54. Deford, 'Georgy-Porgy', 26.
55. Yablonsky and Brower, *Little League*, p.159.
56. M. Chass, 'When a Girl Picks Baseball over Ballet, Her Team Gains', *New York Times* (6 June 1977), 34.
57. L. Ames, 'Girls Playing Heads Up Ball', ibid. (17 July 1977), xxii.
58. Deford, 'Georgy-Porgy', 28.
59. Treaster, 'Town's Little League', 33.
60. Deford, 'Georgy-Porgy', 29.
61. M.L. Thornton, 'Healthy Criticism: Little League Baseball: It's Not Good Enough for Girls', *Today's Health* (July 1974), 6. In the author notes, the reader learns that 'Mrs Thornton runs a mile a day. The author himself covers two miles daily, at a brisk pace'. Ibid., 72.
62. See 'People in Sports', *New York Times* (17 May 1973), 58; (26 May 1973), 22.
63. Treaster, 'Town's Little League', 33.
64. Deford, 'Georgy-Porgy', 36.
65. J.B. Treaster, 'Little League Baseball Proving Just a First Step for Girls Athletes', *New York Times* (23 June 1974), 40.
66. L. Saul, 'Little League Gets a New Umpire: the Courts', ibid. (24 February 1974), 63.
67. Peterson, '"You Really Hit That One, Man!"', 37.
68. J.B. Treaster, 'Girls a Hit in Debut on Diamond', *New York Times* (25 March 1974), 67.
69. Deford, 'Georgy-Porgy', 26.
70. W.B. Waggoner, 'Byrne Declares "Qualified" Girls Should Play Little League Baseball', *New York Times* (28 March 1974), 81.
71. 'Little League Battles', *The Sportswoman* (March–April 1974), 7.
72. Deford, 'Georgy-Porgy', 26–37.
73. 'Say It Ain't So, Flo', 75.
74. Gary A. Fine, *With the Boys: Little League Baseball and Pre-Adolescent Culture* (Chicago, IL: University of Chicago Press, 1987), p.1.
75. See M.J. McPhillips, comment, '"Girls of Summer": A Comprehensive Analysis of the Past, Present, and Future of Women in Baseball and a Roadmap to Litigating a Successful Gender Discrimination Case', *Seton Hall Journal of Sport Law*, 6 (1996), 301–39 for a comprehensive history of the Silver Bullets and a discussion of the women who played ball in college.
76. Not all regions, however, equated softball and baseball. In 1977 the New York State Board of Regents allowed girls to try out for baseball and soccer, distinguishing these sports from 'more vigorous contact sports' such as those enumerated in Title IX's regulations. A.L. Goldman 'Regents Let Girls Join Boys' Teams', *New York Times* (19 November 1977), 1. Also, in 1989, a West Virginia court rejected the West Virginia Secondary School Activities Commission (WVSSAC) theory that softball was substantially equivalent to baseball. The WVSSAC had

prevented Erin Israel, a Little League product, from playing on her high school baseball team, even after she had made the team after open try-outs because the WVSSAC said she could play on her school's softball team instead. The court, echoing the attitude of most baseball and softball players, ordered the WVSSAC to allow girls to try out for baseball or to create all-girl teams because the two games were not the same. *Israel* v. *West Virginia Secondary Schools Activities Commission*, 388 S.E. 2d 480 (W.Va. 1989).

77. From 1974 to 1976, the *New York Times* reported on six occasions that the federal courts and the State Division of Civil Rights was threatening Little League teams for non-compliance.

2

Pride and Prejudice:
Reflecting on Sport Heroes, National Identity, and Crisis in Canada

STEVEN J. JACKSON and PAM PONIC

If there is such a thing as a collective social memory then 1988 will undoubtedly feature prominently upon the historical sporting landscape of Canada. While there were a multitude of sporting moments, spectacles, and celebrities that defined the year, including the Calgary Winter Olympics, arguably the lives of two men came to symbolize what has been described as a crisis of national identity.[1] While their individual stories reveal much about their significance to Canada it was the context in which media images and narratives emerged that truly confirmed their place within the Canadian collective consciousness. We speak, of course, of the 'Great One', ice hockey star Wayne Gretzky and the 'Nowhere Man', track athlete Ben Johnson;[2] two very different athletes whose lives in 1988 and beyond provide key cases for an examination of the power and politics of national identity. In Canada in 1988 Wayne Gretzky and Ben Johnson represented episodes of *pride* and *prejudice* within an evolving national social memory.

This chapter explores the media narratives that have constructed a particular social memory for Canadians based upon the lives of two sporting celebrities, one viewed as a hero, the other as a villain. Specifically, we examine the way in which a number of media discourses worked to define a national identity in crisis by relating the fate of particular individuals to wider political, economic, and cultural issues. The role of the media as it interprets and represents particular events highlights the contested nature of social memory.[3] We begin by outlining the context of Canada in 1988 because it is essential for understanding how and why these athletes continue to figure so prominently within the popular consciousness. The significance of context is highlighted by Ben-Amos and Weissberg[4] who note that, 'Memories are shaped within social frameworks – events can be recalled only if they fit into a framework of contemporary interests.' In particular, we highlight the meanings, politics, and effects of crisis, a central concept in the construction of Canadian collective social memory.

SPORT HEROES, NATIONAL IDENTITY, AND SOCIAL MEMORY

As in many other countries, sports heroes in Canada are viewed as representatives of the nation state and play an important role in the social construction of national identity. Historically, perhaps the first such hero to have an impact on Canada's social memory was Edward 'Ned' Hanlan, 'The Boy in Blue'. Hanlan rose to prominence by virtue of his absolute domination of professional rowing between 1877 and 1884. The significance of his international success and his role in defining Canadian social memory is expressed by Metcalfe:

> Canada was a young country struggling to find an identity independent of Britain and the United States. Certainly within the world at large, Canada was regarded as a colony of the mother country, subservient to it with no identity of its own. ... Within Canada itself, the victories of Hanlan, like the first Canada–Russia series, provided a symbol that transcended provincial boundaries and gave the different parts of the country concrete examples of something Canadian. ... It is difficult to judge the real impact of Ned Hanlan on the majority of Canadians, yet he was the most important single symbol of Canada at that time – the greatest salesman of Canada.[5]

Metcalfe's description of Hanlan highlights the importance of one athlete's achievements and notoriety in defining a Canadian national identity. Notably, one of the reasons why he was so significant was because he provided one means by which Canadians could define themselves as different from the British and Americans. As we shall discuss shortly, over one hundred years later the same claims can be made about Wayne Gretzky and Ben Johnson. Metcalfe makes one further comment about Hanlan that is relevant to our study. He suggests that Hanlan's fame was at least partially attributable to the coinciding growth of industrial capitalism and its technological advances, including the national media.[6] Now, over a century later, the media remain just as, if not more, significant in the shaping of how the nation defines and remembers itself.

CONTEXT AND CANADIAN IDENTITY IN 1988

To suggest that there was a crisis of national identity in 1988 that has in some way shaped the Canadian social memory requires at least two issues to be explored. First, we consider the factors that supposedly contributed to the crisis. Secondly, we shall explore the meaning and significance of crisis in shaping social memory. With respect to the first, we suggest that a good starting point is a contextualization of the political, economic, and cultural setting in 1988.

Several seemingly distinct yet interrelated factors may have contributed to Canada's 'year of crisis'.[7] Among these are Canada's popularized historical insecurities about its cultural uniqueness. Dwarfed by its neighbor, the world's most powerful nation, Canada's identity complex has variously been referred to as an 'obsession',[8] 'collective schizophrenia',[9] and the 'unbearable lightness of being'.[10] The veracity of this identity mania was exploited in a recent Molson Canadian beer advertisement known as 'The Rant'. The advertisement, which Garfield argues has become a manifesto of national identity, features a stereotyped Canadian male. It begins with the main character, dressed in a plaid shirt, stepping on to a stage to share politely his views on what it means to be Canadian. In the course of his colorful speech, this individual reveals his identity and patriotism by debunking many of the myths that surround Canadians and by repeatedly identifying those factors that define them as different from Americans. Commencing in a reserved manner, the speech assumes increasing volume and passion as our Canadian, named Joe, reveals that he is:

> not a lumberjack nor a fur trader, doesn't live in an igloo, eat blubber or own a dogsled and that he has a prime minister, not a president, speaks English and French, not American ... believes in peacekeeping, not policing, diversity, not assimilation, that Canada is the first nation of ice hockey and the best part of North America.[11]

The advertisement has been extremely successful and controversial. Although most Americans unfamiliar with Canadians probably would not understand its point, concerns were raised in Parliament by one minister who called for the commercial be banned just in case it might cause offense. In its own humorous way, the advertisement highlights both the long-standing sense of vulnerability that Canadians have felt in relation to the U.S. and their ability to laugh at it. The former sentiment has also been expressed in many scholarly books over the years, including *The Canadian Quandary*;[12] *Neighbors Taken for Granted*;[13] *The Americanization of Canada*;[14] *Life with Uncle*;[15] *On Guard for Thee*;[16] *From Nation to Colony*;[17] *In the Eye of the Eagle*;[18] *The Beaver Bites Back? American Popular Culture in Canada*;[19] and *The House of Difference: Cultural Politics and National Identity in Canada*.[20] Each explores, in its own way, the manner in which Canadian identity has been and continues to be defined as different from the American. A few address direct the crisis of Canadian identity in 1988.

In that year Canadian anxieties about the fate of their cultural identity were exacerbated by the Canada–U.S. Free Trade Agreement (FTA). According to the Progressive Conservative Party, led by Brian Mulroney, the FTA was essential for Canada's future within an increasingly globalizing economy. Conversely, nationalists, including factions of the opposition Liberal and New Democratic Party, feared that the FTA would inevitably translate American economic colonization into the eradication of Canadian sovereignty.[21] The significance of the FTA was highlighted by its pivotal role within the debates leading up to the federal election held later that year. Arguably, the economic and cultural threat posed by the FTA, whether real or imaginary, contributed to a renewed search for anchors of meaning and symbolic markers of difference in order to confirm Canada's culture and identity relative to those of the U.S.[22] It is within this context that the crisis of Canadian identity and the stories of our two celebrities take place. However, before exploring the specific narratives that formed the basis of their role in the crisis we first briefly examine the relationship between crisis and social memory.

CRISIS AND SOCIAL MEMORY

Historians, sociologists, political economists, political scientists, and psychologists have conceptualized the concept of crisis in diverse ways.[23] Wiener and Kahn, for example, have outlined 12 dimensions that they have identified as generic to any crisis. Those most relevant to the 1988 situation include: a turning point, threat, convergence of events, heightened urgency, and increased tensions, especially in political crises involving nations.[24] A cursory look at these characteristics points to the implications of crisis in the development of a particular social memory.

Events and conditions that are defined and represented as urgent, potential threats or even social change are likely to focus attention and heighten emotions. It is at such times that citizens look to their political leaders for answers, guidance, and reassurance. Consequently, those with the most power to disseminate information, through the media and otherwise, are positioned to shape the nature of, and response to, a national crisis. Furthermore, if we view a crisis in a more general sense, that is, as a form of struggle, then we can begin to see how particular interest groups operate within a contested terrain. In 1988 the crisis became a contested terrain that revealed a struggle over the past, present, and future meaning(s) of Canadian identity. Ultimately, the process and outcome of this struggle as articulated through the media has become part of the national social memory.

WAYNE GRETZKY: THE PRIDE OF CANADA

It is difficult to write about Gretzky without appearing to exaggerate in some way, shape or form. Such are his achievements within his sport that he truly is in a class by himself. From the age of six Gretzky has been a national phenomenon in Canada and in many ways his career and life have seemed like a fairy tale. To understand his national significance requires an understanding of both the place of hockey within the Canadian popular imagination but also some sense of his great ability. Putting Gretzky into perspective Beardsley writes that,

> Because hockey so clearly defines the Canadian experience, Wayne Gretzky is the latest in a long line of hockey heroes who personify the hopes, wishes, and dreams of the Canadian people ... by finding greatness in him, we find it in ourselves.[25]

The fact that he is universally known as the 'Great One' is testimony to Gretzky's supremacy within the sporting realm. By the end of his 20-year career in April 1999 he had amassed 61 NHL records, won four Stanley Cups, been awarded nine Hart Trophies as the League's Most Valuable Player, was selected as an All-Star 18 times, lead the league in scoring ten times, and set career points totals that are beyond comprehension. While there have been too many noteworthy moments to mention none can compare to two that occurred in 1988. Specifically, it was Gretzky's engagement and marriage to the American Janet Jones and his subsequent trade from the Edmonton Oilers to the Los Angeles Kings that initiated the sporting crisis of 1988.

From the moment Gretzky announced his engagement on 12 January there was a prevailing anxiety among the Canadian media. Inexplicably, concern was suddenly being redirected from Gretzky's on-ice performance to his off-ice romance. More specifically, the future Mrs Wayne Gretzky was viewed as a double threat to Canada's most prized possession.[26] Janet Jones was described as the Benedict Arnold of Canada, a Jezebel, a Dragon Lady, and another Yoko Ono (in reference to her purported role in the break up of the Beatles)[27]. It seems that many Canadians were uncomfortable with their national hero's choosing an American over one of their own. In the end, the couple did marry but, of course, it was no ordinary wedding as was reflected in such newspaper headlines as 'Canada prepares for royal wedding'.[28] The fact that regularly scheduled Canadian television was interrupted for the ceremony is but one indication of Gretzky's national significance. Moreover, the presence of television at what is considered by most people to be a private event foreshadowed increasing speculation on the part of the media about Gretzky's future. For example, no time was wasted by some in making links between Gretzky's bond of love with a new American wife and Canada's prospective relationship with the United States in view of the pending FTA. As one observer wrote:

> The marriage of the hockey hero and the Hollywood starlet projected an apt symbolism at a time of often-bitter political debate over the proposed Canada–U.S. free trade agreement, which some critics say will tie Canada too closely to the United States.[29]

The implication is that Gretzky's decision to 'tie the knot' represented the political, economic, and cultural noose that would soon strangle Canada. A member of the Canadian public made the point even more explicitly:

> The 'royal' wedding reads partly like the Canada–U.S. free trade deal. Wayne Gretzky's (Canada) gifts to Janet Jones: a very expensive engagement ring (one estimate put the price at $125,000 although Gretzky denies this), a $250,000 car, plus other gifts. Jones' (United States) gift to Gretzky: a kiss.[30]

For the anxious nationalist prognostics the wedding was indeed just the beginning. Within less than a month the unspeakable happened: Gretzky was traded from the Edmonton Oilers to the Los Angeles Kings. It was on 9 August 1988, also referred to as 'Black Tuesday', that this was announced. Not only did the press conference proclaiming the deal interrupt scheduled programming on Canadian television, it was also noted that the trade was the biggest headline for the *Edmonton Journal* since the end of World War II.[31] The following newspaper headlines typify the media's reactions:

> *Globe and Mail*: 'Defection of "national treasure" stuns fans, players, executives'[32]
>
> *Vancouver Sun*: 'Grieving for the Great One'[33]
>
> *Sports Illustrated*: 'A nation in mourning'[34]

The discourse of crisis and its relevance to the threat of Americanization continued. Reflecting on how the trade was interpreted, Gretzky stated that, 'To some Canadians I was just one more thing the Americans had stolen.'[35] On the wider significance of the trade, Quickfall suggested that, 'Canadians are being forced into Americans' way of thinking. This is an example of it.'[36] What is being inferred is that the Gretzky deal symbolized an ideological shift in Canadian values, perhaps underscored by what Kidd refers to as American cultural hegemony.[37] While it may be argued that these remarks are indirectly related to the free trade debate and the threat of Americanization, the following examples are far more blatant in their connections. The first ones focus on the impending economic threat of the U.S. via the FTA signified by Gretzky's move to Los Angeles. One unhappy fan who called the *Globe & Mail* in Toronto said, 'This is what happens with free trade. We export a national hero to the United States. We lose a national treasure to the Los Angeles Kings.'[38] Another said, 'If this is an indication of the free trade between Canada and the U.S., then Canada is in trouble.'[39] And a Canadian sports journalist stated, 'Who cares why Gretzky is gone? He's gone. He's not our star any more, he's theirs. If this be free trade, stuff it.'[40]

Thus Gretzky's fate was articulated by the media, linking that of Canada as a nation to the FTA and the threat of Americanization. But it is the popularized threat of Americanization, whether real or imagined, that has facilitated such discourses in the first place. The notion that Canadian identity is defined out of difference from that of the U.S. has become fundamental to Canadian social memory. Indeed, according to

Mackey, 'The constant attempt to construct an authentic, differentiated, and bounded identity has been central to the project of Canadian nation-building, and is often shaped through comparison with, and demonization of, the United States.'[41] In the fall of 1988 the tension in Canada was mounting, the FTA loomed, Gretzky was being cited by particular interest groups to represent the demise of Canada if the deal went through, and an election loomed. Then, along came Canada's new hero, Ben Johnson.

FROM PRIDE TO PREJUDICE:
BEN JOHNSON AND THE 1988 CRISIS OF CANADIAN IDENTITY

In most respects Ben Johnson's rise to national hero was a complete contrast to Wayne Gretzky's. Johnson was not an 'all-Canadian' hero, did not compete in the national game, indeed, he was not even born in Canada. Yet in many ways he briefly held the potential to represent the image that Canada has of itself and wants the world to see. That is, one of celebrated multiculturalism and difference. However, despite the fact that Canada was the world's first nation officially to legislate a Multicultural Act (coincidentally in 1988), there have been criticisms that it is as much about 'marking' as it is about 'celebrating' diversity. As Mackey notes:

> 'multiculturalism' constructs a dominant and supposedly unified, white, unmarked core culture through the proliferation of forms of limited difference. ... The particular forms of pluralism which have emerged have created a situation in which those who share in the white unmarked core culture conceive of themselves as 'real' and 'authentic' Canadians, who tolerate and even celebrate the 'color' and 'flavor' of multicultural 'others'.[42]

Benjamin Sinclair Johnson, Jr immigrated from Jamaica in 1976, attaining official Canadian citizenship in 1980.[43] Yet, despite some early victories he failed to attract much national attention until 1987. The milestone that put Johnson and Canada on the map occurred on 30 August when he defeated Carl Lewis and set a world record in Rome. However, it was the anticipation and realization of his record-setting performance in the 100-m final at the Seoul Olympics that truly established Johnson as a Canadian hero and an international superstar. Several broad contextual factors have already been outlined to account for the significance of the Johnson affair. However, there are also specific features of the race itself that might explain why this particular 10-sec event was bestowed with such national and international significance. It may have been the fact that the 100-m sprint is considered the premier event of the Olympic Games. It might have been the fact that Johnson was the first Canadian to win a medal in the event since Percy Williams in 1932. Perhaps it was the fact that individuals throughout the world had rejoiced as witnesses to an extraordinary, not to mention historic, demonstration of human potential, only to have their personal memories betrayed. Or maybe it was the fact that Johnson's victory, and the subsequent loss to the American Carl Lewis, was symbolic of a prevailing Canadian anxiety in anticipation of its post-FTA future. In all likelihood it was a combination of these explanations. Whatever the reason, the state, and particularly the Prime Minister, wasted little time in capitalizing on the moment of victory. Immediately following the race the Prime Minister Brian Mulroney made a congratulatory telephone call to Johnson on live television.[44] He expressed his pride on behalf of the entire nation and said that, 'You have made all of Canada proud.'[45]

However, less than 48 hours later the scandal broke: Ben Johnson had tested positive for the use of steroids. A series of official responses emerged from the athlete, his coach, agent, family, and the Canadian Olympic Association. At first there was complete denial. Then, faced with confirmation of the tests, stories began to circulate. First, it was a 'yellow gooey substance', then it was the presence of a 'mysterious stranger near the testing site'.[46] And, while an official admission from Johnson was a long way off, the media certainly reacted.

For example, the *Toronto Star*[47] in an article entitled 'Johnson affair shocks world', featured newspaper headlines from around the globe including: 'Fastest junkie on earth' (*Daily Star* [London]); 'Drugs turn Johnson's medal into a piece of fool's gold' (*Baltimore Sun*); 'CHEAT!' (*Daily Mirror* [London]); and, 'The fastest man in the world – a doping sinner' (*Abendzeitung* [Germany]). In effect, the Canadian press took the liberty of showing how Johnson's actions, and, by association, Canada's identity, were being represented around the world.[48]

Domestically, the Canadian press repeatedly attempted to capture and circulate the 'affective' response of the nation. Indeed, a complex set of images and meanings of the Canadian collective experience was represented and reproduced through a combination of the media's own reports and editorials as well as their attempts to express the view of the 'everyday' Canadian.[49] The latter tactic was seemingly employed to provide the illusion of a national voice. For example, the *Toronto Star* operated a telephone answering service that enabled people to call in and record their opinions and feelings regarding the Johnson incident. Among the personal responses were cases of anger, confusion, disappointment, embarrassment, compassion, pain, guilt, and contempt. While the majority of responses tended to fall within these categories, there were definitely instances where individual Canadians completely rejected any responsibility for Johnson's actions.[50] In any case it was noteworthy to find that the vast majority of interpretations of the incident contrasted the heights of adulation and the depths of despair, reinforcing the notion of a national, affective response, implying that the nation was experiencing an emotional trauma. Five general categories of affective response to Johnson's disqualification were represented within the media, including, shock and disbelief, humiliation, despair, mourning, and tragedy.[51] Notably, all may be viewed as representing aspects of a crisis of identity. Just as significant is the fact that the media were relating the discourses surrounding Johnson to the previous crisis linked to Gretzky. Consider the following examples, each of which demonstrates aspects of the association, 'The shame sent shock waves across Canada, where Johnson was on his way to supplanting Hollywood-bound hockey star Wayne Gretzky as the national idol.'[52] Johnson's transgression had sent an emotional wave sweeping over the country. Some Canadians treated Johnson's expulsion as high treason, some as raw tragedy. Children wept and sportswriters anguished over the disgrace of the man who had become the nation's number-one hero in the wake of the departure of Gretzky to Los Angeles.[53] 'Canadian officials were particularly stung. With Wayne Gretzky traded recently by the Edmonton Oilers of the National Hockey League to the Los Angeles Kings, Johnson was one of the few remaining Canadian athletic superstars.'[54] 'There's no proof whatsoever that Ben wasn't set up. What a wimp of a country we are. We've given up Wayne Gretzky, now we've given up the gold medal. If this is a precursor to free trade, I hate to see what will happen.'[55]

Each of these examples reveals evidence of the media's attempting to capture the significance of Johnson's downfall by, in part, identifying the key role he played as a heroic substitute for Gretzky. If nothing else, they reinforce the significance of sporting heroes in the construction of Canadian national identity and, arguably, its social memory. Moreover, as revealed in the last quotation, the media clearly linked the Johnson and Gretzky discourses to those of the Canada–U.S. FTA. The impact of the crises of these sporting heroes upon the Canadian collective social memory was expressed by Wayne:

> Above all, 1988 will probably be forever remembered as a very difficult, if not the most difficult year for Canadian heroes. As if the Gretzky trade wasn't bad enough, Scarborough's Ben Johnson was forced to return the gold medal he won in the men's 100 meters at Seoul after testing positive for steroids. The Gretzky and Johnson affairs brought more than just intense disappointment to Canadians. There was an irreconcilable sense of loss. The public had heavy emotional investments in both athletes. But Canada lost more than a couple of superstars in 1988. It was the year the nation lost its innocence.[56]

These observations underscore a national 'affective' response which he describes as a 'heavy emotional investment', to the Gretzky and Johnson cases. The Johnson incident, according to Wayne, compounded the earlier national loss of Gretzky. Moreover, Johnson's downfall signalled a year in which 'the nation lost its innocence'. Thus 'the nation' is used to signify Johnson's corrupt behaviour. It had become a national responsibility.

Gretzky himself spoke about the Johnson issue, linking himself to Johnson and the national significance of the event:

> He was the first guy people rallied around in Canada. I've never seen people [feel] like this about him. Canadians are reserved people. He was our guy. It might have been the beginning of something new for us. I've never seen an Olympic athlete idolized the way he was ... he's a nice guy, he should know the consequences. The doctors ... the people around him have to be at fault too.[57]

Gretzky's statements are revealing, and in and of themselves bestow a special type of significance on the incident. For example, he reinforces the connection made between Johnson, the Canadian people, and the nation through the use of such terms as *our* and *us*. At the same time he uses these terms to identify himself as Canadian, thereby sharing in the collective disappointment and despair.

In summary, Johnson's success and failure arguably attained added significance because of the context in which they occurred; a context that included a nation with a fragile basis of identity, a nation that was characterized as having lost its number-one sports hero and that was supposedly under threat through a pending trade deal with the United States that would threaten its culture and sovereignty. Yet in the wake of the Johnson affair another crisis of identity was emerging in 1988. While some individuals came to his defence, others openly attacked him. Some of these attacks smacked of racism, a feature that Canadians would rather believe to be more applicable to the United States than their own country.

Several articles have outlined the various types of racial-identity politics associated with Ben Johnson both during and after the steroid scandal.[58] In combination these attest to Jackson's argument that Johnson's 'national and racial identities were socially constructed, deconstructed, reconstructed and reproduced through the media.'[59] The racist-based discourses associated with Johnson included a redefinition of his identity, the use of stereotypes including animal imagery,[60] references to his intelligence,[61] racist humour,[62] and overt racism.[63]

Perhaps the most immediate way in which Johnson's 'otherness' was represented was via his transformation from Jamaican immigrant to Jamaican-Canadian, as he became more successful, culminating in his 'achievement' of 'Canadian' status when he became world famous. However, following his disqualification, Johnson was quickly redefined as Jamaican-Canadian. According to the *Sports Illustrated* writer Michael Farber, 'There was a disqualification at Seoul, a qualification at home. Johnson was now a "Jamaican-Canadian".'[64] In losing the gold, he had gained a hyphen, and a silent legacy was established. It appears that Johnson's 'Canadian' identity, which temporarily displaced the hyphenated racial signifier, was contingent upon translating his personal achievements into national sporting pride.[65] Hyphenation, as a specific type of signifying practice is particularly powerful with respect to Jamaican-Canadians. As several authors have argued, in the case of 'Jamaican-Canadians' the hyphen is both a 'national' and a 'racial' signifier. In other words, 'Jamaican', despite the existence of white Jamaicans and black people who are not Jamaican, is a euphemism for 'black' in Canada.[66]

Of course, Johnson's career did not end with his disqualification at the Seoul Olympics. Shortly thereafter the Canadian government established the Dubin Inquiry. The $3.6 million investigation revealed what almost everyone already knew: that Ben Johnson had used steroids and that the use of performance-enhancing drugs was endemic in elite sport. In many ways the Dubin Inquiry was an attempt to cleanse the nation's reputation. However, given its sheer size and significance, the Inquiry served to institutionalize the memory of the Johnson crisis. By institutionalizing the memory we mean that the Dubin Inquiry helped to formalize the documented history of the affair. As a consequence, it contributed to the Johnson drug scandal's becoming the 'watershed of the modern steroid controversy'.[67] In other words, the Johnson affair has become the landmark case upon which all subsequent controversies involving steroids in sports are defined and interpreted. This point was demonstrated in the lead up to the 2000 Sydney Olympics. In a television guide from New Zealand an article entitled 'Faster, further ... higher: Will Sydney 2000 be the ultimate drug Olympics?' featured a half-page photograph of Johnson accompanied by text stating: 'Ever since Ben Johnson crossed the finishing line in Seoul in 1988, fuelled on a cocktail of steroids and corpse-extracted growth hormones, it has been harder and harder to suspend disbelief.'[68] Thus the Johnson saga is not just a social memory within Canada; it is a story that reflects on Canadian identity that is constantly being retold within the context of sport around the world.

Notably, Johnson returned to compete in 1993 only to test positive again, resulting in a lifetime ban by the International Amateur Athletics Federation. It was at this point that Johnson confronted one of the most overt, and admittedly rare, expressions of racism. In his own words, Johnson recounted the 'most disgusting comment I have ever heard' in reference to the suggestion of Pierre Cadieux, the former Canadian Minister of Sports, that he should 'move back to Jamaica, his birthplace, because he had become a disgrace to Canada'.[69] For a second time Johnson played a role in shaping Canada's social memory. It has now been over seven years since his lifetime ban, but he continues a legal battle for the right to compete. In the interim he has been involved in some rather bizarre business and career projects, including serving as fitness advisor to the former Brazilian soccer star Diego Maradona and entering a race where the opponents consisted of a horse and a race car. However, there is perhaps no more striking example of Ben Johnson's sustained position and impact on Canadian social memory than his role as the 'anabolic apparition',[70] a ghost who haunts his 'black' Canadian athletic successors. Here we provide a brief look at how Johnson's legacy has influenced the next generation of Canadian sprinting sensations and, in particular, Donovan Bailey.

Throughout his career, and despite all his success, the Canadian gold medallist and former 100-m world record holder Donovan Bailey has been confronted with the fallout from Ben Johnson's career. A cursory view of the media reports surrounding Bailey reveals the haunting effects of Johnson within the Canadian social memory: 'Donovan Bailey was unbeatable at the world's, but in Canada he can't outrun the shadow of Ben Johnson.'[71] 'Ben Johnson has been erased as Olympic champion everywhere but in his own heart ... he remains a challenge to his country's forgiveness and a phantom who haunts Canada's men of speed.'[72] 'A country forgot about whatshisname. Those demons are exorcised for good, fading like Bailey's jet stream down the straightway.'[73] 'Canadians have much to cheer. Donovan Bailey, with his gold medal in the prestigious 100-metre race, has erased the national shame still lingering from the Ben Johnson scandal.'[74]

The reality is that almost all Black athletes, and in particular those from Jamaica, have lived under a microscope ever since Ben Johnson tested positive in 1988. With every new, rising star, with every victory and with every new record, two questions were being asked. The first was, in effect, silent and focused on whether or not the athlete in question was using performance-enhancing drugs, 'like Big Ben did'. The second focused on which penultimate victory would erase the memory of Ben Johnson. Bailey was particularly hurt by these questions and, as the headlines above demonstrate, they followed him wherever he went. Even after winning an Olympic gold medal and setting a world record, the first issue raised by the media was whether this achievement would finally free him of Ben Johnson. Ironically, it is the media who have been responsible for maintaining the problem.

In the light of the media's relentless pressure and the rather fair-weather attitude of many Canadians, Bailey's success at the 1996 Atlanta Olympics served as poetic justice. For example, when Bailey was questioned at the post-race press conference about whether he would consider sharing his victory with Jamaica he immediately replied, 'It's not even Jamaica sharing. I'm Jamaican, man. I'm Jamaican first. You gotta understand that's where I'm from. That's home. That you can never take away from me. I'm a Jamaican-born Canadian sprinter.'[75] His response expressed both a sense of confidence in his own dual citizenship and identity but also a form of resistance to those Canadians who had questioned his loyalty throughout his career. By consistently acknowledging his dual identity as both Canadian and Jamaican, Bailey appeared to have learned a valuable lesson from Johnson. Well aware of how particular factions of the Canadian public had redefined Johnson into a Jamaican-Canadian following his disqualification, Bailey empowered himself by deliberately and strategically proclaiming a dual identity. Putting it another way, he 'hijacked the hegemonic hyphen' in Jamaican-Canadian.[76] The significance of hyphens within the social construction of identity in Canada is highlighted by Mackey:

> Canada has a proliferation of hyphenated peoples. Many Canadians identify themselves as German-Canadian, Ukrainian-Canadian, Chinese-Canadian, Greek-Canadian, Afro-Canadian, French-Canadian, Native-Canadian, Italian-Canadian and so on. While all these hyphenated forms all have their own histories of constitution, some groups are widely considered more 'ethnic' than others. Others have the privilege of being simply 'Canadian'.[77]

The subtle and not so subtle forms of racism faced by Donovan Bailey and others cannot solely be attributed to Ben Johnson. Certainly his public pronouncements and behaviour since 1988 have not only kept him in the headlines but have also exacerbated the problem for those working most hard to forget him. Nevertheless, to fully understand the complexity of the issues involved requires a more socio-historical and socio-cultural view of identity politics in Canada. Though many Canadians like to think that racism is a problem that exists elsewhere, and in particular in the United States, prejudice remains an important social issue for the nation that prides itself in its inclusion and even the celebration of difference.[78] However, as Mackey[79] notes, the Canadian nation-building project has lived 'with difference' from the outset, and has done so through flexible strategies of managing, appropriating, controlling, subsuming, and often highlighting it.

CONCLUSION: SPORT, IDENTITY, AND SOCIAL MEMORY – YESTERDAY ONCE MORE

We have argued that the media-generated stories of Wayne Gretzky and Ben Johnson represent forms of pride and prejudice with respect to identity politics in Canada. Popular discourses surrounding their lives beginning in 1988 are constitutive and constituting of a Canadian crisis of national identity. To this extent their narratives form part of a Canadian social memory, one that is written in the present based upon a particular version of the past and with distinct views of the future. One constant feature of this evolving social memory is the notion of crisis. The evocation of crisis is important because, as noted earlier, it calls for urgency and demands attention. Moreover, it provides a platform where power can be exercised, expressed, and contested. Politically, the concept of crisis has been used as a means of drawing upon time-honored symbols and meanings which have consistently served to capture and mobilize the national collective in Canada.[80] To this extent crises of national identity in Canada have been argued to be forged by particular interest groups at particular moments of conjuncture.[81] Furthermore, the forging of a national identity crisis has important implications for identity politics. As Mackey asserts,

> contrary to the common sense that circulates about national identity and cultural pluralism in Canada, national identity is not so much in a constant state of crisis, but that the reproduction of 'crisis' allows the nation state to be a site of a constantly regulated politics of identity.[82]

This is being written in 2001 and the crisis continues. The struggle over Canadian identity remains at the forefront of popular debate. Certainly the context has changed but issues such as globalization and free trade, the potential separation of Quebec, and immigration confirm that debates about identity politics are key fixtures within the Canadian popular consciousness. On the sporting front, Gretzky and Johnson may not be the daily headliners they once were, but they are by no means forgotten. Johnson's name emerges from time to time. It is usually due to his continued efforts to return to professional track and field. His most recent legal battles have made the case that he is being unfairly excluded from a career. While Maurice Greene has replaced Donovan Bailey as the world's fastest man, the very possibility that Bailey, Bruny Surin or another black Canadian could have won a medal at the 2000 Sydney Olympics contributed to both an anticipation and a sense of anxiety at the thought of Johnson's legacy resurfacing. In sum, Ben Johnson is neither forgiven nor forgotten.

The 'Great One' retired in 1999 in a final game that celebrated his amazing achievements. Aside from the expected tributes from hockey experts, former coaches, and players, there were some unique twists to this farewell. For example, while it has become traditional for teams to retire the numbered jersey of star athletes at the end of their careers, in the case of Wayne Gretzky they retired his number, '99', from the entire league. Likewise, in an age of professional, commercialized sport it was surprising to see that some NHL teams had given former Gretzky team mates the day off from playing so that they could be in attendance at his grand finale. Perhaps the single thing that most testifies to Gretzky's place within both NHL and Canadian social memory is the fact that both versions (Canadian and American) of the customary pregame national anthems featured modified lyrics to pay tribute to number 99. Now, even after retiring Canadians look to Wayne Gretzky. Most recently, many are hoping that he can provide one more miracle, that is, saving the national game. The flow of Canadian NHL franchises to the United States continues, and, given the distinct tax and other economic advantages, there are real concerns for the future of the national game.[83] Thus, beyond his historic benchmarking within the record books of ice hockey, Gretzky is likely to remain a key figure within debates about sport, culture, and national identity.

The increasing impact of globalization on economies, culture, and people, is likely to have a dramatic impact on how nations see and define themselves in the future. The very idea of homogeneous cultures and national identities has all but vanished. According to Stuart Hall, 'the capacity to live with difference' is the 'coming question of the twentieth century'.[84] With respect to national identity and difference, a major challenge lies ahead for countries such as Canada. For example, there are increasing attempts to draw upon nostalgic visions of an often-mythical past. According to Miles, 'nationalism is a means to sustain a sense of commonality, particularly in periods of conflict and crisis within a nation'.[85] It is at such times that romanticized interpretations of the place of ice hockey and heroes such as Wayne Gretzky are likely to be reproduced as a means of forging a dominant form of white, masculine, heterosexist, anglophone, national identity. Furthermore, the process and politics of constructing this hegemonic national identity will probably occur in response to challenges by cases such as Johnson's. It was not necessarily the crisis of the century, but the 1988 struggle over the past, present, and future of Canadian identity provided a focal point for both the media and its citizens. In doing so it served as a key site for the confirmation of a particular set of images, narratives, and social bodies upon which a selective social memory could be constructed. As Canada enters the twenty-first century the stability and endurance of this memory will remain within the contested terrain of national politics.

NOTES

1. S.J. Jackson, *Sport, Crisis and Canadian Identity in 1988: A Cultural Analysis* (Urbana, IL: University of Illinois, 1992).
2. S.J. Jackson, D.L. Andrews, and C.L. Cole, 'Race, Nation and Authenticity of Identity: Interrogating the "Everywhere" Man (Michael Jordan) and the "Nowhere" Man (Ben Johnson)', *Journal of Immigrants and Minorities*, 17 (1998), 82–102.
3. S. Levine, P. West, and J. Hiltz, *The America's Wars in Asia: A Cultural Approach to History and Memory* (New York, NY: Eastgate, 1999).
4. D. Ben-Amos and L. Weissberg, *Cultural Memory and the Construction of Identity* (Detroit, MI: Wayne State University Press, 1999), p.15.
5. A. Metcalfe, *Canada Learns to Play* (Toronto: McClelland & Stewart, 1987), p.177.
6. Ibid.
7. S.J. Jackson, 'Gretzky, Crisis and Canadian Identity in 1988: Rearticulating the Americanization of Culture Debate', *Sociology of Sport Journal*, 11 (1994), 428–46.
8. A. Chaiton and N. McDonald, *Canadian Schools and Canadian Identity* (Toronto: Gage Educational Publishing, 1977).
9. W. Kilbourn, 'The Peaceable Kingdom Still', *Daedalus*, 117 (1988), 178–84.
10. R. Gwyn, *The 49th Paradox: Canada in North America* (Toronto: Totem Books, 1985).
11. B. Garfield, *Blame Canada and Molson for Brilliant 'Rant' at States*, http://www.adage.com/news_and_features/ad_review/archives/ar20000508.html: 2000
12. H. Johnson, *The Canadian Quandary* (New York, NY: McGraw-Hill, 1963).
13. L. Merchant, *Neighbours Taken for Granted* (New York, NY: Praeger, 1966).
14. S.E. Moffett, *The Americanization of Canada* (Toronto: University of Toronto Press, 1972).
15. J.W. Holmes, *Life with Uncle* (Toronto: University of Toronto Press, 1981).
16. M.M. Bowker, *On Guard for Thee: An Independent Review of the Free Trade Agreement* (Hull: Voyageur Publishing, 1988).
17. M. Scott, *From Nation to Colony* (Lindsay, Ontario: Tri-M Publishing, 1988).
18. J.F. Lisee, *In the Eye of the Eagle* (Toronto: Harper-Collins, 1990).
19. D.H. Flaherty and F. Manning, *The Beaver Bites Back? American Popular Culture in Canada* (Kingston: McGill-Queen's University Press, 1993).
20. E. Mackey, *The House of Difference: Cultural Politics and National Identity in Canada* (London: Routledge, 1999).
21. See Bowker, *On Guard for Thee*; R. Davies, 'Signing away Canada's Soul: Culture, Identity and the Free Trade Agreement', *Harper's* (1989), 43–7; L. Lapierre, *If You Love this Country: Facts and Feelings on Free Trade* (Toronto: McClelland & Stewart, 1987); and Scott, *From Nation to Colony*.
22. S.J. Jackson and K.V. Meier, 'Hijacking the Hegemonic Signifier: Donovan Bailey and the Politics of Racial and National Identity in Canada', in R. Sands (ed.), *Global Jocks: Anthropology, Sport and Culture* (Westport, CT: Greenwood, 1999), pp.173–88.
23. See S. Aronowitz and C. Maccabe, *The Crisis in Historical Materialism: Class, Politics and Culture in Marxist Theory* (Minneapolis, MN: University of Minnesota Press, 1990); F.M. Dattilo and A. Freeman, *Cognitive-Behavioural Strategies for Crisis Intervention* (Guilford: Guilford Press, 1994); C.J. Lucas, *Crisis in the Academy: Rethinking Higher Education in America* (New York, NY: St. Martin's Press, 1998); A. Smith and E. Cox, *The Crisis of 1898: Colonial Redistribution and Nationalist Mobilization* (New York, NY: St. Martin's Press, 1999); A.J. Weiner and H. Kahn, 'Crisis', *International Encyclopedia of the Social Sciences* (1968), pp.510–11; E.O. Wright, *Class Crisis and the State* (New York, NY: Verso, 1996).
24. Weiner and Kahn, 'Crisis', pp.510–11.
25. D. Beardsley, *Country on Ice* (Markham, Ontario: Paperbacks, 1987), pp.109, 111.
26. Jackson, 'Gretzky, Crisis and Canadian Identity'.
27. J. Friedman, V. Sheff, and V. Balfour, 'Trading Places', *People Weekly* (29 Aug. 1988), 38–41.
28. 'Canada Prepares for Royal Wedding', *Montreal Gazette* (19 June 1988), D3.
29. S. Wulf, 'The Great Wedding', *Sports Illustrated* (25 July 1988), 31.
30. V. Ross, 'Cross-border Trading' (letter to the editor), *Macleans* (15 Aug. 1988), 4.
31. W. Gretzky (with R. Reilly), *Gretzky: An Autobiography* (New York, NY: Harper-Collins, 1990).

32. A. Strachan, 'Gretzky Goes to LA', *Globe and Mail* (10 Aug. 1988), A1–2.
33. 'Grieving for the Great One', *Vancouver Sun* (13 Aug. 1988), B1.
34. J. Taylor, 'A Nation in Mourning', *Sports Illustrated* (22 Aug. 1988), 94.
35. Gretzky, *Autobiography*, p.196.
36. J. Quickfall, 'Canadians Are being Forced into American's Way of Thinking', *Edmonton Sun* (11 Aug. 1988), 22.
37. B. Kidd, 'How Do We Find Our Own Voices in the "New World Order"? A Commentary on Americanization', *Sociology of Sport Journal*, 8 (1991), 178–84.
38. Strachan, 'Gretzky Goes to LA', A2.
39. G. Hansen, 'Response to Gretzky Trade', *Edmonton Sun* (11 Aug. 1988), 21.
40. Taylor, 'Nation in Mourning', 94.
41. Mackey, *House of Difference*, p.145.
42. Ibid., p.153.
43. J.R. Christie, *Ben Johnson: the Fastest Man on Earth* (Toronto: McClelland-Bantam, 1988).
44. S.J. Jackson, 'A Twist of Race: Ben Johnson and the Canadian Crisis of Racial and National Identity', *Sociology of Sport Journal*, 15 (1998), 21–41.
45. J.F. Burns, 'Ban Could Cost Plenty to Johnson', *New York Times* (27 Sept. 1988), D31.
46. S.J. Jackson, 'Life in the (Mediated) Faust Lane: Ben Johnson, National Affect and the 1988 Crisis of Canadian Identity', *International Review for the Sociology of Sport*, 33 (1998), 227–38.
47. M. Gorman, 'Johnson Affair Shocks the World', *Toronto Star* (28 Sept. 1998), A28.
48. Jackson, 'Twist of Race'.
49. Jackson, 'Life in the (Mediated) Faust Lane'.
50. Ibid.
51. Ibid.
52. P. Axthelm *et al.*, 'The Doped-up Games', *Newsweek* (10 Oct. 1988), 55.
53. O. Johnson, 'The Games', *Sports Illustrated* (10 Oct. 1988), 38–9.
54. M. Janofsky, 'Johnson Loses His Gold to Lewis after a Drug Test', *New York Times* (27 Sept. 1988), D32.
55. M. Gorman, 'There's No Proof', *Toronto Star* (28 Sept. 1988), A4.
56. J. Wayne, 'Sports: the Year We Lost Our Innocence', *Financial Post* (26 Sept. 1988), 20.
57. 'Gretzky Speaks Out on Ben Scandal', *Toronto Star* (29 Sept. 1988), B2.
58. See Jackson, 'Life in the (Mediated) Faust Lane' and 'Twist of Race'; Jackson and Meier, 'Hijacking the Hegemonic Signifier'; Jackson *et al.*, 'Race, Nation and Authenticity'.
59. Jackson, 'Twist of Race', 28.
60. Janofsky, 'Johnson Loses His Gold'; B. Levin *et al.*, 'The Steroid Scandal', *Macleans* (10 Oct. 1988), 50–3.
61. L. Siegel, 'Ben Johnson Case Questions Validity of IQ Tests', *Toronto Star* (20 June 1989), A15.
62. D. Boyd, 'Canada Waits for Ben to Say It Ain't So after Steroid Controversy', *Vancouver Sun* (27 Sept. 1988), A3; M. Farber, 'Blast from the North', *Sports* Illustrated (22 July 1996), 142–6.
63. S. Blanchard, 'Running from the World', *New York Times* (28 July 1996), 23.
64. Farber, 'Blast from the North', 145.
65. Jackson and Meier, 'Hijacking the Hegemonic Signifier'.
66. C. Foster, *A Place Called Heaven: The Meaning of Being Black in Canada* (Toronto: Harper-Collins, 1996a) and 'Captain Canada: But Will Media Allow Bailey to Escape Johnson's Shadow?', *Toronto Star* (30 July 1996), D3; M. Levine, 'Canadians Secretly Relieved at Johnson's Fall', *New Statesman and Society* (7 Oct. 1988), 8 and 'What if He'd Kept the Gold?', *Globe and Mail* (13 Oct. 1988), A7.
67. Jackson, 'Life in the (Mediated) Faust Lane', 227.
68. B. Zander, 'Faster, Further ... Higher: Will Sydney 2000 Be the Ultimate Drug Olympics?', *New Zealand Listener* (8 July 2000), 26–7.
69. Blanchard, 'Running from the World', 23.
70. Jackson and Meier, 'Hijacking the Hegemonic Signifier'.
71. Farber, 'Blast from the North', 143.
72. C. Kemp, 'Athens to Atlanta: The Olympic Spirit', CBC Television (18 July 1996).
73. C. Young, 'Amid Tackiness, Athletes the Genuine Article', *Toronto Star* (5 Aug. 1996), D3.
74. 'Heroics Overshadow Cowardly Bombing', *London Free Press* (20 July 1996), B6.

75. J. Christie, 'Bailey Satellites Do Damage', *Globe and Mail* (17 July 1996), C2.
76. Jackson and Meier, 'Hijacking the Hegemonic Signifier'.
77. Mackey, *House of Difference*, p.20.
78. N. Bissoondath, *Selling Illusions: The Cult of Multiculturalism in Canada* (Toronto: Penguin Books, 1994); M. Cannon, *The Invisible Empire: Racism in Canada* (Toronto: Random House, 1995); Foster, *A Place Called Heaven*; D. Lazarus, *A Crack in the Mosaic: Canada's Race Relations in Crisis* (Cornwall: Vesta, 1980); Mackey, *House of Difference*; J. McLellan and A.H. Richmond, *Multiculturalism in Crisis: A Postmodern Perspective on Canada* (Halifax: Fernwood, 1994); A.H. Richmond, 'Immigration and Multiculturalism in Canada and Australia: the Contradictions and Crises of the 1980s', *International Journal of Canadian Studies*, 3 (1991), 87–109; V. Satzewich, *Deconstructing a Nation: Immigration, Multiculturalism and Racism in '90s Canada* (Halifax: Fernwood, 1992); R. Walcott, *Black Like Who: Writing in Black in Canada* (Toronto: Insomniac Press, 1997).
79. Mackey, *House of Difference*.
80. J.P. Desaulniers, 'What Does Canada Want?', *Media, Culture and Society*, 9 (1987), 149–57.
81. Jackson, 'Gretzky, Crisis and Canadian Identity'.
82. Mackey, *House of Difference*, p.13.
83. J. Klein and K. Reif, *The Death of Hockey: How a Bunch of Guys with Too Much Money and Too Little Sense Are Killing the Greatest Game on Earth* (Toronto: Macmillan, 1998); D. Whitson and R. Gruneau, *Hockey Night in Canada: Sport, Identities and Cultural Politics* (Toronto: Garamond Press, 1994).
84. S. Hall, 'Culture, Community, Nation', *Cultural Studies*, 7 (1993), 359.
85. R. Miles, *Racism* (London: Routledge, 1989), p.121.

3

Remembering the Black and Gold: African-Americans, Sport Memory, and the University of Iowa

DAVID R. McMAHON

> I wasn't afraid of prejudice, but I didn't want to go looking for it. I wanted to go to school where I could get an education, and where I would be allowed to play football.
>
> Emlen Tunnell
> (UI football player, 1946–47 [1966])

> The University of Iowa has two alternatives: 1. It can be remembered forever as the gatekeeper which opened the gates for black men as head football coaches at major universities; or 2. It can be further remembered as the Big Ten doormat which gets stomped on every Saturday.
>
> Al Schallau
> (from an advertisement in the *Iowa City Press-Citizen* [1978])

> On the sandy, dusty play grounds of West Texas, Hayden had many minority friends, but the teams on which he played were always segregated. He vowed to change that someday, and when he got the chance, he did so, integrating SMU and the Southwest Conference with a gifted black player named Jerry Levias.
>
> Hayden Fry
> (*A High Porch Picnic* [1999])

On Sunday, 9 December 1956, at 11:15 pm, officials from Trans-Canada Air Lines (TCA) listed Flight 810 as overdue. The aircraft left Vancouver at 6 pm, but disappeared into the Canadian wilderness before making it to Winnipeg, its next stop. Less than an hour into the flight, Capt Allan Clarke reported losing the inboard motor on the left side of his aircraft. The pilot feathered the propeller, activated the fire extinguishers, and circled back toward Vancouver through turbulent skies – wind gusts of up to 50 mph were recorded at the time of the plane's last radio contact. The plane crashed somewhere in the Chilliwack Mountain area of south-western British Columbia, killing everyone on board.

The media labeled it the worst commercial aviation disaster in Canada's history. Sixty-two people died in the crash, including Calvin Jones, a former All-American at the University of Iowa and an all-star in his first season in the Canadian Football League (CFL). Jones would have lived had he not missed his plane earlier that morning, one day after starring in his first CFL all-star game. Four other Canadian football players died in the crash.[1]

Before signing with the Winnipeg Blue Bombers in 1956, Jones played guard at Iowa from 1952 to 1955, becoming the only athlete in the university's history to be named first-team All America three years in a row. In 1955 his team mates elected him co-captain; that same year the national media awarded him the Outland Trophy, a prize given to America's outstanding interior lineman. He was the first African-American to be so honored.[2]

His death shocked the university community; indeed, much of the state of Iowa grieved over his passing. His former coach, Forest Evashevski, hoped that he would be found alive: 'Well, if anyone can survive such an accident, Cal can', said Evashevski. He added, as if to reiterate the point, 'He's that tough.' Jones was still enrolled at the University of Iowa at the time of his death. He was finishing a degree in physical therapy, a career he meant to fall back on when his playing days were over.[3]

Newspapers also reported that Jones had been planning a reunion with two of his former team mates Eddie Vincent and Frank Gilliam at the time of his death. They planned to meet at Iowa's Rose Bowl game against Oregon State in Pasadena, California, on New Year's Day 1957. Vincent, Gilliam, and Jones were African-American friends who played on the same high school football team in Steubenville, Ohio. The Iowa media dubbed them the 'Steubenville Trio' upon their arrival on campus in 1952. Jones's death put their plans on permanent hold.[4]

Less than a week after Jones's death, his former team, the Iowa Hawkeyes, left Iowa City to prepare for perhaps the biggest contest in school history: Iowa's first Rose Bowl game. The cartoonist Frank Miller of the *Des Moines Register* gave graphic illustration to the feelings of many Iowans with his ghostly cartoon of Jones hovering above the field under the caption 'Iowa Will Have Twelve Men on the Field in the 1957 Rose Bowl Game'. Playing in Jones's honor, Iowa whipped Oregon State 35–19 in the nation's most prestigious bowl game. Halfback Bill Happel said after the game, 'We dedicated this game to Cal'. 'Our co-captains pick a player to give the ball to after every victory. Today, it was unanimously decided to send the ball to Cal Jones's mother in Steubenville.'[5]

The memory of Calvin Jones lives on in the hearts and minds of Iowa sports fans long after his death. Frank Miller's cartoon helped to give him iconic status, and so did the continual retelling of his story in the athletic histories of the University of Iowa. The university also bestowed upon Jones an even rarer honor: his jersey (number 62) was retired. Nile Kinnick's jersey (number 24) is the other such: Kinnick won the Heisman Trophy in 1939, as the nation's best college football player; he also died in an air crash – a flight-training accident during World War II. Iowa's football stadium was renamed in his honor in 1972.[6]

SPORT AS MEMORY

At least two themes run throughout our history of sports: social circumstances have often allowed or prohibited the participation of an athlete in an event or sport; and the norms of reportage have selectively affected what gets recorded and remembered.

The University of Iowa's athletic history illustrates the interplay of these two themes. A medium-sized university in the Midwest, Iowa is located within the mainstream of college athletics in the United States. As a member of the historic Big Ten Conference and representing a state often associated with the values of average or 'middle' Americans, the university has a long history of African-American participation in intercollegiate athletics. This is true even though blacks have always been a small minority of Iowa's population (never more than 2 per cent of the total).[7]

Despite their enormous achievements on the field, we know little about the social conditions African-Americans experienced off the field. Unlike Arthur Wharton, a pioneering black athlete in Great Britain whose accomplishments on the playing fields were erased from memory because he threatened the white supremacist underpinnings of Victorian England, the athletic achievements of African-Americans at Iowa are well recorded and remembered – it is their race that has been forgotten. Knowledge of the unique circumstances African-Americans encountered as athletes at a predominantly white university is largely missing from Iowa's institutional memory. What remains is a distorted memory, one that emphasizes the positive and ignores the negative aspects of race relations in Iowa's athletic history.[8]

Iowa enjoyed a progressive reputation when it came to black athletic participation in the years before widespread integration in the United States. By the 1950s Iowa had earned a reputation among African-Americans as a haven for black athletes. Ted Wheeler, a former athlete and coach at Iowa, explained in an interview why he came to Iowa in the early 1950s: 'it was the only place a black distance runner could go, back then'. 'As soon as schools found out that I had a real good suntan', he joked, 'and that I was real tall [6 ft 5 in], they lost interest.'[9]

This reputation, however, developed slowly and unevenly over the first five decades of the twentieth century. Participation varied by sport and sex. Black men had played football since Frank Holbrook was the first in 1895, but none played basketball until the 1945/46 season when Dick Culbertson broke the barrier in the Big Ten Conference. In 1957 Simon Roberts became the first African-American to capture an NCAA wrestling title. His feat further enriched Iowa's history of black athletic achievement. But by the late 1960s Iowa's reputation as a haven for black athletes seemed irrelevant as black football players protested against conditions at the university. The mere participation of black athletes was less of an issue as integration became more widespread across the country. As society changed other issues came to the fore, such as athletic eligibility, student support services for athletes, and the hiring of black coaches.[10]

Another important issue was sexual equity. African-American women, like other women, were completely shut out of intercollegiate athletic competition at Iowa until Congress passed Title IX in 1972. This legislation guaranteed women equal access to educational activities, including sports. Although the national implementation of Title IX has been slow, the University of Iowa has built a model program in the years since the landmark legislation was enacted. Under the leadership of Christine Grant, Iowa established a separate athletic department for women. The university's commitment to sexual equity echoed its earlier tradition of racial progress in sports.[11]

While race has been a global issue in sport since the late nineteenth century, the University of Iowa's athletic history shows that race has worked itself out in numerous national, regional, and local contexts. But some key questions remain: do fans and players think deeply about Iowa's tradition of African-American athletes? Have black players influenced the racial attitudes of Iowans? There are no sure answers. One certainty is that the memory of African-American athletes has been put to diverse uses throughout Iowa's athletic history.[12]

Space does not permit a comprehensive history of the African-American athlete at Iowa, but an examination of the stories that have been told (and not told) about black athletes sheds light on the globalizing nature of sport and how the black athlete has been remembered (and forgotten) over time. By focusing on the image of the black athlete in sports publications we learn how amnesia and memory work together to frame our collective memory of sports.[13]

In *Remembering Ahanagran* the historian Richard White confronted his mother's memories of Ireland through historical research. Explaining the dilemma, he wrote:

> I once thought of my mother's stories as history. I thought memory was history. Then, I became a historian, and after many years I have come to realize that only careless historians confuse history and memory. History is the enemy of memory. The two stalk each other across the fields of the past, claiming the same terrain. History forges weapons from what memory has forgotten or suppressed.[14]

The relationship between history and memory is as complex as it is critical. I define history as a dynamic dialog we have with the past through the prism of an ever-advancing present. Only by asking questions and by subjecting vestiges of the past, such as commemorative works on Iowa's athletic history, to rigorous analysis in the present can we rescue our sports memory from the sports reportage of the past. The major obstacle preventing a deeper understanding of our sports history is the reluctance of scholars to journey into this terrain. More work is needed to recover our lost and suppressed memories.[15]

IMAGE AND REALITY OF A UNIVERSITY'S ATHLETIC HISTORY

Sources close to the Iowa athletic department have put forth the idea that the university was a forerunner in the participation of black athletes in college sports. We learn this through sources as disparate as a cartoon, a monograph, a letter from a fan, and various forms of memorialization on campus.

Jack Bender's *A Gallery of Iowa Sports Heroes: Five Decades of Cartoons* (1989) contains one particularly telling illustration. The caption of a cartoon featuring 'Deacon' Davis, an African-American basketball player in the 1950s, offers what is likely to be the dominant interpretation of black athletes at Iowa: 'Racial discrimination has never been a part of the vocabulary at the University of Iowa.' After listing some of the pioneering black athletes at Iowa, Bender adds, 'the annals of early Hawkeye sports are dotted with the exploits of these fine black athletes'.[16]

In contrast to the caption Bender added years later for his 1989 book, a message in the original cartoon supplies a more nuanced story. In the original Bender describes 'Deacon' Davis as the 'Harlem Globetrotter of Big 10 Basketball'. He adds, his 'long arms make him look like Trotters' famed Goose Tatum'. The Harlem Globetrotters, an all-black basketball troupe, are perhaps the world's best known basketball team (besides the Chicago Bulls of the Michael Jordan era). The Globetrotters would never have existed if blacks had not been excluded from playing professional basketball in the early days of the sport. By labeling Davis a 'Globetrotter', Bender unintentionally draws our attention to America's segregated history of sports. Although Iowa helped to break down racial barriers in the late 1940s and the early 1950s by utilizing black basketball players, the fact does not negate the Big Ten Conference's long history of excluding African-Americans from basketball and other sports such as wrestling. Also, informal quota systems remained for many years limiting the number of blacks a coach might play on previously all-white teams.[17]

The caption to Bender's cartoon echoed an interpretation of Iowa athletics written by the historian Leola Bergmann in 1949. Bergmann's *The Negro in Iowa* surveyed African-American history and life in Iowa. She devoted one paragraph to sports:

> In the area of sports, discrimination against the Negroes has been less marked than in many other areas of activity. Through the years the University of Iowa has had several outstanding athletes, among them Edward Gordon who held the national intercollegiate broad jump championship and was on the American Olympic track team in the ninth Olympiad at Amsterdam in 1928. In football some of the great names have been the Negro players such as Wendell Benjamin, 'Duke' Slater, Emlen Tunnell, John Estes, and Earl Banks.[18]

Although years apart, they shared the same view of Iowa athletics. William Naber, a fan of the Hawkeyes for many years, made a similar point in a letter he sent to me in 1997. He said:

I'm sure you're aware of all or most of these [University of] Iowa players but it is fun for me to recollect how the state of Iowa was a forerunner of giving black athletes a chance to perform and earn an education through their talents.

His recollections indicated how African-American athletes became a source of pride for some Iowans:

I've got a strong interest in all black Americans. The majority of black Americans have a heritage in our country that goes back farther than almost any other American group. ... It makes me feel proud that the state of Iowa has been one of the early leaders in letting black Americans become part of the main stream of the American culture. Obviously, there is a long way to go but Iowans should be made aware that their home state can be looked at in a positive way of letting all Americans have the chance to be called simply 'an American'.[19]

Several physical structures on the University of Iowa's campus push a similar theme. In 1972 the university renamed one of its residence halls in honor of a legendary black football player and judge Fred (Duke) Slater. The current outdoor track and field facility was named after a former white track coach Francis X. Cretzmeyer. An inscription on a plaque near the field tells how he was a forerunner in the use of black long-distance runners: 'At a time when American track and field coaches thought that black athletes were genetically inferior and emotionally incapable of running long distances, [Cretzmeyer] accepted them with the same warmth and enthusiasm he showed with all his athletes.'[20]

In 1999 the new women's softball field was named in honor of what was then thought to be the university's first African-American baseball player, Robert L. Pearl. This act of commemoration is a good example of the selective and contradictory nature of memorialization. Pearl was not the first black baseball player, but because of influential donors the name stood. It is an example of feel-good history at its worse. Not only did the athletic department rely on the faulty memory of some important donors, but officials ignored the sound advice of some members of the fund-raising committee that the softball complex should be named after a woman. Apparently one minority was good as another. No change was made.[21]

Memorials paint a positive picture of the university and its athletic history. But the historian David Wiggins used Iowa's athletic history to make his point that predominantly white colleges in the North have often used blacks for athletic glory while neglecting them as students. The example he used was Connie Hawkins, a basketball phenomenon who came to Iowa from New York City in 1960. Off the court Hawkins encountered loneliness and frustration as one of a small number of African-Americans at Iowa. His social isolation was compounded by the fact that he was functionally illiterate. Hawkins was ill-prepared for the academic coursework the university required. Yet everyone had high hopes for him. Iowa fans turned out in droves to watch his dunking artistry during practises and junior varsity games. Hawkins and the white star Don Nelson were the keys to Iowa's national championship hopes.[22]

But when Hawkins became the subject of a New York gambling investigation by the city's police the University of Iowa's athletic department distanced itself from its prize recruit. Boosters had given Hawkins money, but the athletic department moved quickly to cover up any improprieties. They avoided a damaging probe by the NCAA in part by enlisting Hawkins to write a letter exonerating them of any wrongdoing. Meanwhile, Hawkins was thrown to the wolves. In short, he was used by the athletic department, the New York gamblers whom he thought were his friends, and the police who entrapped him. For his trouble he was banned from the NBA for many years despite later being cleared of all charges.[23]

SPORTS JOURNALISM:
THE FIRST DRAFT OF SPORTS HISTORY

None of these portrayals so far adequately encapsulates the complex history of African-Americans and athletics at the University of Iowa. Perhaps the truth is somewhere in between. Iowa was neither radically egalitarian, as Bender would have it, nor intractably racist, as Wiggins implied. Rather, the university reflected the moderate political culture and history of race relations in the state of Iowa and in the Midwest generally.[24]

But how might we explain the difference between the more positive and the more negative accounts? What is the relationship among them? Michael Kammen argued that scholars tend be cynical when writing about 'distortions of our collective memory', often 'ascribing manipulative motives or the maintenance of hegemonic control by dominant social groups'. Like Kammen, I am suspicious of scholars who lean on the conceptual crutch of hegemony and ignore human agency. I suggest a simple sociological explanation: the social situations we inhabit influence the way we write and remember our history.[25]

No group has had more influence than sportswriters in the construction of our sports memory. Recent studies demonstrate how sports reporting was enmeshed with the rise of college sports in the twentieth century. It should surprise no one that formerly sports reporting lacked a critical edge. Academics might have acted as a check on the 'soft' reporting of journalists had not their own norms and status anxieties forced them to abandon the field. Steven A. Reiss described the relationship between sport history and historians: 'Until recently, historians rarely studied sports because it seemed intrinsically trivial, because they considered other topics to be more important, or because they were snobs.' Fortunately, a large body of interdisciplinary scholarship has sprung up to correct the distortions of the past.[26]

How our sports memory has evolved can be seen through a careful study of published sources on Iowa's athletic history. By analysing commemorative books on Iowa football (the sources most often written by sports journalists) along with the few academic studies available on Iowa athletics, we gain a better understanding of how norms of reportage have changed over time on the matter of race. Until the 1960s most journalists and academics ignored a deeper investigation of race in their written histories while scholars mostly ignored sport. But changing attitudes paved the way for the recovery of lost memories as we neared the end of the twentieth century. Now it is common for academics and more popular writers to include a discussion of race in their sports histories, but it was not always so.[27]

COLLEGE FOOTBALL: A METAPHOR FOR LIFE IN IOWA

Loren Hickerson proclaimed Iowa football a metaphor for life in Iowa:

> Iowa football reflects the mores of a greater community which is all of Iowa. There are striking similarities between the uphill fight of the Hawkeyes to win football recognition among the toughest foes, and the uphill fight of the university itself to win a higher place of honor, respect, and proud support among its own people, and the uphill fight of the state itself to become a positive factor among the community of states.[28]

Hickerson's is powerful testimony on how college football can reflect a region's history and culture.[29]

One of the earliest works to shed light on the history of Iowa football is Robert Wilson Meinhard's 'History of the State University of Iowa: Physical Education and Athletics for Men', a master's thesis in history in 1947. His main focus is the development of major and minor sports at Iowa and their eventual bureaucratic control by the university. Although race was not part of his study, his text demonstrates the importance of race and region in the history of Iowa football.[30]

In making a point about the 'ruffianly character' of football in the 1890s, Meinhard described two games between the University of Iowa and the University of Missouri. Each game occasioned violence on the field and off. In 1894 a melee ensued after two players exchanged blows on the field. The Missouri spectators then rushed the field, some of them armed with knives. The Iowa players defended themselves – one player left with a cut lip from a Missouri fan.[31]

But this was nothing compared with what happened two years later when the football team returned to Columbia – this time with a black player on their squad. The author wrote: 'The riot of two years before had only been a preliminary for what was about to happen this November day. Iowa helped furnish fuel for the trouble by taking along Holbrook, a star half-back, who was a negro [*sic*].' Meinhard then quoted large portions of a story from a local newspaper.[32]

According to the press report, Missouri fans spread rumors that Holbrook would be killed. As a crowd milled about outside the team's hotel rooms the night before the game, chants of 'Kill the Negro!' and other insults could be heard. Spectators arrived the next day armed with makeshift clubs spoiling for a fight. The paper reported that the Iowa team protected Holbrook during the game although he hardly seemed to need it: 'At times they [Iowa players] placed themselves near and about Holbrook. Each member of the team seemed to exceed the rest in watchfulness over Holbrook, though he showed no disposition to shield himself back of others.' The game ended after a series of bizarre incidents and plays, including the slugging of an Iowa professor who served as an official during the game. Finally, the Iowa team withdrew from battle after enduring enough abuse. They declared victory and took their lead home with them to Iowa City. Missouri fans pelted their bus with clods of dirt as it departed.[33]

The story made Meinhard's point: sport in the late 1890s was full of violence and race only added to the spectacle. He might have added a point about regional differences in race relations. While the University of Missouri represented a state made famous by the Missouri Compromise of 1820, an agreement admitting Missouri as a slave state, which only postponed a decision on slavery settled by the Civil War, the University of Iowa represented a state that had transformed itself from one of the most racist territories in the North to 'one of the most egalitarian states in the Union'. While Missouri harbored sympathies for the defeated Confederacy, Iowa was a 'bright radical star' on the question of race in the United States.[34]

Although race and violence were important aspects of Iowa's football history, much time elapsed before writers gave these themes serious attention in their athletic histories. In 1953 Robert Rutland, a research associate employed by the state historical society, wrote a special issue on college football for Iowa's popular history magazine the *Palimpsest*. While black players received some mention in the text and were pictured in photographs – including Johnny Bright of Drake, Duke Slater of Iowa, and Sol Butler of the University of Dubuque – Rutland did not make any special mention of their race or interrogate their experience as African-American football players.[35]

Writers lacking Rutland's historical training were no more attentive to race than he had been. Like Rutland's article, Tait Cummins's *Who's Who in Iowa Football*, written in 1948, included some pictures of African-American athletes but contained only a few comments on them in the text. Some of the black Hawkeyes mentioned included 'Ironman' Jim Walker (who played with Kinnick), Homer Harris, Ozzie Simmons, Duke Slater, Archie Alexander, and Kinney Holbrook. The caption beneath a picture of Homer Harris stressed an Iowa first, however:

> Homer Harris holds the unique distinction of being the only Negro in all Western Conference [Big Ten] history to captain a varsity football team. A star on the 1935 and 1936 Hawkeye teams at end, Harris pictured above, was named by his team mates to captain the 1937 team.[36]

He added this final sentence to honor the student-athlete ideal: 'Harris is now a physician in Kansas.'[37]

The caption underneath a picture of the All-American Ozzie Simmons subtly informed the reader of his race: 'Only one Hawkeye ever carried the ball like the swivel hipped [*sic*] fellow above is doing. Of course, it's Ozzie Simmons, *dusky demon* [emphases added] of the 1934–35 era.' Although Simmons experienced troubles with his coach and complained about racism, Cummins made no mention of it. Other black players such as Archie Alexander and C.W. Holbrook were listed as letter winners but he did not identify them as black. If one did not already know they were black the reader would find no confirmation of it here. Also, no mention was made of the contests against Missouri that caused so much trouble for Holbrook; nor did Cummins mention the games that Alexander sat out because of his race.[38]

In 1950s America, college football was king and the Big Ten was the nation's most prestigious conference. Iowa rose near the top of the football world during the decade with two Rose Bowl victories and high national rankings. The formula for success was coach Forest Evashevski and the talents of black players such as Calvin Jones, Frank Gilliam, Eddie Vincent, and Willie Fleming, as well as white players such as Randy Duncan and Alex Karras. More than ever before, Iowa recruited players from outside the state. While other sports would in time get their due, Iowa football's dramatic turnaround in the 1950s helped it to become the leading subject of university-related sports publications in those years. But silence on the matter of race also remained the norm.[39]

A commemorative issue of the state's popular history magazine was published in the wake of Iowa's Rose Bowl victory over Oregon State in 1957. 'University Football through the Years' promised readers an in-depth look at Iowa football. What it showed instead was the growing influence that sportswriters and sports information directors had on the construction of Iowa's sports memory. William Peterson wrote the introduction and was the only non-sportswriter to contribute to the issue. Peterson held a PhD in history and was the superintendent of the State Historical Society of Iowa.[40]

The sportswriter John O'Donnell wrote on the history of the Big Ten; Bert McGrane on Iowa coaches; Tait Cummins on the great Hawkeye teams of the past; Gus Schrader on Iowa's greatest players; and Eric Wilson, Iowa's sports information director, supplied tables and important statistical records. As in the earlier special issue on college football, African-Americans were mentioned in the text and represented in photographs, but no mention was made of their race nor the special circumstances that often accompanied their playing. Also, no attempts were made to go beyond the story of a particular game or season.[41]

This was unfortunate because Iowa had already developed an enviable tradition of black athletes by that time. Why the silence on race by Iowa's sportswriters? David Wiggins labeled this period the romantic era of desegregation. We can speculate that race received no mention because sportswriters shared an inherent belief in integration and in the exceptionalism of American life. The darker side of college athletics was often ignored. College football was seen as proof of the rightness of the American way and an important ingredient in the nation's fight against the Soviet system during the cold war. Problematizing race would have gone against the grain of current thinking, a wet blanket thrown on a marvelous and self-congratulatory celebration of American life.[42]

This continued in 1958 with the publication of *Slater of Iowa*. James Peterson, a lawyer and president of a bottling company in Chicago, published the book honoring Fred (Duke) Slater, Iowa's most legendary African-American athlete. Peterson had previously hosted dinners honoring such football greats as Red Grange of Illinois and George Gip of Notre Dame. Peterson's honorary dinner and book came on the heels of Slater's induction into the Football Hall of Fame. The book heaped praise on Slater from start to finish. Its laudatory tone is best exemplified by a poem included in it:

> Tall as the corn from his native State
> Strong as the best in the Middle West
> True to the word his father taught
> Loved by the team his struggles wrought
> Proud of those who he helped to fame
> Grateful to the sport that built his name
> Modest son of a great University
> Reflecting credit, honor and dignity
> Hailed by the students with great affection
> Forever now a fond recollection
> Humble to the greatness that is his
> Slater of Iowa.[43]

Peterson's poem depicted Slater as an all-American boy, representative of the best in Midwestern heritage. James Shortridge has written that Americans had always associated certain aspects of their national character with regions. Iowa has long been viewed as the cultural core of the Midwest, an indicator of all-American, patriotic values. In Slater's day the Midwest was viewed favorably against the decaying East and the still too wild West. Ever since the 1920s, in periods of disenchantment with urban life or when America faced an external challenge such as World War II, 'Iowa and the Midwest [have been] nostalgically idealized as a rural paradise or America's patriotic heartland'. Slater's Iowa roots undoubtedly reflected and contributed to this image. But more important, it suggested that America was a color-blind society, which it was not.[44]

Peterson's biography is hagiography, not history. It contains the familiar tropes we might expect from the genre. The story begins with Slater facing difficulties imposed on him by poverty. Slater's father, a Methodist minister, had forbidden his son to play football. Like most parents, his father feared that his son would get hurt. But the boy persisted, breaking his proud father's will with a hunger strike. Slater soon showed himself to be a man among boys on the football field. When news of his talent spread, benevolent and influential Iowa alumni came calling. His new friends and mentors helped him to fulfill his dream of obtaining a degree at a time when such a goal was out of reach for many African-Americans.[45]

The biography lacked critical perspective but the photographs and game summaries illustrated how Slater became such a mythical figure. Jim McMillen, an All-American at Illinois, described Slater as a fierce, trash-talking, albeit gentlemanly man: 'As we lined up Duke started a line of chatter that only ended with the final whistle. The theme was mostly what dire things might happen to anyone so bold as to try and get through his side of the line.' McMillen recalled that, by the time the game was over, 'he not only had us brainwashed, but also physically convinced that he just wasn't talking through his head gear.' (Actually, Slater rarely wore a helmet.) McMillen emphasized the giant's chivalrous side: 'As the game progressed it became apparent that the Duke was feeling sorry for our awkward and futile efforts. He began picking the Illinois boys up and sending them back with a friendly pat on the back with words of encouragement.' McMillen ended his vignette with these words: 'This was my introduction to Duke Slater, All-American-gentleman.'[46]

Slater played at Iowa from 1918 to 1921. It was the most successful era in Iowa football to date. Howard Jones was at the helm and molded the Hawkeyes into a national powerhouse. Jones later moved on to the University of Southern California (USC) where he earned even greater fame as a college coach. Slater's greatest moment came during a contest in 1921 against Notre Dame. The Knute Rockne-led Irish were undefeated in 20 games and odds-on favorites to win the mythical national championship annually awarded by sportswriters. Fred Kent's photograph captured Slater's greatness. During a critical play Slater sealed off almost the entire Irish line of defenders while Gordon Locke plunged through the hole to score.[47]

A newspaper report of the game raved about Slater's performance: 'The giant Slater at right tackle was a joy killer for the Notre Dame backs on many occasions and although he carried no ball over for a touchdown he was largely responsible for the Iowa victory.' It was Notre Dame's only loss of the year and kept the Irish from winning the national title. The Hawkeyes finished the season undefeated and won the coveted conference championship. Some experts labeled the Hawkeyes the best team in college football that season.[48]

Slater's career after college also sparkled. After graduating from Iowa in 1921 he played professional football into the 1930s. He also returned to Iowa in the 1920s to study law. He earned his law degree in 1928 and later became a respected judge in Chicago. He returned to Iowa frequently, giving public speeches and attending Hawkeye football games. Slater also helped to recruit black players – by his image and through personal contact. More than just a living legend, he identified and evaluated black talent and sent it Iowa's way.[49]

Slater is arguably the most influential and enduring legend of all African-American athletes at Iowa. In 1972 the university dedicated a dormitory in his honor, Slater Hall. Slater died on 14 August 1966, but not before leaving an indelible mark on Iowa football and the region's history. More than any other player he was responsible for Iowa's reputation as a haven for black athletes. After Slater blacks came to Iowa because they thought they would be given a fair chance to play. One future All-American at Iowa, Ozzie Simmons, called Slater his role model.[50]

SEVENTY-FIVE YEARS OF FOOTBALL AND BLACK ATHLETES AT IOWA

As Iowa approached its 75th year in college football, work was completed on the most comprehensive survey to date. In 1964 Dick Lamb and Bert McGrane's *75 Years with the Fighting Hawkeyes* was published. Lamb was a historian and director of research for the National Football

Foundation; he had previously co-produced and narrated a record on Iowa football. McGrane was a prominent sportswriter for the *Des Moines Register*, Iowa's largest paper and home to one of the premier sports departments in the country (publisher of the 'Big Peach' sports section).[51]

In writing their survey the authors pored over old newspapers and corresponded with as many players, coaches, athletic administrators, writers, and fans as possible. The book placed a positive spin on Iowa football but dealt with the lesser moments as well:

> The glory of victory, conference titles and national championship recognition has more than compensated for the humiliating defeat, the shame of conference suspension or the personality conflicts and internal athletic department struggles which have been a prominent part of the 75-year Iowa gridiron saga.[52]

The book contained some interesting features – such as year-by-year summaries, special mentions of key players and coaches, best-of-decade players, and a list of all-time players. A careful reader would learn that African-Americans had been crucial to Iowa's success. Duke Slater was the only black on the roster from 1918 to 1921; but Forest Evashevski's last team had nine in 1960. The number of African-Americans on Iowa teams continued to grow in later years. African-American players made Lamb and McGrane's best-of-the decade and all-time lists. There were a number of black team captains in the early years: Homer Harris in 1937, William Fenton in 1952, Calvin Jones in 1955, and Larry Ferguson in 1962. The book also established C.W. (Frank) 'Kinney' Holbrook as the first African-American athlete at Iowa: 'Kinney Holbrook, perhaps the state's first Negro gridder, must go down as one of the all-time greats at Iowa. He was a champion sprinter, the most dependable Hawk defensive man, as well as the team's leading scorer.'[53]

The book was a significant improvement over previous surveys and an important contribution to Iowa's sports memory. Its impact is lessened somewhat by the lack of footnotes and a bibliography. But undoubtedly Hawk fans devoured its pages over the years while researchers used it as a work of reference. It demonstrated how sportswriting might use the research methods of academics to create a superior product of sports history. Unfortunately, this type of writing was not yet common in Iowa nor elsewhere.[54]

EMLEN TUNNELL:
RECOLLECTIONS OF AN AFRICAN-AMERICAN ATHLETE

Autobiographies and biographies of sports figures have always been an important genre of sportswriting. Emlen Tunnell's *Footsteps of a Giant* in 1966 recalled his days as a college and professional football player. The book reminisced about the time he spent at the University of Iowa shortly after World War II had ended, an era when increasing numbers of African-Americans played college sports in the Midwest. Tunnell described the day that he showed up for tryouts: 'I had never seen so many Negro guys in all my life.' In terms of numbers he noted that in the fall of 1946 there were '325 candidates for the football team, many of them were war veterans, and fifty-eight were Negroes'. In his autobiography Tunnell also explained why he and others had come to Iowa: 'Most of those Negro boys had come to Iowa for the same reason I had. They knew they would be given a chance to play.' He added, 'Great Negro players were a tradition at Iowa, going back to the days around World War I.'[55]

Before coming to Iowa, Tunnell suffered a broken neck in his only season of football at Toledo. After Toledo he joined the U.S. Coast Guard for military service where he apparently met the former 'Ironman' Jim Walker, who sold him on the University of Iowa. The University of California at Los Angeles (UCLA) also recruited Tunnell. But he disliked the black recruiter who called on him; Tunnell was turned off by a speech the recruiter gave him about the proper way for blacks to behave at UCLA. Tunnell went to Iowa instead; he played two years at Iowa before leaving school and moving on to the NFL.[56]

In his book Tunnell commented on the friendships and opportunities available to him as an African-American student at Iowa. The book showed how networks were important to black students and how they banded together in a mostly white world. Jim Walker persuaded Tunnell to go to Iowa, and his two black friends and team mates, Sherman Howard and Earl Banks, kept him there. Tunnell and his friends often went to a downtown drug store in Iowa City, owned by Jack Lubin, a 'color-blind' white man who once collected donations from customers to purchase eye-glasses for Tunnell.[57]

Tunnell was so enamored with Iowa that he recruited his brother to play on the basketball team. But Stuart Tunnell felt isolated and uncomfortable there, leaving after only a single season. Rather than blame school officials for not doing enough to assure his success, Tunnell reasoned that his brother was too immature for college life. With a bit of humor he noted that his brother's distinctive red hair posed more of a problem than his skin color.[58]

Tunnell painted a rather idyllic picture of Iowa – a place relatively free from racial problems that dogged blacks elsewhere. In a game against the Purdue Boilermakers an opposing player taunted Tunnell with racist insults. The Purdue lineman Dick Barwegan called time-out and forced his team mate to apologize in front of both teams. Tunnell was grateful for this act of sportsmanship, noting that many of the players like himself were veterans of military service and would not put up with disrespectful and racist behavior. It was a message sure to resonate with his readers.[59]

One of Iowa's biggest assets according to Tunnell was its coach Dr Eddie Anderson. Anderson was a physician and war veteran, a native of Mason City, Iowa, and a former Notre Dame football star under Knute Rockne. Anderson played against Slater in the 1921 titanic struggle in Iowa City. Tunnell recalled how Anderson set the tone for the Hawkeye squad: he was 'a sensitive man'. 'And because he had more Negro players than almost any other coach in the nation', Tunnell remarked, 'he found himself in areas of sensitivity, geographical and psychological quite often.'[60]

Traveling on the road held certain dangers for black athletes in the 1940s. But Tunnell gave these potentially sensitive situations a positive spin. When the team went on the road, the African-American players devised a system where they slept three in a room. The idea was not to leave the odd man out and thereby create a racial situation. Tunnell learned later that a white player had already spoken to the coach and volunteered to room with Tunnell if such a situation ever arose. While Tunnell constantly emphasized the positive and the egalitarian nature of Iowa coaches, players, and fans, this particular story suggested that there might be a lonelier side of athletic life for African-Americans.[61]

Tunnell left Iowa after the 1947 season. He later played for 14 seasons in the NFL. He was the first African-American to play for the New York Giants, the first black assistant coach in the NFL, and the first African-American inducted into the Pro Football Hall of Fame. Before retiring in 1961, he played in four NFL championship games (1956, 1958, 1960, and 1961), winning the title in 1956 with the Giants and in 1961 with the Green Bay Packers. He was the leading defensive back and punt returner of his day. Tunnell established all-time marks in both categories. In one season he gained more yards on defense than the league's leading rusher gained on offense.[62]

His accomplishments on the field lend credibility to his recollections. But conditions were not always as good as he made them appear. In the South the major universities and colleges were mostly off-limits to African-Americans well into the 1960s. Blacks were still largely confined to the historically black colleges or to the more egalitarian universities and colleges in the North in the 1940s and 1950s. The South's stand against black players often meant racial conflict when teams from different regions met in bowl games. But for a time it simply meant more talent for northern schools. The monopoly on black players was over by the early 1970s, however. Schools such as Alabama learned that winning came easier when they recruited their own black talent to play football.[63]

IOWA FOOTBALL: HISTORIES FROM THE HAYDEN FRY ERA

While Tunnell's accomplishments were great, his autobiography is not well known. But it was the last significant addition to the sports literature of Hawkeye football until the early 1980s. Hawk fans continued to support their team, but Iowa football floundered in the 1960s and the 1970s. Iowa's demise mirrored college football's fall from grace. Tremendous changes swept American society in the 1960s; while some programs continued to prosper, college football seemed conservative and out-of-step with a generation that embraced the counter culture. But by the 1980s all was right again. College football was more popular than ever. Once again it was at the center of American life.[64]

Like college football, Iowa's football program rose phoenix-like from the ashes of the 1970s. In 1978 a wise-cracking Texan strutted into Iowa City to rescue the program from its doldrums. After 19 long seasons without a winning record, Hayden Fry made Iowa a winner again in only three seasons. The Hawkeyes made their way back to Pasadena and the Rose Bowl in 1981, 1986, and 1991. During Fry's 20 years as coach Iowa fans gorged themselves on a steady diet of bowl games (11 in addition to the three Rose Bowl appearances). They also celebrated three Big-Ten championships and a number of All-Americans and future NFL players. Iowa appeared regularly on national television and were often placed high in year-end polls. Fry was even the inspiration behind a long-

running situation comedy *Coach* that starred Craig T. Nelson as Hayden
Fox. Like Fry, it ended its successful run in the 1990s.[65]

The university may not have had the most successful program in the
nation during the 1980s and the 1990s, but Iowa was not far off the pace
of the elite, big-time programs. Fry led the university into a new era of
sports promotion. He redesigned the uniforms and developed the Tiger-
Hawk logo (the uniforms were modeled after the world-champion
Pittsburgh Steelers of the NFL; the 'Tiger-Hawk' logo became so
popular that a recent attempt to alter it was stymied by students and
fans). The hottest colors in the state were black and gold as merchants
sold Hawkeye apparel everywhere. Fry's tenure also marked an
important building phase in Iowa's athletic history. He left behind new
and remodeled facilities, including one for indoor practise.[66]

Sportswriters took their cue from Fry and refashioned the memory
of Iowa football. The first popular history came early during Fry's reign:
Chuck Bright's *University of Iowa Football: The Iowa Hawkeyes* in 1982.
Bright's book is undistinguished in style and contains only the minimum
features a fan might expect: big-game summaries, photographs, and lists
of All-Americans, captains, and great individual performances. Like the
surveys written in the immediate post-war period, Bright made little
mention of race or the unique circumstances African-Americans faced as
athletes at a predominantly white university campus.[67]

In 1983 Brian and Mike Chapman added their book *Evy and the
Hawkeyes: The Glory Years* to a growing body of literature on Iowa
football. Forest Evashevski's teams had many black stars, such as Calvin
Jones, Earl Smith, Frank Gilliam, Eddie Vincent, Willie Fleming, Bob
Jeter, Joe Williams, Wilburn Hollis, Dayton Perry, Larry Ferguson, and
Al Hinton. But Evashevski's biggest coup was the Steubenville, Ohio
trio of Vincent, Gilliam, and Jones. Jones was a surprise catch. As Ohio's
player-of-the-year he was expected to attend Ohio State and play for
Woody Hayes. But after visiting the Iowa campus with his friends, Jones
decided to enroll at Iowa instead. The future All-American and Outland
Award winner explained his decision: 'I'll tell you why I came here.
They treated me like a white man, and I like it here. I'm going to stay.'[68]

Although a reasonable chronicle of the Evy years, the book fell short
of the new standards of sports history. More critical questions might
have been asked on the subject of race: how did Evy recruit players such
as Calvin Jones and white stars such as Alex Karras? What impact did
black football players have on Iowans' racial attitudes in these early years

of the civil rights movement? In short, what role did African-Americans play in the creation of big-time college football at Iowa in the 1950s?

Evashevski's lasting impact on the program as coach and athletic director merited greater scrutiny as well. Evashevski was a coaching phenomenon who retired young at the age of 41. Had he continued he might have become one of the greatest coaches in college football. (He would always be a legend in Iowa.) Instead of more coaching, he pushed his way into the athletic director's job, ousting the popular Paul Brechler in the process. But his success as athletic director did not measure up to his success as a coach. The sportswriter Maury White summed it up best:

> It is in no way demeaning to say Evy was better at coaching than at directing, for his football teams were joys to behold. But it was when he was athletic director that the Hawkeyes stumbled into that long pre-Hayden [Fry] period of mediocrity.[69]

Although the new books published during the early years of the Hayden Fry era did not show it, writing on sport had become more analytical and scholarly by the 1980s. In the summer of 1985 Iowa football received its first serious analysis, albeit in a popular history magazine. Two articles appeared on Archie Alexander, a former black football player who played at Iowa around 1910. Both were written by professional historians: one on Alexander's business and political life by Charles Wynes; the other on his football career by Raymond Smith.[70]

Wynes's article focused on Alexander's upbringing and business career. A native of Ottumwa, Iowa, Alexander grew up in a town of 14,000, of whom 467 were black. His family later moved to Des Moines, Iowa, which remained his home for the rest of his life. After attending the University of Iowa, Alexander founded what *Ebony* magazine once called 'the nation's most successful interracial business'. Alexander's first white partner was George F. Higbee who died in 1925. He was later joined by Maurice Repass in 1929, a former classmate and team mate at Iowa. Large contracts he received from the University of Iowa helped to build his firm in the early years. They included the university's heating plant (1926), power plant (1928), and a tunnel system (1928) under the Iowa River that piped power to the west campus.[71]

Unlike many blacks of his day, Alexander stayed with the Republican Party even after President Roosevelt was elected in 1932 and began his New Deal programs that were widely viewed as beneficial to African-

Americans. Another president, Dwight Eisenhower, rewarded Alexander's work in the Republican party by appointing him Governor of the Virgin Islands in 1954. The appointment was a disaster, however. Alexander proved to be a better business owner than politician. His values did not mesh well with the traditional politics of the Virgin Islanders. None the less, the appointment was a significant achievement for a black man of modest beginnings.[72]

The historian Raymond Smith focused on Alexander's football career. Smith's article exemplified the methods and goals of the new sports history. Smith detailed how national processes pulsed their way through Iowa and the career of this unique athlete. More than a blow-by-blow description of Alexander's athletic career, the article showed how these years marked a transitional period in college football. Important rule changes modernized the game, making it more similar to the one we see today. Iowa football did not draw the huge crowds it did in later years, perhaps only 2,000 or more regularly attended, but Smith argued that football revenues helped the athletic department to turn a profit and pay for other programs.[73]

Alexander was like other black athletes of the period in that his interests went beyond football. He was intent on getting an education. The same could be said of Duke Slater who arrived seven years later. Unfortunately, Alexander experienced forms of racial prejudice common in his day as well. 'In his three years of varsity football at Iowa', Smith noted, 'Archie Alexander never missed a game because of injuries. He missed three games because opponents refused to play against the Hawkeyes if they put a black man on the field, however.'[74]

A Council Bluffs paper documented one such instance. While extolling Alexander's positive attributes as a player, the writer resigned himself to the inevitable, 'With an ideal build and a good football disposition, Alexander has displayed great possibilities the last week and the coaches hate the idea of relegating him to the side lines for the Missouri and Kansas games.' Why would Iowa leave such a great player on the sidelines? The paper provided the answer:

> the Iowa authorities are anxious to avoid any stirring up of feeling between local institutions and the southern schools and if the request is made that Alexander not be played it will undoubtedly be willingly granted, though a severe blow to the local eleven.[75]

Alexander's predicament was typical. While having access to education and football, blacks could be forced off the field at will. During his career Alexander missed two games against Missouri and one against Washington of St. Louis. One of the Missouri games was even a home game played in Iowa City. This unfair treatment certainly upset Alexander but he was undeterred. In 1905 he tried out for the football team at Highland Park College in Des Moines, Iowa, only to have the college president tell him to forget about getting an education. Better to find more suitable employment like that of a janitor, he was told. Alexander ignored the advice.[76]

The year 1989 marked the centennial of Iowa football. Such occasions often produce 'memory spasms' and the publication of sports histories. This one was no exception. Al Grady added *25 Years with the Fighting Hawkeyes* to the list of previously published histories of Hawkeye football. A local sportswriter, his book was packaged by the Iowa athletic department with Lamb and McGrane's book *75 Years of the Fighting Hawkeyes*, to complete a two-volume set for the centennial. Perhaps one of the most important controversies that occurred in the intervening years was the black boycott of spring practise in 1969. Fortunately, Grady wrote almost an entire chapter on it. His version was a dramatic improvement over brief comments made by Bright in his 1982 book.[77]

Grady's analysis of the boycott demonstrated how sportswriting had changed since the 1950s and the early 1960s. As consciousness of the plight of African-Americans grew in the United States, race could no longer be ignored in popular sportswriting. Unlike some of the other surveys, Grady provided the historical context for the events he covered. For example, his treatment of the boycott began with a survey of the turbulent 1960s: the sit-ins at a lunch counter in Greensboro, North Carolina in 1960, the assassination of Martin Luther King Jr, and the raised fists of Tommie Smith and John Carlos at the Olympics in 1968. Grady then analysed the racial turmoil coach Ray Nagel found himself in the spring of 1969.[78]

Nagel's problems began when he dismissed two black football players, Greg Allison and Charles (Doc) Bolden, following the 1968 season. Academic problems claimed Allison, while Bolden found himself in trouble with the law, ostensibly for writing bad checks. Nagel had apparently derided the two black players in front of the others before dismissing them. This angered many black players on the team. The

Afro-American Student Association got involved and the seeds of the boycott were sown. When rumors of a boycott surfaced, Nagel threatened to dismiss anyone from his team who did not attend the first day of spring practise in 1969. When this opened 16 black players boycotted, firing the first salvo in what became a highly publicized media war. By the time the fall practise opened, the excitement was over. After a team meeting some black players were 'elected' back on to the team while others were sent packing. Only seven of the original 16 were on the team when the season began.[79]

Ray Manning was one of four black players who did not participate in the boycott. In an interview years later he said that he thought Jerry Stevens, the head of the Afro American Student Association, had taken advantage of the situation. Stevens wanted the athletic department to pay for a special house for African-Americans on campus. He argued that the university owed them as much for using blacks as 'gladiators'. Manning was ambivalent about the whole protest movement, but he was an admirer of Harry Edwards, the black sociologist and chief spokesman for the black athletic revolt in the 1960s. Manning felt that the coach had no way of understanding what the black players were going through at the time – he was something of a victim, too. Manning decided not to boycott because he felt that he could do more for his people by staying on the team and in school.[80]

The first black player voted back on to the team was the tailback Dennis Green. A native of Harrisburg, Pennsylvania, Green later became an assistant coach at Iowa in the early 1970s. He was also the first black head coach in Division I college football, the first black head coach in the Big Ten Conference, and the second black head coach in the NFL. In his 1997 book *No Room for Crybabies* Green reminisced about the boycott in 1969: 'I endured one of the most frustrating times of my life as a college player after being labeled a radical and an agitator for joining fifteen black team mates in a boycott of spring practise', he wrote. Describing both the excitement of the times and the price he paid for his protest, he said,

> We were caught up in the times of the revolt of the black athlete. I'll never say it was a mistake to stand up for your principles. But the protest designed to get more respect as individuals from coaches, additional black assistant coaches, and better academic counseling – didn't turn out the way any of us hoped.[81]

The boycott ultimately led to another spoiled season. But Grady noted its positive effects: 'The interesting thing to note is that most of the items the blacks demanded were implemented at Iowa, and throughout the Big Ten, within a few years, and a couple of them, within a few months.' Yet the black players' demands also revealed ironies and contradictions inherent in many protest movements of the 1960s. In the 1930s black players such as Ozzie and Don Simmons had no choice but to room in off-campus housing such as the Alpha House, an all-black fraternity. Ironically, in the era of integration blacks demanded separate housing for black athletes. At least this time segregation would be on their terms.[82]

When players called for more black assistant coaches in 1969, Iowa was one of two teams in the Big Ten Conference who employed one. The assistant coach at Iowa was Frank Gilliam, one of Evashevski's former players from the 1950s. He recruited Dennis Green to play for Iowa and, later, was the director of player personnel for the Minnesota Vikings when Green was hired as head coach. (Ironically, Green replaced a former Hawkeye assistant and head coach, Jerry Burns.) Green's tenure as the Vikings' head coach must be deemed a success although he has not yet won a Super Bowl. As coach of the Vikings in the 1990s, he earned acclaim for resurrecting the careers of black athletes such as Chris Carter, Randall Cunningham, and Randy Moss.[83]

The black boycott symbolized a period of shifting memory. It occurred because expectations had outpaced conditions. The university had not changed as much as the times had. The image of Iowa as a haven for blacks apparently had been forgotten or had become irrelevant by the late 1960s. While continuity still existed, a chasm between generations of African-American athletes and officials had apparently developed that only widened in later decades. Scholars have pointed out that a disconnection from the past was a common trait of the 1960s generation in America. Students believed that they were making history rather than passively living through it. Their conceit was a familiar one of youth.[84]

While the revolutionaries largely ignored the triumphs of earlier generations, their actions changed the academy. Academics began to realize that sports were central to American life and that the study of sport and race could be a useful avenue of research. After all, what political figure or intellectual commanded the world's attention like Muhammad Ali? Beginning in the 1960s and extending through the 1970s and the 1980s, a new literature sprang up chronicling the achievements of black athletes. Sports journalists also gave greater attention to black issues in their articles. A new era of racial awareness had been ushered in by the 1990s.[85]

In 1995 Maury White wrote an article on the history of black athletes in Iowa. White was a retired sportswriter for the *Des Moines Register* and curator of its Iowa Sport Hall of Fame. His article chronicled the careers of early black athletes at Iowa colleges and provided the most thorough biographical treatment of Frank Holbrook, the first African-American to participate in intercollegiate athletics in Iowa. White was careful to explain the difficulties and the value of this type of research. He noted 'firsts' were slippery, since nobody thought to pay attention to them at the time they happened. His article drew heavily but critically on the work of Arthur Ashe whose popular history of the black athlete had altered the landscape of America's sports memory.[86]

White's article is a good example of how the history of race and sport was taken more seriously in the 1990s. Academics and popular writers were hard at work excavating the hidden history of the African-American athlete. Others subjected the contemporary sports scene to uncharacteristic levels of analysis as well. Tom Witosky of the *Des Moines Register* investigated the graduation rates of college athletes. He also reported on sports scandals and the pernicious influence of sports agents in college athletics. For example, Witosky covered the story of the Iowa running back Ronnie Harmon who received $54,000 from sports agents while he attended the University of Iowa. While older sportswriters had helped to establish the myth of the student-athlete, writers such as Witosky exposed it for what it was – a myth.[87]

While these trends would in time shape the way the University of Iowa's athletic history was remembered, syrupy reflections continued to roll off the presses. Mark Dukes and Gus Schrader published their *Greatest Moments in Iowa Hawkeyes Football History* in 1998. The slick, coffee-table book consisted mostly of previously published stories taken from the *Cedar Rapids Gazette*. The book celebrated Iowa's great victories but did little to place Iowa football in historical perspective. The volume included stories on African-American athletes such as Slater and Jones. Although the book did not go beyond what we already knew about these athletes, it probably helped to preserve their memory for another generation.[88]

In 1999 Fry's memoir was published, *Hayden Fry: A High Porch Picnic*. While entertaining, it epitomized a genre that suffered from the bad habits of the past. Written in a folksy style that favored description over analysis, Fry's book offered useful tidbits but did not add up to a serious work of history. Organized around obvious lines, the book contained chapters for each rung of the ladder and season-by-season summaries of Fry's career. Three chapters at the end discussed such topics as Fry's retirement in 1998, Iowa fans, and the implementation of Title IX.[89]

Ironically, race was the underlying theme of the book. The foreword was written by Jerry Levias, the first black player at Southern Methodist University (SMU). Fry recruited Levias to integrate the Southwest Conference in 1966. He said Levias was the player he most admired during his coaching career. Early in the book we learn about Fry's views on race: 'Our first home in Odessa (Texas) was on the south side of the tracks ... We lived there long enough for me to make some friends – many of them what we call today minorities.'[90]

A whole chapter is devoted later in the book to the integration of SMU and the Southwest Conference by Fry and Levias. Fry recalled how he told administrators during an interview for the job that he would not accept the position if he could not integrate the team and the Southwest Conference. After some debate the administration hired Fry with one stipulation: the first black player had to be exemplary in every way. Fry found his Jackie Robinson in Jerry Levias. His first major recruit at Iowa was the thunder-footed Reggie Roby, a black high school player from Waterloo, Iowa. Roby became an All-American punter at Iowa and played for many years in the NFL.[91]

Fry's tenure marked an important era in Iowa athletics. The participation of black athletes in college sports became less of an issue as the South integrated its colleges in the late 1960s and the early 1970s. Since 1970 the important issues in sports have been the implementation of Title IX, the commercialization of athletics, the debate over athletic eligibility and standards such as Proposition 48, the hiring of black administrators and coaches, and the growing influence of sports agents in college athletics. Fry's career embodied all these trends.[92]

A media darling when he came to Iowa, Fry occasionally found himself on the wrong side of the press. The trial of two notorious sports agents Norby Walters and Harold Bloom threatened to undue the positive work Fry had done. The scandal exposed the poor academic record of Devon Mitchell and Ronnie Harmon, two outstanding Iowa football players in the 1980s. Both had received payments from agents while they attended the University of Iowa. Fry was not implicated in the scandal but it showed that his players had violated NCAA rules. The bad publicity from this episode encouraged Hunter Rawlings III, the president of the university, to make some hasty remarks about barring first-year students from playing sports at Iowa. Fry reacted with great emotion, claiming that the unilateral action of the president would doom the recently revived football program. Why should Iowa establish standards that none of its competitors had to live by? Rawlings backed down. And like other college presidents who flirted briefly with athletic reform, Rawlings left Iowa for greener pastures before anything was done about it.[93]

OTHER MILESTONES: BLACK COACHES AT IOWA

Before Fry was hired a five-column advertisement appeared in the *Iowa City Press-Citizen* on 23 November 1978, promoting the candidacy of a black man Eddie Robinson. Grambling's legendary black coach was then on his way to becoming America's most successful coach, a mark he reached in 1985 by surpassing Paul 'Bear' Bryant. Al Schallau, an attorney in Los Angeles who grew up in Iowa City, had paid for the advertisement. In his open letter he voiced his opinion that Robinson was needed to turn the moribund program around. He cited Robinson's coaching ability and argued that 'The University of Iowa has the opportunity to be remembered forever as having opened the gates for black people as head football coaches at major universities.'[94]

Grambling was not a major football program of the caliber of Notre Dame, Ohio State, or even Iowa. But this small, traditionally black college, had produced more than its share of professional players. Robinson's name circulated in the media in the mid 1970s as a likely person to become the first black head football coach in the NFL. The advertisement reminded readers that Robinson had earned his master's degree in physical education at Iowa in 1954. Iowa accepted Robinson even though his credentials could not be verified. His alma mater had closed during World War II and all his records were lost.[95]

Robinson spent five summers at Iowa between 1948 and 1958. In four semesters he earned his master's degree in physical education while picking up football tips from the Iowa coaching staff. Dr Eddie Anderson and Forest Evashevski tutored Robinson on the finer points of the game while he was there. Robinson later used Iowa's single-wing offense at Grambling until he learned that Evashevski had scrapped it. Robinson later returned to Iowa to pursue a PhD but his real purpose was to learn Evy's new wing-T offense. Jerry Burns, an assistant under Evy, offered Robinson access to game films in exchange for teaching one his classes. Robinson later returned to Grambling, installed the wing-T, and used it until he retired. When his fellow coaches chided him about being behind the times he responded by saying, 'How many games have you won'?[96]

Robinsion was never interviewed for the job but Iowa hired its first black head coach in 1978. Ted Wheeler was tapped to lead the track program. Wheeler was a former long-distance runner and Olympic athlete at Iowa in the 1950s. In 1983 Iowa scored a 'triple achievement' in minority relations by hiring a black man and a black woman to lead the men's and the women's basketball program. Like Wheeler in 1978, George Raveling and C. Vivian Stringer were the first African-Americans to head their own programs in the Big Ten Conference. These milestones once again gave the impression that Iowa athletics was a special place for African-Americans. The experiment resulted in long tenures for Wheeler and Stringer but not for Raveling.[97]

Not long after Raveling began coaching at Iowa, a Seattle newspaper reported that Iowans disliked Raveling because he was black. The story had hardly died down when Raveling accepted a job at the University of Southern California, a step down in the basketball world, but away from the fishbowl of Iowa basketball. Raveling's departure exemplified the perils of big-time sports. When given an opportunity one had to make good or be scorned. While Raveling was an excellent recruiter, his teams did not do as well as expected. By replacing the legendary Lute Olson, who had taken Iowa to the Final Four and who looked like the stereotypical Iowan, Raveling had walked into a minefield. Iowa basketball, like athletics in general in the 1980s, was a media frenzy where every activity of a coach or player was scrutinized. In a way, he fell victim to the new global capitalism that was then transforming sports into the world's biggest form of entertainment.[98]

Walter LaFeber explained the global rise of basketball in his 1999 book *Michael Jordan and the New Global Capitalism*. LaFeber described what he called the 'Faustian bargain' of this new era: corporations and individuals who profited handsomely from the new global media could just as easily be destroyed by it. Jordan's first departure from basketball in 1993 was caused by the media's close examination of his personal life, including his apparent gambling addiction and his father's murder.[99]

Raveling's departure was a direct consequence of intense media scrutiny. He felt extra pressure as a black coach in a mostly white state. Iowa fans may have been upset at Raveling's use of black players and Iowa's new style of play, but what angered Iowans most (besides the losses) were the sweatsuits Raveling and his assistants wore during basketball games. Suits and ties were the required apparel for college coaches at the time. But Raveling was prone to hyperventilating during games and so he donned a sweatsuit instead. The outcry was immediate and vicious. Fans did not hesitate to voice their opinion that the sweatsuits had to go. Understandably, Raveling was defensive. But he stubbornly persisted in wearing the sweatsuits. He resigned in 1986 before his contract was up. Leaving the hassles of Iowa behind, he took a position where he could be 'alone among four million people'.[100]

CONCLUSION

In the 1970s and the early 1980s one of the most popular television programs in the United States was 'M*A*S*H'. This portrayed the men and women of the U.S. Army who belonged to a mobile hospital unit near the front line in the Korean War. One episode featured a story about a former black football player Billy Tayler, who was wounded in the leg during combat. When he arrived at the M*A*S*H 4077 doctors were forced to amputate his leg. When Tayler awoke from surgery he learned what had happened. Knowing that his playing days were over, he contemplated suicide. Only Radar O'Reilly, the naive and kindly corporal from Ottumwa, Iowa, was able to soothe his pain. Radar found an old copy of *Life* magazine featuring an Iowa–Minnesota football game. Tayler was the star that day and recounted to Radar how difficult it was to win over the Golden Gophers. In the end, Tayler decided not to give up on his life, just like he and his team mates did not give up against Minnesota on that autumn afternoon before the war.[101]

This touching episode is just one example of how the history of the black athlete at Iowa has found its way into the media. It is fertile with symbolism: the white fan and the black athlete. Although it was fictional, the episode contained a kernel of truth – much as the self-congratulatory tales of black athletes memorialized in Iowa's athletic history contained some measure of truth. But the real story is more complicated. The

University of Iowa was neither radically egalitarian in its convictions nor intractably racist. Rather, it reflected the moderate political culture of Iowa and the region's history with race. The University of Iowa, located in the heartland of America, was neither immune from the globalizing influences of sport nor completely dominated by them. University officials and students demonstrated ability in shaping their own institution's history.

The argument of this chapter is that sport functions as a way of remembering. Too often our sports histories have ignored the larger picture because writers have erased racial conflict from their works. While sports reporting has evolved over the years – becoming more analytical and less descriptive – much of our sports memory remains in a fog. More work needs to be done to salvage it from the sports reporting of the past. More research is needed to recover the history of the black athlete in the United States and throughout all of North America. One way this might be done is for scholars to integrate the scholarship on memory with the scholarship on sports. What better way is there to deliver our memory from the amnesia of the past?

NOTES

1. See Calvin Jones file in Alumni Vertical Files, University of Iowa Archives, Iowa City, Iowa (hereafter UIAVF).
2. Ibid.
3. Ibid.
4. Ibid.
5. Ibid. The quotation from Happel may be found in M. Finn and C. Leistikow, *Hawkeye Legends, Lists and Lore: The Athletic History of the Iowa Hawkeyes* (Champaign, IL: Sports Publishing, 1998), p.101.
6. For a brief sketch of Jones's career see D.L. Porter (ed.), *Dictionary of American Sports: Football* (Westport, CT: Greenwood, 1987), p.297. For more on Nile Kinnick see P. Baender, *A Hero Perished: The Diary and Selected Letters of Nile Kinnick* (Iowa City, IA: University of Iowa Press, 1991) and D.W. Stump, *Kinnick: The Man and the Legend* (Iowa City, IA: University of Iowa Press, 1975).
7. The best survey of the university's history is S. Persons, *The University of Iowa in the Twentieth Century: An Institutional History* (Iowa City, IA: University of Iowa Press, 1990). For insights on the history of African-Americans at Iowa, see P. Hubbard, *New Dawns: A 150-Year Look at Human Rights at the University of Iowa* (Iowa City, IA: Sesquicentennial Committee, 1996) and *My Iowa Journey: The Life Story of Iowa's First African-American Professor* (Iowa City, IA: University of Iowa Press, 1999). For a brief overview of blacks in Iowa see D.E. Motten, 'Iowa', in J. Salzman *et al.*, *Encyclopedia of African-American Culture and History*, Vol.3 (New York, NY: Simon & Schuster, 1996), pp.1395–7. For comparative histories of black athletes at other predominantly white institutions see D. Spivey and T. Jones, 'Intercollegiate Athletic Servitude: A Case Study of the Black Illinois Student-Athletes, 1931–1967', *Social Science Quarterly*, 55 (1975), 939–47; D. Spivey, 'Sport, Protest, and Consciousness: The Black Athlete in Big-Time Intercollegiate Sports, 1941–1968', *Phylon*, 44 (1983), 116–25, and 'End Jim Crow in Sports: The Protest at New York University, 1940–1941', *Journal of Sport History*, 15 (1988), 282–303;

D. Wiggins, 'Prized Performers but Frequently Overlooked Students: The Involvement of Black Athletes in Intercollegiate Sports at Predominantly White University Campuses, 1890–1972', *Research Quarterly for Exercise and Sport*, 62 (1991), 164–77; and J. Behee, *Hail to the Victors! Black Athletes at the University of Michigan* (Ann Arbor, MI: Swink-Tuttle, 1974).

8. P. Vasili, *The First Black Footballer – Arthur Wharton, 1865–1930: An Absence of Memory* (London and Portland, OR: Frank Cass, 1998). For an excellent introduction to the historiography of African-American athletes see D.K. Wiggins, *Glory Bound: Black Athletes in a White America* (Syracuse, NY: Syracuse University Press, 1997).

9. See Finn and Leistikow, *Hawkeye Legends*, p.103; and the Ted Wheeler file in Faculty Vertical Files, University of Iowa Archives, Iowa City, Iowa (hereafter UIFVF).

10. The best source on black athletes at Iowa is Finn and Leistikow, *Hawkeye Legends*. For an examination of black student life at Iowa in the 1930s see H. Jenkins, 'The Negro Student at the University of Iowa: A Sociological Study' (MA thesis, University of Iowa, 1933).

11. Finn and Leistikow, *Hawkeye Legends*, p.139. For more on women's athletics at Iowa see M.K. Lienau, 'The Metamorphosis of the Department of Intercollegiate Athletics for Women at the University of Iowa, 1974–1984' (PhD thesis, University of Iowa, 1989) and Hubbard, *New Dawns*, pp.60–62. See also P. Vertinsky and G. Captain, 'More Myth than History: American Culture and Representations of the Black Female's Athletic Ability', *Journal of Sport History*, 25 (1998), 532–61 and P. Vertinsky, 'Gender Relations, Women's History and Sport History: A Decade of Changing Enquiry, 1983–1993', ibid., 21 (1994), 1–25.

12. For more on race and sport in a variety of contexts see Vasili, *Black Footballer*; J. Polumbaum and S.G. Wieting, 'Stories of Sport and the Moral Order: Unraveling the Cultural Construction of Tiger Woods', *Journalism and Communication Monographs*, 1 (1999), 69–118; J. Bale, 'Capturing "The African" Body? Visual Images and "Imaginative Sports"', *Journal of Sport History*, 25 (1998), 234–51; B.Wilson, '"Good Blacks" and "Bad Blacks": Media Constructions of African-American Athletes in Canadian Basketball', *International Review of the Sociology of Sport*, 32 (1997), 177–89 and S. J. Jackson, 'Life in the (Mediated) Faust Lane: Ben Johnson, National Affect and the 1988 Crisis of Canadian Identity', ibid., 33 (1998), 227–38 and 'A Twist of Race: Ben Johnson and the Canadian Crisis of Racial and National Identity', *Sociology of Sport Journal*, 15 (1998), 21–40.

13. Consult the University of Iowa's Main Library and archives for the most complete collection of sports publications on the University's athletic history.

14. R. White, *Remembering Ahanagran: Storytelling in a Family's Past* (New York, NY: Hill & Wang, 1998), p.4.

15. The French sociologist Maurice Halbwachs was the pioneering scholar of collective memory. An excellent introduction to his thought is L.A. Coser (ed.), *Maurice Halbwachs on Collective Memory* (Chicago, IL: University of Chicago Press, 1992). Little of the burgeoning memory scholarship includes sports. Some scholars who have used the concept of nostalgia in their works include E. Snyder, 'Sociology of Nostalgia: Sport Halls of Fame and Museums in America', *Sociology of Sport Journal*, 8 (1991), 228–38 and C.F. Springwood, *Cooperstown to Dyersville: A Geography of Baseball Nostalgia* (Boulder, CO: Westview Press, 1996). The growing body of literature on war and memory might provide useful models for scholars seeking to apply the idea of collective memory to sports. Exemplary studies include P. Novick, *The Holocaust in American Life* (Boston, MA: Houghton Mifflin Company, 1999); K. Savage, *Standing Soldiers, Kneeling Slaves: Race, War, and Monument in Nineteenth-Century America* (Princeton, NJ: Princeton University Press, 1997); J. Winter, *Sites of Memory, Sites of Mourning: The Great War in European Cultural History* (New York, NY: Cambridge University Press, 1995); G.K. Piehler, *Remembering War the American Way* (Washington, DC: Smithsonian Institution Press, 1995) and G.L. Mosse, *Fallen Soldiers: Reshaping the Memory of the World Wars* (New York, NY: Harper Collins, 1992).

16. J. Bender, *A Gallery of Iowa Sports Heroes: Five Decades of Cartoons* (Cedar Rapids, IA: Voice of the Hawkeyes, 1989). p.31. See also G.L. Lee, *Interesting Athletes: A Newspaper Artist's Look at Blacks in Sports* (Jefferson, NC: McFarland, 1990), pp.110–11, 120, for cartoons of the Iowa athletes Fred (Duke) Slater, Ozzie Simmons, and Emlen Tunnell. Lee was a prominent African-American illustrator. His cartoons give us an insight on who was considered a sports hero in the African-American community.

17. Bender, *Gallery*, p.31. For more on basketball see R.W. Peterson, *From Cages to Jump Shots: Pro Basketball's Early Years* (New York, NY: Oxford University Press, 1990) and N. George, *Elevating the Game: Black Men and Basketball* (New York, NY: Harper Collins, 1992).

18. L.N. Bergmann, *The Negro in Iowa* (Iowa City, IA: State Historical Society of Iowa, 1949; reprinted 1969), p.88.

19. W. Naber to the author, 30 April 1997.

20. See Slater Hall Vertical File, University of Iowa Archives, Iowa City [hereafter, UIVF], and the Fred (Duke) Slater file, UIAVF. The Francis X. Cretzmeyer field is located on the campus of the University. See also M.White, 'Cretzmeyer Chose Coaching over Medicine – and Won', *Des Moines Register* (11 July 1993).

21. Information about this controversy was provided by R. Breaux and a member of the committee who wished to remain anonymous. Breaux is an African-American student who is researching the history of black students at the University of Iowa. He corresponded with university officials about the erroneous designation of Robert Pearl as the first black baseball player.

22. Wiggins, 'Prized Performers', 164–5.

23. For more on Connie Hawkins see D. Wolf, *Foul!: The Connie Hawkins Story* (NewYork, NY: Holt, Rinehart & Winston, 1972), especially pp.58–91; D.L. Porter (ed.), *Biographical Dictionary of American Sports: 1989–92, Supplement* (Westport, CT: Greenwood, 1992), pp.288–9; A. Grady, 'The Field House I Remember', in Irving Weber *et al.*, *1927–1982 Remembered: 55 Years, Iowa Field House* (Iowa City, IA: Goodfellow Sports Promotions, 1982), p.6 and; M. White, 'Iowa History Honored by 3 Honorees', *Des Moines Register* (19 April 1992).

24. For more on African-Americans in Iowa sports history see the author's chapter, 'Pride to All: African-Americans and Sports in Iowa', in *Outside-In: African-American History in Iowa, 1838–2000* (forthcoming, 2001). My understanding of Iowa's history with respect to race leans heavily on R. Dykstra's interpretive perspective. See Dykstra's *Bright Radical Star: Black Freedom and White Supremacy on the Hawkeye Frontier* (Cambridge, MA: Harvard University Press, 1993) and 'Iowans and the Politics of Race in America, 1857–1880', in M. Bergman (ed.), *Iowa History Reader* (Ames, IA: Iowa State University Press, 1996), pp.129–58.

25. M. Kammen, 'Some Patterns and Meanings of Memory Distortion in American History', in M. Kammen, *In the Past Lane: Historical Perspectives on American Culture* (New York, NY: Oxford University Press, 1997), p.200.

26. S.A. Reiss (ed.), *Major Problems in American Sport History* (Boston, MA: Houghton Mifflin, 1997), p.vii. For more on sports reporting and the rise of big-time college sports in the United States see M. Oriard, *Reading Football: How the Popular Press Created an American Spectacle* (Chapel Hill, NC: University of North Carolina Press, 1993); and M. Sperber, *Onward to Victory: The Crises that Shaped College Sports* (New York, NY: Henry Holt, 1998).

27. The best book on Iowa's athletic history is Finn and Leistikow, *Hawkeye Legends*. The volume is attentive to race and sex. Construction is also under way on a new Hall of Fame and Visitors' Center. An exhibition now pending would commemorate the history of African-American athletes at Iowa.

28. The quotation from Loren Hickerson may be found in A. Grady, 'Hawkeyes: The Pride of Iowa', in M. Dukes and G. Schrader, *Greatest Moments in Hawkeyes Football History* (Chicago, IL: Triumph Books, 1998), p.13.

29. For more on region and college football see B. Rader, *American Sports: From the Age of Folk Games to the Age of Televised Sports* (Englewood Cliffs, NJ: Prentice Hall, 1996), especially Ch. 11: 'Intercollegiate Football Spectacles', pp.172–89.

30. R.W. Meinhard, 'History of the State University of Iowa: Physical Education and Athletics for Men' (MA thesis, University of Iowa, 1947).

31. Ibid., p.84.

32. Ibid., p.85. The paper was the *Vidette Reporter* (10 Nov. 1896).

33. Meinhard, 'History of the State University of Iowa', pp.85–6.

34. D. Schwieder, *Iowa: The Middle Land* (Ames, IA: Iowa State University Press, 1996), p.87. Schwieder quotes Dykstra, 'The Issue Squarely Met: Toward an Explanation of Iowans' Racial Attitudes, 1865–1868', *Annals of Iowa*, 47 (1984), 431. See also Dykstra, *Bright Radical Star*.

35. R. Rutland, 'College Football in Iowa', *The Palimpsest*, 34 (1953), 401–32.

36. T. Cummins, *Who's Who in Iowa Football* (Cedar Rapids, IA: Stamats Publishing, 1948), p.24.

37. Ibid.
38. Ibid., p.27.
39. For a biographical sketch of Evashevski see T. Cohane, 'Forest Evashevski: Iowa Head Coach Had Fierce Compulsion to Excel', in Dukes and Schrader, *Greatest Moments*, pp.84–9.
40. W. Peterson *et al.*, 'University Football through the Years', *The Palimpsest*, 38 (1957), 389–447.
41. Ibid.
42. See Wiggins, 'Prized Performers', 171–2. For more on the construction of college football's image in America during the 1940s and the 1950s see Sperber, *Onward to Victory*.
43. J.A. Peterson, *Slater of Iowa* (Chicago, IL: Hinckley & Schmitt, 1958).
44. See J.S. Shortridge, *The Middle West: Its Meaning in American Culture* (Lawrence, KS: University of Kansas, 1989); and M.S. Knepper and J.S. Lawrence, 'Visions of Iowa in Hollywood Film', *Iowa Heritage Illustrated*, 79 (1998), 158.
45. Peterson, *Slater*, pp.8–13.
46. Ibid., p.32
47. Ibid., pp.25–7.
48. Ibid., p.22.
49. See Slater file, UIAVF. A. Ashby recalled how Archie Alexander and Duke Slater recruited blacks to play for Iowa in his 'Views and Reviews', *New Iowa Bystander* (4 Feb. 1982).
50. 'UI Slater Hall Dedicated, Family Attend Homecoming', *Daily Iowan* (30 Oct. 1972) [Slater file, UIAVF]; M. Trowbridge, 'The Man behind Floyd of Rosedale', *Iowa City Press-Citizen* (25 Nov. 1989) [Ozzie Simmons file, UIAVF].
51. D. Lamb and B. McGrane, *75 Years with the Fighting Hawkeyes* (Dubuque, IA: Wm. C. Brown Co., 1964). For more on the 'Big Peach' see M. White, 'Sports Editor Sec Taylor Was Champion of Iowa Coverage', *Des Moines Register* (27 June 1999).
52. Lamb and McGrane, *75 Years*, p.vi.
53. Ibid., p.11.
54. More studies on Iowa sportswriters are needed. See D.R. McMahon, 'The Newspaperman and the Historian: Maury White and the Making of Iowa Sports History', paper presented at the Annual Northern Great Plains History Conference, 7 Oct. 1999.
55. E. Tunnell (with B. Gleason), *Footsteps of a Giant* (Garden City, NY: Doubleday, 1966), p.68.
56. Ibid., p.69
57. Ibid., pp.70, 87–8.
58. Ibid, pp.85–6.
59. Ibid., p 72.
60. Ibid., p.84. For more on Eddie Anderson see T. Cohane, *Great College Coaches of the Twenties and Thirties* (New Rochelle, NY: Arlington House, 1973), pp.6–10.
61. Tunnell, *Footsteps*, p.84.
62. See D.L. Porter (ed.), *African-American Sports Greats: A Biographical Dictionary* (Westport, CT: Greenwood, 1995), pp.607–8; M. White, 'Iowa, Pro Star Tunnell Joins Register Hall', *Des Moines Register* (30 March 1975) and 'Iowa Varsity Club to Induct Six', ibid. (14 July 1998).
63. For more on integration and sports in the South see C.H. Martin, 'Integrating New Year's Day: The Racial Politics of College Bowl Games in the American South', *Journal of Sport History*, 24 (1997), 358–77; J. Paul *et al.*, 'The Arrival and Ascendance of Black Athletes in the Southeastern Conference, 1966–1980', *Phylon*, 45 (1984), 284–97; R.E. Marcello, 'The Integration of Intercollegiate Athletics in Texas: North Texas State College as a Test Case, 1956', *Journal of Sport History*, 14 (1987), 286–316; C.H. Martin, 'Jim Crow in the Gymnasium: The Integration of College Basketball in the American South', *International Journal of the History of Sport*, 10 (1993), 68–86; R. Pennington, *Breaking the Ice: The Racial Integration of the Southwest Conference* (Jefferson, NC: McFarland, 1987).
64. See M. Sperber, *Beer and Circus: How Big-time College Sports Is Crippling Undergraduate Education* (New York, NY: Henry Holt, 2000).
65. For a brief sketch of Fry see M. Dukes, 'Hayden Fry: A Hero to Hawkeyes Found His Treasure in Iowa City', in Dukes and Schrader, *Greatest Moments*, pp.216–23.
66. Ibid. More information can be found in a file on Hayden Fry in the author's possession.
67. C. Bright, *University of Iowa Football: The Hawkeyes* (Huntsville, AL: Strode Publishers, 1982).

68. B. and M. Chapman, *Evy and the Hawkeyes: The Glory Years* (New York, NY: Leisure Press, 1983), p.75.
69. M. White, 'Brechler Left Mark on Iowa', *Des Moines Register* (24 Sept. 1997). See also R. Maly, 'Forever an Iowa Legend: Evashevski to Be Honored', *Des Moines Register*, n.d. [in author's files].
70. C.E. Wynes, '"Alexander the Great", Bridge Builder', *The Palimpsest*, 66 (1985), 78–86 and Raymond A. Smith, 'He Opened Holes Like Mountain Tunnels', ibid., 87–100.
71. Wynes, 'Alexander', 78–81. Wynes erroneously identifies Alexander as the first African-American football player at Iowa. The first was Frank Holbrook. See his file, UIAVF.
72. Wynes, 'Alexander', 81–6.
73. Smith, 'He Opened Holes', 87–90.
74. Ibid., p.99.
75. Ibid. See the *Council Bluffs Nonpareil* (3 Oct. 1909).
76. Smith, 'He Opened Holes', 99 and Wynes, 'Alexander', 86.
77. A. Grady, *25 Years with the Fighting Hawkeyes: Fourth Quarter, 1964–1988* (Iowa City, IA: University of Iowa Athletic Department, 1989), pp.22–42; Bright, *The Hawkeyes*, pp.234–5. For more reflections on Iowa football during its centennial year see C. Harker, '100 Years of Iowa Football', *Iowa Alumni Review*, 42, 5 (Sept. 1989), 16–33 and 42, 6 (Nov. 1989), 16–31; M. White, 'Hawkeye Football in the '90s', *Des Moines Register* (12 Sept. 1989).
78. Grady, *25 Years*, p.22.
79. Ibid., pp.23–7.
80. Ibid., p.28.
81. D. Green (with G. McGivern), *No Room for Crybabies* (Champaign, IL: Sports Publications, 1997), p.4. See the Dennis Green file, UIAVF.
82. Grady, *25 Years*, p.28.
83. For the University of Iowa's connection to the Minnesota Vikings see M. White, 'Vikings Rely on Hawkeyes', *Des Moines Register* (14 Jan. 1992).
84. For a discussion of the new scholarship on the 1960s see R. Perlstein, 'Who Owns the Sixties? The Opening of a Scholarly Generation Gap', *Lingua Franca*, 6 (1996), 30–7. For more on the black athletic revolt of the 1960s see Wiggins, *Glory Bound*, pp.104–74.
85. For historiographical overviews see J. Sammons, '"Race" and Sport: A Critical Examination', *Journal of Sport History*, 21 (1994), 203–98 and D. Wiggins, 'From Plantation to Playing Field: Historical Writings on the Black Athlete in American Sport', *Research Quarterly for Exercise and Sport*, 57 (1986), 101–16.
86. White, '100 Years of Black Athletes'; A. Ashe, *A Hard Road to Glory: A History of the African-American Athlete*, 3 vols (New York, NY: Warren Books, 1988).
87. The author's impressions are based on a lecture given by Maury White and Tom Witosky, 'From Stone Age to Stonewalling: Half a Century of Sports Journalism', Iowa City, 17 June 1996.
88. Dukes and Schrader, *Greatest Moments*, especially pp.18–19, 60–1.
89. H. Fry (with G. Wine), *Hayden Fry: A High Porch Picnic* (Champaign, IL: Sports Publishing, 1999).
90. Ibid., p.6.
91. Ibid., pp.67–71. See Reggie Roby file, UIAVF.
92. For more on the Fry years see Grady, *25 Years*, pp.88–138.
93. H. Fry, *Hayden Fry*, pp.167–9. Ronnie Harmon's reputation took a hit in Iowa after he admitted accepting $50,000 while a player at Iowa. Some Hawkeye fans believed that Harmon threw the 1986 Rose Bowl because he fumbled four times in the first half of a game Iowa was heavily favored to win; Iowa lost 45–28 to UCLA. For more on this see T. Witosky, 'Was '86 Rose Bowl Fixed?', *Des Moines Register* (13 Jan. 1998).
94. A. Schallau, 'The One Coach Who Could Turn Around Iowa Football Fortunes, Eddie Robinson, Head Coach, Grambling University', an adverisement in the *Iowa City Press-Citizen* (23 Nov. 1978). See the following stories: 'Robinson Coaching a Possibility', *Iowa City Press-Citizen* (23 Nov. 1978) and 'UI Hasn't Talked to Robinson', ibid. (24 Nov. 1978).
95. O.K. Davis, *Grambling's Gridiron Glory: Eddie Robinson and the Tiger's Success* Story (Ruston, LA: M & M Printing, 1983), pp.33–4 and B. Austin, 'Robinson has Hawkeye Roots', *Iowa City Press-Citizen* (27 Dec. 1996).

96. Ibid.
97. Hubbard, *New Dawns*, pp.62–3; Finn and Leistikow, *Hawkeye Legends*, p.166. See also the George Raveling and C. Vivian Stringer files, UIFVF.
98. See B. Plaschke, 'Seattle Newspaper Blasts Iowa', *Daily Iowan* (12 April 1986) [Raveling file, UIFVF]. For more on Iowa basketball's rise to prominence see R. Miller, *Spanning the Game* (Champaign, IL: Sagamore Publishing, 1990), especially Part III: Coaching at Iowa, pp.79–110; G. Schrader and F. Thompson, *Lute-Lute-Lute* (Topeka, KS: Josten/American Yearbook Co., 1981) and R. Lester (with B. Loomer), *Ronnie #12* (Iowa City, IA: Sports Promotions, 1983).
99. W. LaFeber, *Michael Jordan and the New Global Capitalism* (New York, NY: Norton, 1999), p.121. See the author's review of LaFeber in the forthcoming *Minnesota Journal of Global Trade*, 10 (2000).
100. See M. Hansen, 'Iowa Coach Raveling Takes Basketball Post in Southern California, *Des Moines Register* (28 April 1986) [Raveling file, UIAVF].
101. The episode 'End Run' was shown on 25 Jan. 1977. It was written by J.D. Hess, directed by H. Morgan and starred Henry Brown as Billy Tyler. For more on the sitcom see J.H. Wittebols, *Watching M*A*S*H, Watching America: A Social History of the 1972–1983 Television Series* (Jefferson, NC: McFarland, 1998).

THE BODY IN MEMORY AND REPRESENTATION

4

Tobacco, Health, and the Sports Metaphor

MICHELLE McQUISTAN and
CHRISTOPHER SQUIER

First used in ritual and as a medicinal herb by the natives of north and central America, tobacco has since been blessed and cursed by peoples world-wide. After its introduction to England in the sixteenth century, James I declared it to be 'a custom loathsome to the eye, hateful to the nose, harmful to the brain, dangerous to the lungs'.[1] In *My Lady Nicotine* (1900) J.M. Barrie describes the anguish of a pipe-smoker who must choose between his habit and his fiancée, a decision which delays his marriage for six months.[2] As we enter the new millennium, the romance with tobacco is ending; the World Health Organization estimates that the number of people world-wide who die each year from tobacco-related disease will rise from the current 3.5 million to 10 million by 2025. A mounting challenge that the tobacco industry has faced since its products became widely available at the beginning of the twentieth century is to market successfully a product that ultimately kills or severely compromises the user. An early approach in the mass advertising of tobacco was to couple products with metaphors for health, beauty, purity, and freedom. Attractive and vigorous models, scenes of rustic beauty or vast landscapes and, of course, sports have been common features of tobacco advertisements. The effort to inculcate positive images of the relationship between smoking and athletics has become a major strategy as the adverse health effects of tobacco become more widely known. Increasingly, the tobacco industry has reinforced its link with sports through official sponsorships, lending brand names and large subsidies to tennis, golf, motor racing, and other events. As nations restrict the advertising of tobacco products in the mass media and on billboards, sponsorship keeps brand names and logos in front of the public and provides a powerful vehicle for introducing new products into the emerging markets of eastern Europe, south-east Asia, and China.

CIGARETTES AS A VEHICLE OF GROWTH

Although tobacco has been used for over 2,000 years, its widespread use is a relatively new phenomenon that was facilitated by the introduction of cigarettes. Until the middle of the eighteenth century tobacco was smoked in pipes and cigars. During the Crimean War (1853–56) English, French, and Piedmontese soldiers copied the habit of their Turkish allies by rolling tobacco in paper (*Papirossi*) which was cheaper than prefabricated cigars. After the war, these soldiers took cigarettes back to their own countries. At the French court Louis Napoleon, Emperor of France, became 'an enthusiastic devotee' of the cigarette. In Britain army officers introduced the cigarette into London clubs. In 1865 the 'double cigarette' was introduced in Austria. This was perhaps the first one to resemble modern cigarettes. It had a mouthpiece at either end and was three times as long as the modern cigarette. Before smoking, it would be cut in half.[3]

In the United States, following the end of the Civil War in 1865, there was a demand for 'exotic' Turkish cigarettes. Since these were hand-rolled by 'cigarette-girls', they were expensive and the market was small. This changed on 30 April 1884 when W. Duke and Sons of North Carolina were able to use the first cigarette-rolling machine, which was capable of producing as many cigarettes in a minute (200) as a worker could roll by hand in an hour. Now, cigarettes, which were already cheaper than cigars, could be mass-produced and the industry was born.[4]

Early cigarette advertisements were directed primarily at men, for tobacco use by women was considered abhorrent and unladylike. These advertisements had bucolic beginnings depicting men, women, and children in verdant settings. For example, a 1907 advertisement by W.D. & H.O. Wills promoting 'Wild Woodbine' cigarettes shows a man in a powdered wig conversing with an attractive woman in a pastel painted park. A more pointed theme is evident in a 1906 advertisement for 'Tuxedo' tobacco. A young, well-dressed couple sit on the deck of a large yacht; as the woman's dress blows in the breeze, she holds a package of 'Tuxedo' tobacco away from her companion. Holding a pipe in his hand, he reaches out towards the woman as she flirtatiously resists his request by placing her other hand on his arm. The caption beside the woman reads, 'Beg for it'. This double entendre presented a more blatant use of sexuality for selling tobacco that was to be repeatedly exploited in the years that followed.

Print advertising of tobacco boomed with the introduction of color printing at the end of the nineteenth century. Before then tobacco companies used coupons and tobacco cards to entice male consumers to purchase their products. After the end of the American Civil War tobacco companies started inserting tin tags into plug tobacco, which could be exchanged for items such as pocket knives or diamond pins. Other items included cards depicting actresses, colored sheets of costumes of foreign lands, silk flags, and sports cards.[5] Tobacco cards related to sports first appeared in the nineteenth century. In addition to baseball cards, these portrayed a variety of sports, including boxing, horse racing, the Olympic Games (reintroduced in 1896), automobile racing, and cycling. In fact, tobacco cards were first issued in Britain, where soccer and cricket ranked as the most popular sports, so that cards depicting these sports, and not baseball, were the most popular.[6] Tobacco cards often came in series, thus prompting the consumer to stay loyal to one brand of cigarettes to complete a series, which could result in an individual having to smoke substantial numbers of cigarettes. For example, in 1908 Ogdens Tobacco Co. in England printed a 50-card set named 'Pugilists and Wrestlers'. In 1911 Mecca Cigarettes put out a set of boxing cards called 'Mecca Cigarettes Champion Athlete and Prize Fighter Series'. Each card was set up in a similar fashion. The front of each displayed the picture of a famous athlete and the back contained statistics about him. Perhaps the most controversial card was that of the baseball star Honus Wagner, issued by Piedmont Tobacco in 1910. From 1903 to 1909 Wagner won six batting titles and helped the Pittsburgh Pirates to win the 1909 World Series. In addition to being a great baseball hero, Wagner was notorious for his love of cigars and chewing tobacco. Although he enjoyed tobacco, he did not want young children to purchase tobacco products in order to obtain his tobacco cards and he demanded that they be withdrawn from the market.[7]

Although it was commonplace at the beginning of the twentieth century to use women in tobacco advertisements to attract men's attention, smoking by women was not socially acceptable. Indeed, before World War I films and plays used cigarettes as props to identify the 'female villain' of their shows. As late as 1922 an 18-year-old female student at Michigan State Normal College was expelled for smoking in class. The student brought a suit against the college president, but the Michigan State Court upheld the school's ruling.[8]

SOCIAL CHANGE AND THE WOMEN'S MARKET

With the passage of the 19th amendment to the U.S. Constitution on 26 August 1920, tobacco companies gained a large new population on which to focus their advertising strategies: the emancipated woman. Views on women's smoking began to change during the 1920s, and 'flappers' were the first to symbolize the female use of cigarettes. As Lehman Brothers stated, cigarettes were a 'required accessory for the flapper of the twenties'.[9] Women had been freed from male domination and cigarette smoking gave them some of the privileges and freedom that had previously been reserved for men. In 1926 Bryn Mawr College, an all-female college, allowed its students to smoke. The following year Philip Morris ran an advertisement that stated, 'Women, when they smoke at all, quickly develop discriminating taste.' A 1929 Liggett and Myers advertisement depicted a woman asking her male companion to 'Blow Some My Way'. By 1934 Eleanor Roosevelt was known as 'the First Lady to smoke in public',[10] and many advertisements featured eminent society women lauding the benefits of a particular brand.

It was not long before tobacco companies used images and slogans associated with sports, health, and fitness to attract women to their products. During the Victorian era and into the mid-twentieth century, women were not encouraged to participate in team sports requiring physical contact. However, individual sports such as tennis, golf, and swimming were considered acceptable if a woman chose to indulge in them for personal pleasure or to improve her health.[11] Tobacco advertisements followed these social norms and showed women involved as spectators or participants in sporting activities. For example, a 1927 Players' advertisement displayed an image of Helen Wills, a tennis champion who won seven national tennis titles at Forest Hills in New York City and eight British championships at Wimbledon.[12] Here was a famous, healthy, attractive female associating sport with cigarettes. The implicit message was that well-known women athletes were associated with cigarettes, so they must be a healthy habit for you too.

In the 1920s the American Tobacco Company's 'Lucky Strike' brand launched a campaign that has only been rivaled for its cynicism and dishonesty by the 'Virginia Slims' advertisements of recent decades. The theme behind this promotion was that smoking would help to keep a woman fit and trim. One of the most controversial advertisements suggested 'Reach for a Lucky Instead of a Sweet'. In a 1936 article

Fortune magazine explained how Percival Hill, son of George Washington Hill, the president of American Tobacco, had seen a 'fat girl munching something and a svelte girl in a taxi lighting up a cigarette', and this was the inspiration for Hill's famous campaign.[13] The slogan led to vigorous protests from the U.S. sugar and candy industries which objected to the implication that their products led to obesity, and subsequent 'Lucky Strike' advertisements suggested 'Reach for a Lucky Instead'. Through the unscrupulous use of attractive, thin, women athletes, tobacco companies were able to market their products to women.

As well as capturing the newly emerging market of female smokers, tobacco companies used sports to maintain brand allegiance by men. In *American Sports*, Rader refers to sports in the post-1920 period as the 'Age of the Spectator'.[14] Major League Baseball, college football, and basketball changed their games, their stadiums and their images to attract more spectators. As a relief from the boredom of the office and in opposition to old Victorian values, consumers eagerly adopted spectator sports as a form of entertainment. Sports 'enhanced the sense of individual identity' and could 'furnish a more satisfactory set of compensatory heroes'.[15]

TOBACCO SEIZES THE MALE SPORT SPECTATOR

Tobacco companies exploited the American male's new-found interest in spectator sports to promote their products. 'Camel' advertisements from the late 1920s and the 1930s focused on crowds of spectators at football games. In a 1929 advertisement a young woman stands up in the crowd cheering on her team. The caption reads, 'More genuine pleasure ... more hearty cheer ... Camel gains on every play, Go into a huddle with yourself and a pack of Camels ... and you're all set!' This advertisement allows the male spectator to be part of the action as he goes 'into a huddle' with his pack of 'Camels'. Furthermore, if he partakes in the action, a lovely lady might give him a 'hearty cheer'. Similar advertisements for 'Camels' appeared throughout the 1930s.

As the decades pass, so do the links that tobacco companies develop between sports, sports heroes, and smoking. A 1938 Joe DiMaggio 'Camels' cigarette advertisement shows DiMaggio telling a group of fans that he has smoked 'Camels' steadily for five years. In another 'Camels' advertisement Glen Hardin, the world's champion hurdler, claims 'Camels are the favorite cigarettes of athletes'. Once again, the companies were associating their products with an image of health. By the 1950s a new genre of sports advertisements appeared. Rather than focusing on tobacco use by spectators, these suggest that smoking is an 'after-sport' activity. In 1950 'Lucky Strike' ran an advertisement which said, 'Light up a Lucky ... it's light up time!' In this advertisement a stylish looking man sits casually next to a tennis court with a racket dangling between his legs as he holds his cigarette. An equally stylish woman gazes at him longingly. Not only is this suggesting that the man may get 'lucky', it is strongly encouraging smoking as a form of relaxation after participating in sporting activity.

Although the tobacco companies were actively trying to promote positive images of tobacco use, and little was known until the middle of the twentieth century about tobacco-related diseases, the industry's strategy was not unopposed. As early as 1870 Harry Wright, a Boston baseball team manager, advised a young boy aspiring to become a professional player that he must 'abstain from intoxicating drinks and tobacco'.[16] In the 1880s a Cleveland baseball writer 'attacked tobacco chewers and attributed their "dulled perception or even stiff arms" to the use of such "narcotics"'.[17] Other forms of opposition came from doctors, educators, and the Women's Christian Temperance Union (WCTU). In the early 1900s some physicians spoke out, including a Dr Tidswell, who suggested that female sterility was the result of smoking by men. In 1907 *Education* magazine wrote that boys who were habitual smokers would remain 'physical and mental dwarfs'.[18] The WCTU distributed posters that conveyed their message by simply depicting a woman with an infant in her arms and a cigarette in her mouth. By 1909, 12 states had legislation that banned tobacco. Kansas was the last of these to abolish this restrictive legislation in 1929.[19]

The opposition to tobacco during the late 1800s and the early 1900s was based more on moral reasoning than medical evidence. Consequently, when the tobacco industry supported the efforts of the Western allies in both world wars, moral taboos disappeared and the industry gained thousands of new consumers who were rapidly addicted. During World War I General John J. Pershing cabled Washington in order to request thousands of tons of tobacco for his soldiers. By 1918 cigarettes were a daily ration, and Allied soldiers smoked 60–70 per cent more tobacco than they did as civilians.[20] As Lehman Brothers succinctly stated, cigarettes were 'the weary soldier's relief, the worried man's support, and the relaxing man's companion'.[21]

FIGURE 1

FOR DIGESTION'S SAKE... SMOKE CAMELS

"That's what I do — and my digestion goes along O.K.," says Glenn Hardin, world's champion hurdler

"I'M A GREAT BELIEVER in the way Camels help to ease strain and tension," says Glenn, one of America's great athletes. "It's no wonder Camels are the favorite cigarette of athletes. Take my own case. It wouldn't do me much good to eat and not digest properly. So I smoke Camels with my meals and after. Camels give me an invigorating 'lift.' And you'll notice, the same as I do, that Camels don't get on your nerves." Camels set you right! Choose Camels for steady smoking.

A feeling of well-being comes after a good meal...and plenty of Camels

FOR that luxurious feeling of ease so worth-while at mealtime — light up a Camel. Fatigue and irritability begin to fade away. The flow of digestive fluids — *alkaline* digestive fluids — speeds up! You get in the right mood to *enjoy* eating. Camels at mealtime and afterwards help to keep digestion on its proper course. You'll welcome Camels between meals too! They are milder — better for steady smoking.

In a series of advertisements appearing in the 1930s, tobacco companies used images and testimonials of famous athletes to link their products to health.

FIGURE 2

This is one of a series of advertisements associating thinness and youth with smoking. The slogan 'Reach for a Lucky instead of a sweet' was changed to 'Reach for a Lucky instead' after vigorous protests from the candy and sugar industries who objected to the implication that their products led to obesity.

FIGURE 3

Whereas in the past women were frequently spectators in sporting activities, today's tobacco advertisements depict women actively participating in sports.

FIGURE 4

In the 1980s the use of oral snuff rose substantially among professional athletes following a tobacco industry marketing campaign to link its use with high level athletic performance and virility. This advertisement depicts several famous athletes promoting smokeless tobacco as a healthy alternative to smoking.

Rather than the traditional image of the Marlboro Man as a cowboy on a horse, Marlboro 'Motorcycle' advertising presented a more modern Marlboro Man.

Just as moral reservations associated with male smoking disappeared during World War I, female smoking became an accepted habit during World War II. As the U.S. war effort grew, the number of female workers increased from 12 to 16.5 million, making up 36 per cent of the civilian labor force. Although women's entrance into the workforce entailed only light jobs at first, they eventually began to replace men in heavy industry.[22] The tobacco industry embraced this opportunity to reflect the changes taking place in the workforce. In a 1943 'Chesterfield' advertisement a beautiful woman wears a welding mask flipped up above her head; behind her is a large sign that says 'Buy War Bonds'. Although she is involved in heavy industry, the woman has painted nails, wears lipstick, and looks glamorous. She also has a cigarette casually dangling from the corner of her mouth, and a pack of 'Chesterfield' cigarettes conspicuously hangs out of her coat pocket. Not only is this woman helping the fight for freedom, she is gaining her own freedom to work outside the home. Like the emancipated women of the 1920s, those of the 1940s could use the cigarette to display their independence.

HEALTH CONCERNS AND TOBACCO CONSUMPTION

An important development during the 1950s was the growing realization that there was a health risk associated with smoking. Although concerns had been raised by anti-tobacco groups about the health effects associated with smoking since the beginning of the twentieth century, there was limited scientific evidence to support such views. This ignorance allowed the tobacco industry to launch an insidious campaign in the 1940s, using doctors to promote their products. In one such advertisement a male physician is sitting with an attractive woman and her daughter. The caption reads, 'More Doctors Smoke Camels Than Any Other Cigarette!' Another advertisement from this time shows a picture of a physician with the caption, 'Not One Single Case of Throat Irritation due to Smoking Camels'. Throat irritation from smoking was a concern for both consumers and tobacco companies, and there were frequent attempts to develop products that were less irritating. Fortunately, the use of physicians for the endorsement of tobacco products was short-lived as the health effects of tobacco use became widely accepted by the medical and the scientific community in the 1950s.

The first definitive epidemiological studies linking cigarette smoking to lung cancer appeared during this decade and were followed by reports from the Royal College of Physicians in England in 1962 and the U.S. Surgeon General in 1964. As the health risks became better known, the government became more involved with tobacco advertising. The Federal Trade Commission first started regulating its advertising in 1955 by asking for voluntary compliance from the industry to stop printing advertisements that made reference to health benefits and positive physical effects, such as lower throat irritation as a result of smoking a particular brand of cigarette. In July 1965 the U.S. government issued the Cigarette Labeling and Advertising Act which mandated that, starting on 1 January 1966, all cigarette packages must include a warning that cigarette smoking might be hazardous to health. The Public Health Cigarette Smoking Act of 1969 mandated the elimination of all television and radio broadcasting of cigarette advertising after 1 January 1971 and required stronger and more specific warnings on cigarette packaging.[23]

With the elimination of cigarette advertising from television and radio in the U.S., tobacco companies lost valuable advertising exposure. To compensate for this, companies began using indirect advertising in the form of sports sponsorship to keep their names before the public and to promote an association between tobacco and health. The first sport to accept such sponsorship was motor racing. In 1968 Colin Chapman's Formula One Team Lotus in the United Kingdom carried advertisements for Imperial Tobacco's 'Players Gold Leaf' cigarettes on its cars.[24] In 1971, the same year that cigarette advertising was banned from television and radio in the U.S.A., the National Association for Stock Car Auto Racing (NASCAR) followed suit when it accepted sponsorship from R.J. Reynolds (RJR), the first non-automotive sponsor in U.S. motor racing. What started as 'moonshine racing in the hills' developed into the fastest growing sport in the United States as a result of tobacco sponsorship. RJR recognized the potential to use motor racing as a marketing tool for its product and invested millions of dollars in the sport. With increased prize money from RJR, teams were able to increase their size and produce better cars, which led to more exciting competitions, a greater number of fans and more teams.[25] As NASCAR racing increased in popularity, fans began to identify drivers more and more with their sponsors as they made personal appearances and gave press conferences wearing the colors and logos of their sponsors on uniforms, hats, and coats.[26] According to Barrie Gill, CEO of Championship Sports Specialists, motorsport racing is 'the ideal sport of sponsorship – it's got glamour and world-wide television coverage. They're there to get visibility. They're there to sell cigarettes.' Indeed, sponsorship has provided an invaluable tool for advertising tobacco products. For example, during the 1989 Indianapolis 500 Marlboro received over $2.6 million worth of advertising exposure.[27]

Sports sponsorship was not limited to male events such as motor sports. In 1971 Philip Morris Tobacco Co. decided to underwrite the Virginia Slims Tour as a separate professional tennis tournament for women. This tournament, using the slogan 'You've Come a Long Way, Baby', was intended to capitalize on the feminist liberation movement of the 1960s and the 1970s. Up to 1970 prize money for women's tennis was only 10 per cent of that of their male counterparts, and several tennis tournaments barred women competitors because they might not be as profitable as men. The Virginia Slims Tour challenged these views. In 1971 Billie Jean King, one of the country's most famous tennis stars, became the first female athlete to win $100,000 in a single year. In 1973, wearing 'Virginia Slims' colors, she defeated Bobby Riggs, a triple crown winner at Wimbledon, in front of 30,472 people at Houston's Astrodome and an estimated television audience of 50 million.[28] Philip Morris's sponsorship of women's tennis helped the feminist movement during the 1970s by opening the doors for women to make a profitable living from sports, while the association of 'Virginia Slims' with tennis implied to the public that cigarettes were healthy. At the same time, sponsorship allowed Philip Morris to circumvent the government's restrictions on television advertising by associating its name with a sporting event and, in doing so, to cause thousands of women to become addicted to cigarettes and give rise to an epidemic of lung cancer.[29]

Tobacco sponsorship and advertising continue to play critical roles in involving women in sport competitions and activities. For example, Imperial Tobacco has sponsored the du Maurier LPGA competition in Canada since 1985. Unlike men's golf, which attracts $136 million in television contracts, women's golf depends on companies such as Imperial Tobacco to sponsor its tournaments. However, Imperial Tobacco may discontinue this as a result of a 1997 ban which, from 2000, allows tobacco sponsors to advertise only on site and print their name on the bottom 10 per cent of billboards. As the du Maurier spokesman Michel Descoteaux said, 'It is difficult to imagine how we could remain associated. This is the reason you sponsor an event, to be seen doing it.'[30]

Current tobacco advertisements also depict women in sporting activities, but they appear more frequently as spectators than as participants, a situation reminiscent of the 1920s when males were represented as sports spectators. Such an approach may be an outcome of the Master Settlement Agreement that tobacco companies signed in November 1998. This states that 'Cigarette advertising shall not depict as a smoker anyone who is known as an athlete, nor shall it show any smoker participating in, or having participated in, a physical activity requiring stamina or athleticism beyond that of normal recreation.'[31]

Smoking rates among males began to decline in the United States during the late 1960s as a result of increased public awareness regarding the health risks associated with cigarette use. In response to this decline, tobacco companies began a new campaign in the 1980s that linked the use of smokeless tobacco (moist oral snuff or chewing tobacco) to high-level athletic performance and virility. An advertisement from U.S. Tobacco showed a group of well-known male athletes and the phrase 'We love tobacco. We don't smoke', reflecting the growing public concern about smoking and second-hand smoke as a health risk and promoting smokeless tobacco as a harmless alternative. Perhaps the most pervasive use of smokeless tobacco occurred in Major League Baseball. Baseball cards showed images of American heroes with huge wads of chewing tobacco bulging in their cheeks. One could rarely watch a baseball game on television without seeing players chewing and spitting. Although tobacco companies were not advertising their products direct, they were benefiting from the image of health and athleticism that had been coupled with the widespread use of smokeless tobacco in baseball. The promotion of snuff as a healthy alternative to cigarettes had significant economic benefits for the industry. According to the U.S. Department of Agriculture, moist snuff consumption in the U.S. increased almost every year between 1981 and 1991, rising from approximately 30 million to 48 million lbs in 1991.[32] By the 1990s 10–12 million Americans used snuff, nearly all of them male and most between the ages of 18 and 24.[33] Furthermore, in January 2000 the American Center for Disease Control and Prevention reported that, according to a 1999 survey, 11.6 per cent of high school males and 4.2 per cent of middle school males had reported using smokeless tobacco on one or more of the 30 days preceding the survey.[34]

NORTH AMERICAN CHALLENGES TO SPORTS SPONSORSHIP

During the 1990s governments and sporting agencies in Canada, the United States, and Europe started to challenge sports sponsorship. In 1996 Health Canada proposed *Tobacco Control: A Blueprint to Protect the Health of Canadians*. This involved restrictions on sponsorship by tobacco companies, including prohibition of the use of brand-identifiable elements on non-tobacco promotional items associated with a sponsored activity and of testimonials and personal endorsements by athletes and celebrities.[35] However, in November 1997 Canada's Health Minister agreed to permit tobacco companies to continue the sponsorship of motor racing as allowed by the 'Grand Prix amendment'.[36] This was in contrast to the United States and countries in the European Economic Union which do not allow tobacco logos to appear in motor races. Whereas tobacco advertising is to be banned in Europe from 2001, the EU has allowed an exception for Formula 1 racing, permitting sponsorship to continue until October 2006. Sponsorship legislation in the United States is different from that of the EU. While sponsorship of events in which the young are a significant percentage of the intended audience are prohibited by the Master Settlement Agreement, tobacco companies merely face limited sponsorship restrictions on events such as NASCAR. Furthermore, events in adult-only facilities are exempt from sponsorship prohibitions and limitations.[37]

Although exceptions have been made regarding sponsorship, the end of sponsorship is near. This is due in part to research findings such as that provided by the British Cancer Research Campaign in 1997, which revealed that 'boys are twice as likely to become regular smokers if they are motor racing fans', since 'tobacco sponsorship encourages young boys to take up smoking ... and ... encourages brand recognition.' Tobacco companies deny that the goal of sponsorship is to encourage young boys to smoke, but under recent agreements in accordance with the Master Settlement Agreement, the companies have started to withdraw their support of certain sporting events. For example, U.S. Tobacco Company announced on 16 November 1999 that it was ending its Skoal team sponsorship in the NASCAR Winston Cup Series.[38] Additionally, R.J. Reynolds Tobacco Company announced on 12 October 1999 plans to withdraw its sponsorship of the NASCAR Winston Racing Series, a weekly, short-track, race program, because 16-

and 17-year-olds are allowed to participate in the races. RJR also announced that it would not renew its contract with Travis Carter Enterprises after the 1999 NASCAR Winston Cup Series season. However, RJR has not completely terminated its motorcar sponsorship. Instead, the company intends to focus its efforts on the sponsorship of the 'largest and fastest-growing series in motorsports'.[39] For example, it posted $300,000 in the point fund for the 1998 NASCAR Winston West Series.[40] RJR also sponsors the Winston No Bull 5 competition, where five Winston Cup drivers compete for $1 million. Five spectators can also win the same amount, depending on which driver wins. While the Master Settlement Agreement prohibits the distribution of free samples of tobacco products through the mail, samples are still allowed in 'adult-only' facilities.[41] Consequently, 'Winston' cigarettes and other promotional items can be distributed near racing events. Although the states are attempting to eliminate tobacco sponsorship, RJR continues to find loopholes in restrictions so as to promote its products to racing fans at NASCAR events.

As tobacco companies are phasing out their sports sponsorship in the United States and Europe, they are infiltrating new markets in low- and middle-income countries by using the strategies that were successful in the U.S. and Europe. Sports sponsorship has led the way into these new markets. Soccer is one of the most popular sports in Asia, and in China Marlboro sponsored the Chinese National Football League for five years. Similarly, the Chinese basketball team was sponsored by Hilton, part of the British American Tobacco Company. Sponsorship of tennis tournaments such as the Marlboro Open and the Salem Open in Hong Kong has provided companies with other venues to promote their products and, at the same time, images of health and goodwill.[42] In Malaysia the Minister of Information allowed the broadcasting of the Atlanta Olympic Games to be sponsored by Peter Styvesant, admitting that the government needed the tobacco money to support the broadcast. Additionally, Malaysia hosted its first Formula 1 race in 1999. One reason for Formula 1's move to this area was to avoid the European bans on tobacco sponsorship.[43] In India tobacco companies sponsor cricket matches, an enormously popular game in the subcontinent. A study by the National Organization for Tobacco Eradication discovered that '15–20 per cent of students surveyed felt that smoking and "ghutka" [a form of powdered tobacco used in India] improves memory. Students also believed that if you smoke, you will become a better cricketer.'[44] In

South Africa Rembrandt sponsors rugby events and Rothmans sponsors soccer, horse racing, and yacht racing. A Swedish yacht sponsored by Nicorette, a nicotine replacement, was banned from competition as it was believed to represent a threat to the sponsoring tobacco company.[45] Although many low-income countries originally accepted tobacco sponsorship of sporting events, they, like the richer ones, have begun to place restrictions and bans on the sponsorship of sports.

CONCLUSION

Throughout the 1900s tobacco companies used extensive advertising strategies to attract consumers to their products. What started as a male activity grew to encompass the female smoker during the 1920s with the emancipated woman. Advertisements linked cigarette smoking to wealth, health, and glamour, and this image continued throughout the century. As the tobacco industry faced opposition from American federal and state governments, tobacco companies further emphasized 'health' aspects by linking tobacco products to sports sponsorship in the 1970s, the 1980s, and the 1990s. When the adverse effects of smoking became more publicized to the general public, the companies shifted their marketing strategies to promote smokeless tobacco in the 1980s, especially among baseball players. As foreign markets opened in low-income countries such as China, the industry used sports sponsorship as a means to establish its products within those new markets. However, as governments continue to restrict the advertising strategies of the tobacco industry they will be forced to come up with new ways in which to sell their products.

NOTES

1. James I, *A Counterblaste to Tobacco* (1604).
2. J.M. Barrie, *My Lady Nicotin* (1900).
3. Count Corti, *A History of Smoking*, trans. Paul England (New York, NY: Harcourt, Brace, 1932), pp.252–3.
4. Ibid, p.254. E. Whelan, *A Smoking Gun: How the Tobacco Industry Gets Away with Murder*, (Philadelphia, PA: George F. Stickley, 1984), p.xiii.
5. Lehman Brothers, *About Tobacco* (n.p., 1955), pp.26–7.
6. http://home.earthlink.net/~cardking/sports.htm
7. B. Diskin, *Easy-going Honus Was a Pirates Icon* (ESPN Internet Ventures, 1999).
8. Whelan, *Gun*, p.61.
9. Lehman Brothers, *About Tobacco*, p.31.

10. Whelan, *Gun*, p.61.
11. B.G. Rader, *American Sports: From the Age of Fold Games to the Age of Spectators* (Englewood Cliffs, NJ: Prentice-Hall, 1983), p.166.
12. Ibid., p.221.
13. Whelan, *Gun*, pp.53, 62.
14. Rader, *American Sports*, p.196.
15. Ibid., p.198.
16. D.Q. Voigt, *American Baseball: From Gentleman's Sport to the Commissioner System* (Norman, OK: University of Oklahoma Press, 1966), p.41.
17. Ibid., p.173.
18. Whelan, *Gun*, pp.48–9.
19. Corti, *History of Smoking*, p.266; Whelan, *Gun*, p.48.
20. Ibid., p.50.
21. Lehman Brothers, *About Tobacco*, p.30.
22. R. Polenberg, *War and Society: The United States 1941–1945* (New York, NY: Lippincott, 1972), p.146.
23. K.M. Friedman, *Public Policy and the Smoking-Health Controversy: a Comparative Study*, (Lexington, MA: Lexington Books, 1975), pp.38, 58–60.
24. http://ourworld.compuserve.com/homepages/john_hopkinson/lotus.html
25. M. Howell, *From Moonshine to Madison Avenue: A Cultural History of the NASCAR Winston Cup Series* (Bowling Green, OH: Bowling Green State University Popular Press, 1997), pp.ix, 11.
26. Ibid., p.11.
27. http://metalab.unc.edu/boutell/infact/youth.html; A. Blum, *New England Journal of Medicine*, 324, 13 (28 March 1991), 913–16.
28. Rader, *American Sports*, pp.343–4; L Schwartz, *Billie Jean Won for All Women*, ESPN Internet Ventures (1999), http://espn.go.com/sportscentury/features/00016060.html
29 C.G. Husten, J.H. Chrismon, and M.N. Reddy, 'Trends and Effects of Cigarette Smoking among Girls and Women in the United States, 1965–1993', *Journal of the Medical Women's Association*, 51, 1 and 2 (Jan./April 1996), 11–18.
30. D. Ferguson, *Loss of du Maurier Would Be Major Blow to LPGA*, Associated Press (28 July 1999).
31. http://www.jrjt.com/CO/pages/COHowWeThink_smokinghealth.asp
32. 'Surveillance for Selected Tobacco-Use Behaviors – United States, 1900–1994', http://www.cdc.gov/mmwr/preview/mmwrhtml/00033881.htm (18 Nov. 1994), pp.1–32.
33. 'Surveillance for Selected Tobacco-Use Behaviors – United States, 1900–1994', *Morbidity and Mortality Weekly Report*, 43 (18 Nov. 1994), pp.25–27.
34. Center for Disease Control and Prevention, 'Tobacco Use among Middle and High School Students, United States, 1999', *Morbidity and Mortality Weekly Report*, 49, 3 (28 Jan. 2000).
35. J. Barker, 'New Research Focuses on Tobacco Sponsorship', *Canadian FundRaiser* (13 Nov. 1996).
36. *Health Groups Condemn Government's Cave-in to Auto Racing*, Ottawa, http://www.seercom.com/airspace/cave.html
37. http://www.philipmorris.com/tobacco_issues/link9.html
38. *R.J. Reynolds Tobacco Company withdraws NASCAR Winston Racing Series* (Winston-Salem, NC, 12 Oct. 1999); *Winston to Leave Carter at End of Season* (Winston-Salem, NC, 10 June 1999); *NASCAR Winston West Series Quick Facts* (http://www.nascar.com/touring/nww/facts.html), *Skoal Racing: Atlanta Is the End* (Hampton, GA, 16 Nov. 1999).
39. *Winston to Leave Carter at End of Season* (Winston-Salem, NC, 10 June 1999).
40. *A Packed House for the Winston West* (Scotts Valley, CA, 8 January 1998). NASCAR Winston West Series Public Relations; http://www.racingwest.com/news/1998/01-08entries.html
41. http://www.tobaccowars.com/tw3_news.asp?article=560
42. C. Homes, *Cash Cow on Its Last Breath*, http://lists.essential.org/intl-tobacco/msg00052.html

(22 Feb. 1999).
43. CAP SIDE, *Put Health before Profits* (http://www.sousthside.org.sg/souths/cap/title/put.htm); Reuters, *Tobacco Pushes F1 to Middle East* (London, 27 Oct. 1999).
44. F. Noronha, *India: a Doctor Takes on Big Tobacco* (Third World Features, May 1999).
45. N. Zuma, 'South Africa: Taking a Stand', in R. Hammond (ed.), *Addicted to Profit: Big Tobacco's Expanding Global Reach*, http://www.essentialaction.org/addicted/country.html (1998), pp.20–4.

5

Drugs and Number in the Reporting of U.S. Sports

MICHAEL A. KATOVICH

The universe of sport consists of two vital temporal dimensions – uncertainty in the present and careful, meticulous recording of accomplishments in the past. Of all American sports, professional baseball has forged a powerful allegiance to what has been described as a common stock of knowledge, and what I will refer to as an intersubjective past.[1] People in a community share an intersubjective past that they define as factual, valid, and recognizable. Such a past applies to baseball, especially in reference to numerical accomplishments. Owing to its statistical data, baseball statisticians agree that players from the past can be compared to current players through reference to numbers. Comparisons on the basis of numbers become the basis of intersubjective pasts among baseball fans – and the numbers themselves become memorized as significant symbols to which fans, commentators, and historians can make quick reference.[2]

People forge communal bonds as they make reference to and share intersubjective pasts. But they stay connected as they anticipate a future together in reference to their shared pasts. Mead[3] pointed out that the communal connection people feel toward each other requires not only agreement on factual and valid things from the past, but also on a narrative about which any particular past can be recalled. Along with sharing an intersubjective past, people also share a moral past, or a past in which metaphor, character, and emotional storytelling can provide a context for their community data.

In baseball, moral pasts represent idealized versions of the game and the character of the participants who play the game as they accumulate numbers.[4] As with all professional sports, baseball observers and participants regard the accumulation of numbers without consideration for team goals as untoward. Beyond the numbers, accomplishments in baseball should honor the values and beliefs that make up the idealism of the game, what Halbwachs described as a collective memory of agreed upon standards.[5] Baseball's status as an American pastime is an on-going focus on such idealism that fans and reporters share. This focus incorporates both intersubjective and moral memories of accomplishments, character, and the meaning of any particular number.[6] In this chapter I discuss the reporting of numbers and drugs in professional baseball as validating the game's intersubjective and moral pasts. I shall emphasize that these pasts allow baseball fans and reporters to engage in boundary maintenance that separates the honored place of extraordinary accomplishments in the form of numbers from dishonorable acts and deeds that should have no place in baseball.[7] Intersubjective and moral pasts are used to recall honored accomplishments and dishonorable deeds by which future players become measured and evaluated. In this regard, I shall pay attention to selective reports of two honorable accomplishments, Joe DiMaggio's 56-games consecutive hitting streak in 1941 and Cal Ripken's consecutive game playing streak established in 1995. In contrast, I discuss the comments on the suspension of Darryl Strawberry who tested positive for cocaine and was suspended for the entire 2000 season. Comments regarding such positive or negative acts validate two key purposes associated with the game's idealism – to play in order to accumulate numbers (an intersubjective past) and to play out of an authentic love for it (moral past).

In assessing reports and comments on these feats and the ignoble suspension I link moral and intersubjective pasts to star and shame narratives. Star narratives refer to storytelling about an athlete that demonstrates the idealism of the game's collective memory. The star narrative represents a modified version of what Huizinga described as 'pure play', or engaging in activity for the joy it brings the self and others.[8] Shame narratives employ sticky labels as keys[9] for journalistic comment that allows for righteous indignation on the part of commentators, beyond ordinary anger and criticism. Shame narratives employ a form of direct labeling in that comment about a fallen star becomes a blunt, harsh accusation that the rule-breaker has acted against the game's moral past.[10] Through the shame narrative, reporters view the fallen star as an evil threat to the community spirit.[11]

PURE PLAY AND ACCUMULATING NUMBERS

Owing to its status as 'America's pastime' and its rich past transmitted via oral, printed, and video media, baseball has become equated with a salient and obdurate moral order. More than any other professional sport in America, it represents a commitment to a mythological ideal emphasizing fair competition and a sacred commitment to tradition.[12] Central to its tradition and order is attention to a spirit of pure play which Huizinga described as carefree and spontaneous.[13] It implied a horizontal structure in that all players become involved equally in their on-going activity.

Reminiscent of Max Weber,[14] Huizinga felt that bureaucratic constraints would eventually doom pure play in sport. Concomitant with rapid institutionalization and routinization, a methodical and rigorous 'work ethic' transforms pure play into competitive game. This transformation brings about an emphasis on specific outcomes rather than the processes of playing. Increased pressures to engage in systematic preparation and to make sport conform to the business-like mentality of corporations signaled the demise of the sacred quality of pure play and ushered in a profane devotion to victory at all costs. It further contributed to the vertical structure of the contest, separating the great from the near-great and inferior as well as professionals from amateurs.

Even so, baseball fans and commentators still feel able to appreciate the spirit of pure play. While pure play loses its integrity when it becomes more vertical through distinction – as people become to be perceived and known as 'better than others' – fans of particular sports and their commentators still honor the 'spirit' of such play. They center on acts performed out of love for the process of competition which become interesting to fans, reporters, and players by the very act of 'playing fair' and taking and giving one's best.[15]

Despite Huizinga's dire warnings and current evidence that reporting on baseball (as well as other professional sports) has taken on a more ironic and cynical presentation, newspaper and broadcasting journalists have continued to romanticize baseball as played for the love of the game itself, often in sentimental and even maudlin terms.[16] Through a focus on specific outcomes – numbers – baseball fans and commentators not only share intersubjective pasts as they commit them to memory, but also share moral pasts as they identify heroes who conduct themselves as committed to the love of the game. As

Durkheim[17] noted about objects in general, honoring the status of numbers in baseball as sacred allows for a collective orientation to the difficulty and hard work associated with accomplishing what everyone in the baseball universe understands as great. Understanding the sacredness of numbers is further enhanced by the realization that, among an elite cadre of the highly gifted, only a select few can achieve the understandable goals. Just as Ulysses was the man among all men of strength who could string the bow and shoot the arrow through ax heads to hit a bull's eye, so those who put up significant numbers become honored as people who help reporters and fans to keep their faith in the spirit of pure play.

Believers with faith in this spirit can anticipate sacred things to come as well as believe that such things will occur with great difficulty and through great sacrifice. What Huizinga lamented as the demise of a present centered pure play becomes a collective orientation (or perhaps an illusion) toward a future for the spirit of pure play. Numbers do not simply represent a work ethic but call out responses that unify people in the baseball universe. They become the basis for narrative storytelling among fans and commentators, or the process of weaving intersubjective and moral pasts together.

NARRATIVE STORYTELLING IN BASEBALL

Most fans would agree that storytelling and retrieving the past are important to appreciate the game. Through narrative storytelling people create systems of retention[18] that allow for shared recognition of the significance of events. Passionate baseball fans can remember and agree upon significant details of games and dramatic moments that led to their outcomes.

Establishing an oral tradition through storytelling narratives situates fans and reporters as sharing pasts about the game's on-going commentary.[19] Shared pasts further facilitate intense interactions between people even if they do not know each other all that well. Passionate fans who remember the stories told to them by others and can engage in garrulous talk with one another demonstrate their competence as storytellers and as memorizers of important social facts. Their conversations and retrieval of important bits of information and the morals of stories make the oral tradition of baseball as important as the game itself and that is always in 'restorable reach'.[20]

The more poetic commentators such as Roger Angell[21] also feel that baseball's rich oral tradition is enhanced by some of the unique characteristics of the game itself, including its democratic-like line-up, the slower rhythm of the game that permits on-going talk about the various confrontations, the ritualized conflicts between managers and umpires, and the finality of substitutions (contributing to the chess analogy). The repeated confrontations between pitchers and batters not only establish a coherent past of plate appearances and sequences of pitches, but also turn the narrative of the game into a one-on-one drama.

Baseball storytelling also allows for a shared mythology that created the foundation for immortality. As Schmitt and Leonard have noted,[22] 'the post self' as one who becomes presented in history, is linked to the several present-centered 'footprints' players leave as they make themselves knowable in history's light. DiMaggio's famous rationale for playing 'all out' in every game was that he always considered the possibility that someone in the audience had not seen him play before. In effect, the good baseball story, the story with a moral past, centers on the self-conscious player who actively demonstrates that he is taking this past seriously.

Baseball storytelling and the establishment of a moral past through an oral tradition can occur with reference to print and video media. While some legendary feats remain almost exclusively oral, such as Babe Ruth's 'called shot' in the 1938 World Series, radio, print, and video recounting of events have contributed to an oral tradition rather than obliterated it. Fans continue to talk about dramatic moments that they either saw themselves or on television; that they experienced as it happened or after it happened via a replay. Even in the video age of baseball, oral storytelling about feats and misdeeds contributes to the collective bonds between those who share the same interests in baseball and who share its moral past.[23]

Through narrative storytelling, moral and intersubjective pasts become fused together. Baseball fans and reporters share the opinion that statistics represent an authentic summary of achievement and commitment to the spirit of pure play. Through repeated storytelling and enthusiastic references, particular numbers stand out as pinnacles of baseball's intersubjective past that become linked to honoring the game's moral past. The numbers themselves attain a sacred status, even after becoming surpassed. Fans and reporters remember Ty Cobb's 4,117 hits (surpassed by Pete Rose who ended with 4,256 hits). Even though Roger

Maris (in 1961), Mark McGuire (1998, 1999) and Sammy Sosa (1998, 1999) surpassed 60 home runs, fans and reporters still revere 60 as Ruth's home run number. Cal Ripken's consecutive game streak number has surpassed but not diminished the 2,130 games played consecutively by Lou Gehrig.

With attention to and validation of sacred numbers, baseball reports provide intense intersubjective and moral pasts filled with obdurate markers that avid and even casual fans commit to memory. For good or ill, fans and reporters create a type of moral intersubjectivity when recalling numbers and creating a place for those who establish great numbers. In treating particular numbers as sacred and linked to the moral past, some players become treated as paradoxical scapegoats who are honored and castigated simultaneously.[24] The feat by the individual warrants attention as legitimate, but the feat also undermines an endeared marker that people in the community regard as necessary to maintain an oral tradition. Suspicion toward a person's accomplishments by breaking a record became evident in 1961, when Maris finally broke Ruth's season home run total by hitting 61. Commissioner Ford Frick, a sports reporter during the days of Ruth, ordered that Maris's record be accompanied by the soon-to-be famous asterisk indicating that he broke the record by playing in 162 games rather than Ruth's total of 154.

Another sacred number associated with Ruth, his career total of 714 home runs, also became protected in several ugly ways. Hank Aaron's 755 total home runs surpassed Ruth's total, yet Ruth's figure seems more memorable than Aaron's. Beyond this, Aaron's home run record became notable in that some despised him for his pursuit of Ruth's record. The more odious critics shared their racist and derogatory words with Aaron, who began to collect statements written to him and about him as he neared and then broke Ruth's record. Other non-racist but nostalgic reports questioned the validity of Aaron's record. Critics mentioned that he played many more games than Ruth, hit most of his home runs for losing or mediocre teams, had a convenient 'launching pad' in Atlanta's Fulton County Stadium (with a high sea level), and went up to the plate only to hit home runs. The tone of this criticism suggested that Aaron may have been overly motivated by the record and not motivated intrinsically. Even so, most writers and commentators have dismissed these criticisms and now applaud Aaron's persistence. His 715th home run in April 1974 is now considered remarkable and is replayed as one of the stellar moments in the history of the game.

DiMaggio's 56-game consecutive hitting streak and Ripken's 2,131st consecutive game, breaking Lou Gehrig's 2,130, did become seen as honorable in their pursuit. Although each player endured intense scrutiny and, especially in the case of Ripken, endured continuing questions relating to his motivations for breaking the record, both established their records while accompanied by positive reporting and admiration on the part of fans.

DIMAGGIO'S 56 AS A SACRED NUMBER

Joe DiMaggio's 56-game hitting streak in 1941 became of the more notable and romantic quests defined by a number. DiMaggio himself has come to represent the romance of the game and to epitomize its moral past. Paul Simon wondered 'where have you gone Joe Dimaggio?' and Halberstam[25] called him 'the perfect Hemingway hero' who 'exhibited grace under pressure'.

DiMaggio's accomplishment, amid growing concerns over war in Europe, a still shaky U.S. economy, and an apparent gap in great achievements by popular figures, became a shared focus for sports fans across the nation. As the streak became more and more noticeable and a subject of newspaper stories, it began to eclipse the pennant races and any other accomplishment by other individual players. It is noteworthy that in the same year of DiMaggio's achievement Ted Williams hit .406, the last man in baseball to hit over the .400 mark. Even Williams's extraordinary hitting during the 1941 season became secondary news during DiMaggio's hitting streak.

DiMaggio and his streak characterized a star narrative, portrayed as a noble quest for a record by a team player who always played to win and demonstrated an undying love for the game he played. DiMaggio cultivated a meticulous reputation throughout his playing career and retirement of a player who never took the goals of the team and the team's fan base for granted. One of the more famous remarks attributed to him came in response to an observation that he always played 'all out', never letting up. 'Someone may be in the stands watching who has never seen me play before,' he said.

As the quest became a subject of intense scrutiny, the individualistic (rather than the team) orientation of the star narrative repeatedly made DiMaggio the center of media attention. While such an orientation may promote the idealism of intersubjective and moral pasts, it requires the individual to pronounce his efforts as secondary to the greater good. DiMaggio did his part by stating that, 'It'll suit me fine if my streak ends [with] us winning a ball game. That's all that matters.'[26] Reporters also tended to agree with DiMaggio. When one described 'a lucky bad hop single' that kept DiMaggio's streak alive at 30 games, he added that 'Joe would have probably given up even that though for the chance to spear Myril Hoag's looping single which drove in the winning run for the [Chicago White] Sox in the ninth.'[27]

DiMaggio's hitting streak characterized a star narrative in that neither the accomplishment nor the man became defined as flukes. Reporters remained vigilant about any potential fluke hits. When DiMaggio set the all-time record by a Yankee for hitting in consecutive games (30), he did so through an infield single. One report said that the grounder 'took a horrible hop and bounced off the Chicago shortstop's shoulder. There was no way Appling could field the ball.'[28] When DiMaggio broke the modern record of hitting in 42 consecutive games, a *New York Daily News* reporter observed that 'both hits were well thumped blows ... there were no flukes about these blows, they were record breakers.' After DiMaggio broke Willie Keeler's record of hitting in 44 consecutive games, the same reporter assured his readership that 'there were no fluke blows that kept the streak intact.'[29]

The test of the star narrative is revealed in the individual's ability to confront difficult tasks and to demonstrate skill in dealing with them. The star reveals a will to overcome real obstacles, rather than any magical or mystical obstacles. This is important in baseball with its many documented superstitions.[30] The star neither accepts fate as determining success nor as an excuse for failure. DiMaggio lived up to this narrative through direct responsibility for his acts. In replying to a reporter's question 'whether he felt it jinxed him to talk about the streak?', DiMaggio answered, 'Heck no. Voodoo isn't going to stop me. A pitcher will.'[31]

Another important part of a star narrative requires the acknowledgement of the player's achievement as outside the bounds of normal success. The acknowledgement should occur through a proclamation by someone respected other than by the person who accomplishes the feat. Self-proclamation of one's greatness may work in other sports but not in baseball. Greats of the past and observers with remarkable reputations confer the honor accorded to a star. Many others agreed that DiMaggio's streak and his play were worthy of a sacred place in the community. After stretching his streak to 48 games a *New York Daily News* reporter proclaimed that, 'DiMaggio was a Superman. Not content with spanking three singles and a double in the first game and a 410-foot run scoring triple and single [in the second game], he robbed the A's of as many hits as he made.'[32] Ty Cobb said that he wanted to see DiMaggio establish the record so that 'a genuine star can break it and not a fly-by-night sensation'.[33] Further, after the streak reached 30, one pitcher, Bob Muncrief of the St. Louis Browns, did not issue an intentional walk to DiMaggio when he came to bat with the lead run in scoring position and first base open. DiMaggio had gone hitless in his first three at bats and this fourth at bat could very well have been his final one of the day. DiMaggio singled during this at bat. When asked about his decision Muncrief said, 'That wouldn't have been fair – to him or me. Hell, he's the greatest player I ever saw.'[34]

Although fans and reporters demonstrated great enthusiasm over DiMaggio's quest for 56, it had its share of scrutiny as to whether it could be seen as a legitimate star narrative. Pitchers such as Muncrief decided to pitch 'to' rather than 'around' DiMaggio in crucial game-deciding situations. Some hits were described as lucky. One report stated that

> DiMaggio went without a hit into the seventh inning, then slammed a hard grounder toward third base, where it was stopped but not handled or thrown by Dario Lodigiani, an old family friend from San Francisco. The official scorer decided that the ball was too tough to handle, and the streak reached 25.[35]

Another retrospective account of a hit early in the streak implied brotherly intervention, stating that 'in the sixth inning Dominic DiMaggio had all sorts of trouble with a long fly Joe hit to center, perhaps sensing with brotherly intuition the birth of a streak no one else had yet noticed.'[36] The drama of the streak, and the assurance that the streak contained legitimate hits, became more intense as it surpassed the 30-game mark. By game 35 hourly wire reports became routine features as baseball fans around the country paid attention. Decisions regarding hits versus errors also became more scrutinized. During game 38 DiMaggio grounded to the St. Louis Browns' shortstop who muffed the play. Several Yankees rushed out of the dugout to see that Dan Daniel, the official scorer, had ruled an error. Many voiced and showed their displeasure non-verbally, but, as Seidel noted, 'Daniel … had no choice. Any other call would have been a travesty.'[37]

But as the streak became a shared focus for fans and reporters, attention to the motivations of other players and managers began to intensify. During game 38, for example, as a hitless DiMaggio stood on deck to bat in the bottom of the eighth inning, Joe McCarthy ordered Tommy Heinrich (who preceded DiMaggio in the batting order) to bunt in a non-bunt situation. McCarthy did not want Heinrich to hit into a double play and end the inning before DiMaggio could come to the plate. With two outs, DiMaggio did come to the plate and he ripped a clean single to the outfield, prompting the Yankee bench to rush out into the field as if one of their team mates had ended the game with a dramatic home run.

The motives of the official scorer also became a topic of reports. Dan Daniel, mentioned earlier and described as 'the leading partisan of the DiMaggio mystique', became the subject of more than one news story.[38] In game 42 of the streak, with DiMaggio on course to break Keeler's record of 44, DiMaggio grounded to the Red Sox third baseman who could not make a clean pick up and threw late to first. Daniel ruled it a base hit which 'offended the purists'.[39]

DiMaggio's streak not only went on to define the man, but to become part of baseball lore. It exhibits consistency, dedication, duration, and a willingness to play with grace in the face of on-going and intense scrutiny. When it was over a report simply stated that, 'One of the greatest feats in the history of baseball … ended under the gleaming arc lights of Municipal Stadium.'[40]

RIPKEN'S BREAKING OF GEHRIG'S RECORD

Cal Ripken's consecutive game record, breaking the famous 2,130 streak held by Lou Gehrig, typifies the spirit of pure play, not only with regard to love of the game but also to a day in and day out proof of one's commitment to the game over an extended period. A consecutive game playing streak embodies a type of duration that fans and reporters admire increasingly over time. Ripken's spirit of pure play and playing out of love for the game became linked to his 'calling' as a ballplayer. As Ripken noted, 'I have no secrets other than to say that I've learned a work ethic from my father and think it's important to the team and to my team mates to be in the line-up every day.'[41] Ripken's approach of the record commanded on-going print and televised attention, including the broadcasting of the 2,131st consecutive game on national television

(ESPN). But even though this record was made in a different era than Dimaggio's streak, the allusion to a moral past became clear. One such allusion equated Ripken's streak with the hard-working people of the country who show up everyday for work and do with their jobs with little fanfare. As one reporter noted, 'But through it all the Oriole shortstop has continued to show up for work every day, joining legions of blue collar workers in America, workers like postmen, pizza makers and auto mechanics, who also showed up for work every day.'[42] In this light, some reports focused on the contrast between the immense publicity given to Ripken's streak and the relative anonymity of his hard-working fans:

> [Gehrig's] record fell Wednesday night at Baltimore's Camden Yards when Ripken ... played in his 2,131st straight game. The achievement commanded a presidential visit, the presence of many celebrities both inside and outside of the sport, and most importantly, a sellout crowd whose numbers must have included average working stiffs who toil daily – as Ripken does – without promise of much more than a gold watch when they retire.[43]

As the possibility of Ripken's breaking the streak became more apparent, reporters repeatedly posed questions that asked him to evaluate the significance of the streak and to put its meaning in terms of a moral past. Ripken became baseball's version of a looking-glass self[44] who lived up to personal and collective expectations and continually confronted the image he projected as the streak wore on. Sensitive to the fact that he was breaking a beloved man's record, a man whom the adoring press dubbed 'the Iron Horse', Ripken became a self-conscious and reflective version of a contemporary Lou Gehrig. In turn, his presentation of this image became judged by fans and reporters as confident, modest, and responsible. Ripken's self became referential in terms of the spirit of pure play. He echoed its sentiments by saying, 'I believe in my heart that our true link is a common motivation: Love of baseball, passion for your team, and a desire to compete on the very highest level.'[45]

Aside from the theme of love for the game and a referential looking-glass self who let others toot his horn, loyalty also applied to Ripken's streak. Ripken is one of the few superstars who has stayed with the one team. His longevity as a Baltimore Oriole made him a familiar presence during a time when other players resembled temporary and even imaginary contributors. Ripken's streak symbolized an important stability in a disturbing world of change.[46] In the era of free agency, when teams become built and rebuilt without a sense of continuity, few fans can recall the line-ups of their team from year to year. One reporter wondered

> how many Reds fans can give an accurate Cincy line-up? Not many … Any old Cub fan worth his salt can recall the Wrigley Field line-up when they were kids too. Baseball should be thankful for a guy like Cal Ripken – for both his durability and his stick-to-it-iveness. Certainly he had been more reliable than the game he plays …[47]

Ripken suffered during the streak. Reports of how friends and family even put pressure on him to continue the streak began surfacing as he approached the 2,000 consecutive game mark. Other reports noted how his hair had fallen out, which seems to be the key sign of a baseball player's stress – the same thing apparently happened to Roger Maris when he was in the process of breaking Babe Ruth's record in 1961. In the light of such accounts, not all reporters saw in Ripken's achievement the sort of spirit of pure play that I have tried to demonstrate. One critic of Ripken noted that,

> Ripken to me is one of the most overrated players of his time. There's no doubt he would have been a better player had he taken a day off every now and then. He played through injuries and hurt his team for years, then ended his streak on a whim in a nothing game. Reporters nationwide hailed him for his class.[48]

Despite this criticism, Ripken's achievement became the subject of good press and fan adoration. Still, the end released him from the pressure to endure. As Ripken participated in the celebration of his achievement, taking a lap around Camden Yards, after being removed from the game in which he was the star player, he noted that, 'It was the closest thing to an out-of-body experience that I'll ever have.'[49]

STRAWBERRY'S SUSPENSION

Commissioner Bud Selig suspended Darryl Strawberry for the entire 2000 baseball season after he tested positive for cocaine on 19 January. As this was the third violation of Strawberry's drug aftercare program, reporters regarded the suspension as a fair and justifiable act. One reporter noted that, 'Selig is wary of protecting the integrity of the game and believes that Strawberry must be punished.'[50] Another was more emotionally direct: 'For once, somebody told Darryl Strawberry no. We must applaud baseball commissioner Bud Selig for that.'[51]

With little disagreement as to whether or not Selig should have suspended Strawberry, the journalistic focus seemed to be on how Strawberry the person allowed the events leading to the suspension to happen. How to regard him became the issue and how to explain his acts became the subject of journalistic commentary. In the main, differences between local coverage and that elsewhere seemed to differ along the lines of whether to try and understand Strawberry and salvage his commitment to a moral past or to skewer him as an enemy of such a past and an enemy of the spirit of pure play.

Local coverage emphasized the tragic qualities of a man who had jeopardized his future with the game and wasted his potential as a player once compared to the all-time great Ted Williams. As one editorial put it, 'There is something terribly sad about Darryl Strawberry.'[52] This same local coverage couched its assessment of Strawberry's tragedy in the therapeutic rhetoric of our times. This assigns blame to the fallen star, but, importantly, also blames the system that permits, often unintentionally, a 'disease'.[53] The editorial stated that, 'The truth is that baseball has been an enabler in Strawberry's addiction ... shielding him from the need to confront the truth about his addiction.'

Another columnist echoed the therapeutic rhetoric by emphasizing the loss of control themes that dominate such rhetoric. 'What was initially a moral transgression in using drugs has raged into a terrible fire. Strawberry is ravaged by an urge he cannot control, a habit he cannot kick and a game he emotionally can neither do with nor without.'[54] Shifting the focus from the man to the craving for the substance and underscoring a common with-or-without theme of the tragic view at least attempted to make Strawberry into a sympathetic figure despite the commonly accepted agreement that what he did was wrong.

Still other local writers noted the disappointment in losing Strawberry as someone who could accumulate important numbers to help the Yankees in their quest for the championship. One reporter, commenting on his comeback season last year, maintained that, 'His bat speed was incredible ... Bernie Williams and others spoke of him hitting perhaps 25 to 30 home runs during the 2000 season.'[55] In this vein, Strawberry's contribution to an intersubjective past became noteworthy.

In turn, his inability to keep contributing to this past signified another sad part of the story – his eventual lack of the numbers he should have been able to accumulate were it not for his apparent addiction. In the words of another local reporter,

> Maybe Strawberry will finally realize that the addictions that long ago robbed him of the chance to hit 600 homers and get into the hall of fame have turned him into another Steve Howe and, quite possibly, have killed the last stages of his perplexing career.[56]

Earlier I noted that the star narrative relies on a variation of Huizinga's notion of pure play. In a similar manner, the reporters' use of the fallen star narrative discussed Strawberry's emotional commitment to the game. They noted how much he loves to play baseball,[57] how he rebounded from colon cancer to return to the sport he loved,[58] and how, even at the ripe age of 38, he was in the process of dedicating himself to be the designated hitter so as to contribute to another championship season.

Whereas local reports relied on the fallen star narrative by employing the dramatic device of tragedy, outside reporters used a shame narrative to label the fallen individual as disgraceful and to cast him as an enemy of the pure play spirit. The basis of the shame narrative resides in the current language of anti-drug discourse, emphasizing the responsibility of individuals to abstain, and the promotion of the notion of individuals' taking responsibility for their actions. Whereas the fallen star narrative employs a therapeutic code that places the individual within a system that may be enabling the individual's demise, the shame narrative is used as an angry reaction to the individual as one who has violated the sacredness of the spirit of pure play and as one who should judge himself as harshly as others do.[59]

One outside reporter, commenting on the reports that his team mates appreciated his love for the game, sneered, 'For the life of me, I can't understand when in his scarred baseball career, Darryl Strawberry lapsed from home run hitter to pinstriped Mother Theresa. Team mates babble dotingly about the guy.'[60] Another editorialist mentioned that,

> Most people who have serious problems with booze or drugs quickly find themselves out of work and out of options ... [and] as someone who hasn't had a drink in almost 18 years after nearly destroying my life with alcohol, I can't help wonder why Darryl Strawberry can't pull himself together and deal with his problem.[61]

Outside reporters were not the only ones who employed the shame narrative. Some local commentators also expressed anger that Strawberry was useless to his team and antagonistic to a moral past. One, emphasizing the theme of boundary maintenance, remarked that

> I kind of liked having Strawberry around as an example of the damage and waste that drugs can bring. The improvident Strawberry has been sent away, perhaps forever, for the good of the game, and as an example for the country's imitative youth.[62]

Other local and outside reporters used Strawberry as a metaphor for another popular topic in the press: the overpaid and pampered athlete who lacks discipline, inner strength, and moral direction – or who is personally unable to contribute to a moral past. One stated that, 'For all of his trouble, Strawberry has never lost his sense of entitlement.'[63] Another drew upon the weakness of some athletes as moral men asked, 'How can they be so strong when they put on the armor and so weak when they take it off?'[64]

But in the main, outside commentators seemed to emphasize that the therapeutic language of understanding the person as having some sort of death wish and being unable to control an addiction could not suffice as appropriate explanations of and commentary on the person himself. They treated Strawberry as an embarrassment to the game in that his acts interrupted faith in the game's moral past.[65] The skewering of Strawberry as an enemy of the moral past and of the pure play spirit became charged with the emotional fervor against an evil force.[66] As one commentator put it,

> Those who will defend him ... talk about what a disease cocaine addiction is and how sick Strawberry must be. An addict, they say, just can't help himself. But Strawberry never looked like a drug addict. Never talked like a drug addict. Never appeared to be strung out, or desperate or even sick, except when he was fighting cancer. No, what Strawberry appeared to be was a man who had everything, but who still wanted more ... He was addicted, all right, but it was to doing whatever he wanted to please himself.[67]

Another columnist resorted to a more folksy put down: 'Darryl Strawberry is a drug loser ... who can't say nope to dope.'[68]

CONCLUSION

This essay has examined journalistic reports on numbers and drugs that indicate sacred accomplishments and profane violations by individual athletes in professional sports. In this light numbers signify the future of the sacred and the romance of play while drugs as signify an interruption in observer celebration of faith in the future of the sacred. Journalists' writings on the romance of sport involve an emphasis on the individual as noble achiever. The person rather than the contest itself becomes the center of attention. The individualistic orientation allows for the maintenance of idealism in sport, even in the face of growing concerns over contests', both collegiate and professional, becoming corrupted by television and high financial stakes. However, this orientation can become a renewed source of cynicism and despair when individuals within the sport break rules or violate codes and standards that observers deem as central to the spirit of pure play. While an emphasis on the individual as one who accomplishes great deeds can encourage observer idealism, the same approach can create renewed cynicism when an individual fails to live up to the responsibility of being a noble competitor.

The enthusiasm expressed by journalists and fans for sport as play centers on the creation of a star narrative or an emphasis on the heroic individual who plays out of love for the game. My reading of this narrative is that it represents an adjustment on the part of fans and journalists. Acknowledging that pure play does not exist in sport as presently constituted, observers maintain at least the appearance of pure play in sports. The star narrative allows for the mythology of pure play in that its spirit becomes apparent by and through the star's heroic and creative performance.

Obviously, the keying of the star's performance contradicts one ingredient of pure play in that it elevates him over other participants. But this contradiction becomes resolved by transforming the quality of pure play from the activity to the individual engaged in it. Instead of focusing on the contest when assessing whether or not it exhibits characteristics of pure play, observers can key on a particular individual 'superstar' as exhibiting these characteristics and preserve at least the illusion that pure play exists.

Numbers become central to the contradiction of preserving pure play by emphasizing the thing (individual performance) that threatens the integrity of such play. Hitting streaks and games played in succession are two numbers that serve as markers to distinguish the extraordinary from the mundane. This distinction, while apparently antithetical to the spirit of pure play, becomes the seed of pure play's mythology. Whereas the play itself has become a corporate game within a bureaucratic system, the individual player towers over the game as a symbol of the play itself. The great achievements of the individual become viewed as transcending the profane mechanisms of the contest. As revealed in numbers, an individual's greatness becomes honored by a sacred enumerated code – the numbers themselves become revealed as sacred, emphasizing the individual's labor of love.

Sports journalists have reported on numbers and provided a memory of such numbers for decades. The reports, and the subsequent collective memory of such numbers, celebrate the individual accomplishment as an indication of the player's love and dedication to playing the game. The accomplishments also become encoded in the game as boundaries that define the commitment to play and challenge individuals to exceed the commitments. The early boundaries themselves are remembered and romanticized as reflecting a time in which players dedicated themselves to pure play – motivated intrinsically by the accomplishment rather than external rewards and monetary incentives.

In baseball, honoring numbers allows for a collective experience of the sacred as figurative or implied in the activity itself. This in turn provides believers with faith in or anticipation of sacred things to come. When this faith or figurative sense of the sacred is somehow challenged a collective experience of something being violated emerges. Feats such as DiMaggio's 56-game hitting streak or Cal Ripken's record for consecutive games allows fans and reporters to reference achievements as validating their shared intersubjective and moral pasts. Identifying a fallen individual such as Strawberry, while problematic, nevertheless provides an opportunity for fans and reporters to define a misdeed as antagonistic to the honored pasts and to cement a commitment to such pasts.

NOTES

1. A. Schutz, *The Phenomenology of the Social World* (Evanston, IL: Northwestern University Press, 1967).
2. See G.H. Mead, *Mind, Self, and Society* (Chicago, IL: University of Chicago Press, 1934).
3. G.H. Mead, 'The Nature of the Past', in J. Coss (ed.), *Essays in Honor of John Dewey* (New York, NY: Henry Holt, 1929), pp. 161–73.

4. J. Tygiel, *Past Time: Baseball as History* (New York, NY: Oxford University Press, 2000).
5. L. Coser, 'Introduction: Maurice Halbwachs 1877–1945', in Maurice Halbwachs, *On Collective Memory* (Chicago, IL: University of Chicago Press, 1992), p.21.
6. See B. Shwartz, 'Iconography and Collective Memory: Lincoln's Image in the American Mind', *Sociological Quarterly*, 32 (1991), 301–19.
7. M. Douglas, *Purity and Danger: an Analysis of the Concepts of Pollution and Taboo* (Boston, MA: ARK Paperbacks, 1966).
8. J. Huizinga, *Homo Ludens: a Study of the Play Element in Culture* (Boston, MA: Beacon Press, 1950).
9. E. Goffman, *Frame Analysis: an Essay on the Organization of Experience* (Cambridge, MA: Harvard University Press, 1974).
10. T.A. Hayes, 'Stigmatizing Indebtedness: Implications for Labeling Theory', *Symbolic Interaction*, 23 (2000), 29–46.
11. See R. Stivers, 'The Concealed Rhetoric of Sociology: Social Problems as Symbol of Evil', *Studies in Symbolic Interaction*, 12 (1991), 279–99.
12. D.Q. Voight, *America through Baseball* (New York, NY: Nelson Doubleday, 1976).
13. Ibid, p.197.
14. M. Weber, *The Protestant Ethic and the Sprit of Capitalism* (New York, NY: Scribner's, 1958).
15. See R. Callois, *Man, Play, and Games* (New York, NY: Schocken Books, 1961), pp.82–7.
16. See M. Crispin-Miller, 'Deride and Conquer', in T. Gitlin (ed.), *Watching Television* (New York, NY: Pantheon Books, 1986), pp.183–228.
17. E. Durkheim, *The Elementary Forms of the Religious Life* (New York, NY: Free Press, 1915 and 1960).
18. See C.J. Couch, *Information Technologies and Social Orders* (New York, NY: Aldine de Gruyter, 1996) and A. Kleinman and J. Kleinman, 'How Bodes Remember: Social Memory and Bodily Experience of Criticism, Resistance, and Deligitimation following China's Revolution', *New Literary History*, 25 (1994), 707–23.
19. M.A. Katovich and C.J. Couch, 'The Nature of Social Pasts and Their Uses as Foundations for Situated Action', *Symbolic Interaction*, 15 (1992), 25–48.
20. A. Schutz and T. Luckmann, *The Structure of Life Worlds* (Evanston, IL: Northwestern University Press, 1974).
21. R. Angell, *Five Seasons* (New York, NY: Simon & Schuster, 1976).
22. R.L. Schmitt and W.M. Leonard, II, 'Immortalizing the Self through Sport', *American Journal of Sociology*, 92 (1986), 1088–1111.
23. See C. Einstein (ed.), *The Baseball Reader: Favorites from the Fireside Books of Baseball* (New York, NY: McGraw-Hill, 1980), pp.14–15.
24. See R. Girard (trans. P. Gregory) *Violence and the Sacred* (Baltimore, MD: Johns Hopkins University Press, 1977) and R. Girard (trans. Y. Freccero), *The Scapegoat* (Baltimore, MD: Johns Hopkins University Press, 1986).
25. D. Halberstam, *Summer of '49* (New York, NY: Morrow, 1989).
26. *New York Daily News Legends Series. Joe Dimaggio: an American Icon* (Sports Publishing Co., 1999), p.56.
27. Ibid., p.53.
28. M. Seidel, *The Streak: Joe DiMaggio and the Summer of '41* (New York, NY: McGraw Hill, 1988), p.123.
29. *New York Daily Legends Series*, p.58.
30. See G. Gmelch, 'Baseball Magic', *Transaction*, 8 (1971), 286–9.
31. Seidel, *The Streak*, p.142.
32. *New York Daily Legends Series*, p.63.
33. Ibid., p.54.
34. Ibid., p.57.
35. J. Durso, *DiMaggio: the Last American Knight* (Boston, MA: Little-Brown, 1995), p.127.
36. Seidel, *The Streak*, p.65.
37. Ibid., p.147.
38. Durso, *DiMaggio*, p.122.
39. Ibid., p.134.

40. *New York Daily News Legends Series*, p.67.
41. *Los Angeles Times* (7 Sept. 1995), B.1.
42. *Indianapolis News* (7 Sept. 1995), C.1.
43. *Indianapolis Star* (7 Sept. 1995), F.1.
44. C.H. Cooley, *Human Nature and Social Order* (New York, NY: Scribner's, 1902).
45. *St. Louis Post Dispatch* (7 Sept. 1995), D.5.
46. See Schutz and Luckmann, *Structure*, pp.25–8.
47. *Indianapolis News* (7 Sept. 1995), C.1.
48. *Cleveland Plain Dealer* (30 April 1999), D.1.
49. *St. Louis Post Dispatch* (7 Sept. 1995), D.1.
50. *New York Times* (25 Feb. 2000), D.1.
51. *Fort Worth Star Telegram* (1 March 2000), C.1.
52. Editorial Desk, *New York Times* (1 March 2000), A.22.
53. See T. Szasz, *Ceremonial Chemistry: the Ritual Persecution of Drugs, Addicts, and Pushers* (revised edn) (Holmes Beach, FL: Learning Publications, 1985).
54. *New York Times* (26 February 2000), D.1.
55. Ibid. (29 Feb. 2000), D.1.
56. Ibid. (24 Feb. 2000), D.3.
57. Ibid. (29 Feb. 2000), D.1.
58. Ibid. (24 Feb. 2000), D.3.
59. T.J. Scheff, 'Shame and Conformity: The Deference-Emotion System', *American Sociological Review*, 53 (1988), 395–406.
60. *Fort Worth Star Telegram* (1 March 2000), C.1.
61. Ibid. (1 March 2000), B.13.
62. *New York Times* (28 Feb. 2000), D.1.
63. Ibid., 3.
64. *Fort Worth Star Telegram* (29 Feb. 2000), C.2.
65. See E. Gross and G. Stone, 'Embarrassment and the Analysis of Role Requirements', *American Journal of Sociology*, 70 (1964), 1–15.
66. A. Delbanco, *The Death of Satan: How Americans Have Lost the Sense of Evil* (New York, NY: Farar, Straus, and Giroux, 1995).
67. *Fort Worth Star Telegram* (27 Feb. 2000), C.6.
68. Ibid. (24 Feb. 2000), C.1.

Curling in Canada

STEPHEN G. WIETING and
DANNY LAMOUREUX

North American fans of sport long have recognized the prominence of Canadians in ice hockey. Ever since cable television services expanded in the 1980s to offer both U.S. and Canadian viewers programs with live coverage of the other countries' sporting events (and as this television industry capital allowed Canadian Football League franchises to bid for American college stars), U.S. football fans have admired the wide–open style of the Canadian Football League. These presumed dominant Canadian sports aside, the rink of Sandra Schmirler, the four-member team she led to the 1998 gold medal in Nagano, was named 'Canada's Team' in 1998 instead of the Grey Cup champion Calgary Stampeders, of the Canadian Football League and Canadian hockey franchises within the National Hockey League.[1]

World championships have been contested for men in curling since 1959 and women since 1979, and there are few sports of any kind that have witnessed so commanding a dominance by a nation of a sport as Canada in curling. The long and venerable tradition of curling there is relatively unknown to fans and sport scholars outside that country. This general gap in international attention to the sport and its very uniqueness suggest its potent value as a resilient example of sport and cultural memory – that is, how parts of Canada's cultural legacy are remembered in sports writing, idealized athletic images, and national celebrations of a sporting endeavor. The recent emergence of the sport on to an international viewing stage provides in sharp detail as well a record of how the history of a national sport and the special features of its performers negotiate the necessary but often treacherous channels leading to global attention. In this essay possible reasons for the popularity in and success by Canada in curling are explored, details of the selection of curling as an Olympic sport are noted, and the special atmosphere surrounding the sport and its participants are reviewed.

Within the central themes of this volume, a conclusion notes the tension that persists between the need to maintain the purity of the sport's history and integrity in Canada (and other countries where it is a durable sport) and the attempts to make it a popular and marketable sport in other countries.

CANADA AND CURLING

Curling, a sport possibly invented as early as the first part of the sixteenth century in Scotland, appeared in a first literary reference in a poem in 1638. Curling is known to have been played by a Scottish regiment stationed in Canada in 1789. Due to the immigrant flow of Scots supported by the Canada Land Company, curling clubs were established by the settlers in North America in Kingston (1820), Fergus (1834), West Flamborough (1835), Toronto and Milton (1836), Galt and Guelph (1838), and Scarborough (1839). Curling interest and participation expanded along lines of the western movement of the railroad in the later part of the nineteenth century. The sport is documented to have first appeared in the United States in 1832 in the Orchard Lake Curling Club. A national championship was established in Canada, the Brier, in 1927, with winners coming mainly from the Western provinces of Manitoba, Alberta, and Saskatchewan. The game has been played for a considerable time within Europe in Denmark, Germany, Austria, Italy, Holland, France, Finland, Norway, and Sweden; and in England and Wales in the United Kingdom; now 34 countries are members of the World Curling Federation.[2] Despite this geographical spread, the notion of a world championship has always been restricted to Canada, with a gradually expanding group of national competitors. Such a championship was first instituted between Scotland and Canada as the Scotch Cup (eventually including the U.S.). This was replaced as the Air Canada Silver Broom in 1968 with teams from ten countries. It now is the Ford World Curling Championship and includes ten countries (Canada, United States, Finland, Norway, Sweden, Austria, Switzerland, Germany, Scotland, and Denmark). The International Curling Federation (now the World Curling Federation) was founded in 1966. A continuing international effort led to full inclusion of curling into the winter Olympic Games held in Nagano, Japan in 1998, where Canada won the men's silver medal and the women's gold medal, further establishing that country's world prominence.

While a tantalizing question persists over why the Scots should have invented curling, a somewhat more accessible project and one of greater interest to students of contemporary sport patterns concerns the reasons for the astonishing popularity and success of curling within Canada.

With a population of 29,200,000 and an area of nearly 10 million sq km (2.9 persons per sq km), Canada is relatively small (with slightly over one-tenth of the population of the United States) and possesses a relatively large body of natural resources for sport and recreation. Canada is sixteenth in the medals won in the summer Olympics and tenth in the number won in the winter games. Only Sweden, Hungary, Finland, Australia, and Romania, smaller in size than it, have higher medal totals in the summer Olympics. But five of the nine countries above Canada in the winter Olympics medal totals (Norway, Austria, Finland, Sweden, and Switzerland) are smaller. So, by virtue of the support from a population that can provide a talent pool, Canada is not exceptional. By the standard of living only the United States has a higher GNP per capita than Canada of the 15 countries ahead in the number of medals won in the summer Olympics. Canada, with $24,400 per capita, is just below Norway ($24,500) and some $4,000 below the U.S. per capita income, making its individual wealth greater than seven of the nine countries that rank higher in the yield of winter Olympic medals. World class sport requires some mechanism for a select populace to train exclusively, furthermore, a country must invest in development programs. All of this is a national expense that favors more affluent and developed national sponsors. The success of other countries with considerably lower standards of living than Canada suggests that these monetary resources cannot account clearly for the standing in world competition.

One cannot argue, then, on the basis of relative population resources or standard of living, that Canada is an especially productive site for producing successful competitors in summer or winter Olympic events. But the success of Canada in curling does raise the question of why, over such a long period, Canada has sustained such a level of excellence and competitive advantage in that sport in particular. In the 41 world championships held since 1959 the Canadian men have won 25 championships; others with multiple wins are far in the distance, with the U.S. having won four and Scotland, Switzerland, Sweden, and Norway three each. Women's world championships began in 1979, and through 1999, Canada has won ten of the 21, and the next highest, Sweden, only five.

Four main factors are associated with the dominance of curling in Canada. First, because for centuries the sport required a solid sheet of ice over lakes and rivers, weather has been a necessary though not a sufficient condition. Secondly, while there is debate about the true origin of the sport – in its fundamental activity ice blocks or stones could be thrown across the ice for a variety of reasons – Scotland shows the strongest claim, based on both literary and archaeological evidence. And because of the long period of Scotch settlement in Canada, the importation of its curling heritage seems to have been an important contribution to Canada's own culture and national identity. Thirdly, the very nature of the available land and the emergence of the railroad allowed expansion of the sport from east to west in the territories that became the provinces of Canada. Fourthly, there is a long history of benefaction coming from the W.L. Mackenzie Company who were the representatives for Macdonald Tobacco in western Canada. George L. Cameron, president of Mackenzie early in the twentieth century, was himself a curler and sought to advance the sport. When the founder of Macdonald Tobacco, Sir William Macdonald, died, he left the company to Walter M. Stewart. Stewart, as part of his personal and the company's agenda, invested heavily in projects that would promote the future of Canada. He believed sport was a potent vehicle for such promotion, and through Cameron's prompting gave curling especially strong support. He saw it as a force to unite the provinces.

CURLING BECOMES AN OLYMPIC SPORT

One of the earliest inventories of sport, in the *Iliad* of Homer, included a chariot race, boxing, wrestling, a footrace, javelin and discus throwing, archery, and a type of sword fighting. Fifteen men's events have remained continuously in the modern summer Olympic Games since 1896, 12 of which were track and field, two fencing, and a 1500-m freestyle swimming competition (there being no women's events in the first Olympics). Rowing, with two events of single sculls and eight oars with cox, were scheduled but cancelled due to inclement weather. The first winter Olympics in 1924 included six sports and 14 events, with bobsled, ice hockey, figure skating (men, women, and pairs), speed skating (four men's events), and Nordic skiing (four men's events), and, notably, curling as a demonstration sport. In this first competition, in Chamonix, Great Britain, with Scots comprising the winning rink, defeated France 42–4 and Sweden 38–7. Canada and the U.S. did not attend and Switzerland withdrew late.

Many other events have been added to the Olympics and separate divisions within these have been included. In the 1996 summer Olympics there were listed 33 distinct sports, with 165 events for men, 97 for women, and seven which were mixed. In the 2000 Sydney Olympics, to show the degree of fluidity of the Games roster to reflect sexual balance, commercial potential, and interest group pressures, both new sports and new events were added. Taekwando was added as a new sport with four classifications for men and women, as was the triathlon for men and women. In the interest of sexual balance, several new events within existing sports were added for women, including trap and skeet shooting, water polo, the 500-m cycling sprint, seven divisions of weight lifting, the pole vault, the 20,000-m walk, and the modern pentathlon. Trampoline for men and women as a gymnastics event and synchronized diving (platform and spring) were added to the diving agenda. In the 1998 winter Olympics, there were 11 distinct sports with 38 events for men and 35 events for women.

The vagaries of event and sports selection show that commercial factors, tastes, and regional preferences are variables that must be managed to get one's sport into the Olympics and to keep sports from being discontinued. Seven entire sports have been dropped (including golf and cricket). Within sports a quite remarkable distribution of events shows the highly variable if not capricious bases for selection or discontinuance. In shooting for men 20 events once in play have been discontinued; in men's cycling there have been 17 events contested at one time and then discontinued.

Curling was a demonstration sport in 1924, 1932, 1988, and 1992. Several key steps in the process for full Olympic sanction included the formation of the International Curling Federation in 1966 (later the World Curling Federation, WCF), and substantial increases in the number of countries promising international membership and investment in team development. A key strategic factor as well lay with the vigorous lobbying by Gunther Hummelt, past president of the WCF from 1990 to 2000.[3] The sport is on the Olympic schedule for the 2002 Games in Salt Lake City and for the 2006 Games. The factors that led to the entrance of the sport in 1998, such as world-wide participation, will continue to be crucial, there now being 34 national members of the WCF. Both the Canadian Curling Association and the United States

Curling Association are candid in acknowledging the necessity to show commercial interest in the 2002 Games in order to ensure inclusion beyond 2006. A major concern in the aftermath of the 1998 games was that there was no network coverage by U.S. stations. Plans are established now that International Sports Broadcasting will produce coverage in Salt Lake, with NBC having contracted for coverage and the Canadian Broadcasting Corporation subcontracting from NBC.

THE IMAGE AND STYLE OF THE CURLING ATHLETE

There has been a vast amount of difference in the bodily definition and comportment of athletes within sports over the last 100 years. There have, as well, been different norms of embodiment of the athletic performance between sports. This variability has challenged students of sport over the last ten years especially, as discussed in the introduction to the volume and in the closing essay. Curling in the bodily shapes, comportment, and training styles of athletes brings a new exemplar to this variability. John Hoberman and others have documented the often contradictory forces that drive perfection in sport, all part of the Enlightenment impulse not only to improve but also to bring human performance more systematically under the control of scientific products and tutelage.[4]

Despite the general patterns Hoberman describes, the long cultural histories of separate sports continue to display unique and at times mystical features of sport conduct, preparation, and success. Within swimming, for example, there has long been a belief in the inestimable value of the long build-up and then the 'taper'. While the taper includes a rest period with a smaller amount of training, there are also associated with the taper ritualized aspects of removing bodily hair and dead skin (shaving), body spray to reduce drag, and now the elimination of the vagaries of the body entirely through the employment of the body suit (which was authorized by the International Olympic Committee for 2000).

With the dominance of Kenyans from the early 1960s (first men and more recently women) in middle-distance and distance events in track, many speculations about the 'secret' have been floated by journalists, scholars, and athletes, such as altitude effects, diet (some of the tribes from which groups of elite Kenyan riders originate are pastoralists), and being required to run daily to school.[5] Wrestlers have an elaborate mythology about losing weight. Cyclists almost beyond comprehension in the Tour de France find it all but impossible to escape the oppressive force of the *peloton*, or major grouping of riders in each stage of the race, which seems to wield a force sufficient to keep a single rider from 'escaping' into a solitary lead.[6] Curling has its own cultural heritage that adds new illustrative material to what might be called these extra-kinesthetic aspects of bodily style, comportment, and training. There is a long history of sociability associated with bonspiels, or matches, wherein each one is associated with liberal hospitality by the host rink or club. This has by repute often involved much alcohol consumption.[7] Historical reviews of major events of the sport in Canada such as the Brier (named originally for a brand of tobacco produced by the Macdonald Company), the men's national curling championship, recount heavy partying and alcoholic consumption associated with the performers.[8]

There are differences in the modern tournament opportunities for women, not being part of the Brier, and starting their international championship later. But there is a national championship now, and international championships began in 1979. Pictures of women indicate participation in early bonspiels. The earliest record of an all-female contest is from 1823. The image of men depicted in Canadian national events such as the Brier is of a hard-partying group of athletes. There is no such image presented of women. Nor is there evidence of the eroticized images of women described for a number of modern sports such as gymnastics and figure skating.[9] If there is any regularized portrayal of a non-sporting image of the female athlete in curling, it is in terms of customary roles of wife and mother (Schmirler and her rink) and as professionals attempting to juggle work and the demands of training and competition. Such is *Sweep*'s (a Canadian curling magazine) characterization of Elisabet Gustafson, a surgeon from Sweden who has skipped four world championship teams.[10]

Curling is a very old sport in Europe and in North America. But attendant with growing world competition and the prospects for commercial success in cash bonspiels, government training monies, and a professional tour, the stakes for higher performance levels potentially drive participants to improve. This occurs at the levels of recruitment where the training of the young is being refined, and it occurs at the levels of junior championship competition where contenders for the men's Brier, the women's Tournament of Hearts, and the World Ford

Championships receive early exposure to national and international competition. The pre-season training program within Canadian curling includes considerable flexibility training, aerobic conditioning, and some anaerobic conditioning suitable for bursts of work, such as the 26 sec needed of hard sweeping to support a shot. Personal attributes that can be refined with training that are important include pacing and concentration which are required, since single matches may last for six hours and even up to eight or nine hours in a championship. The duration of the national championships is nine days; professional events and some bonspiels may continue for four days. Within the elite performance training programs the priorities stressed include resiliency, visual acuity, and knowledge of force vectors and friction – skills analogous to those of golf. There is a premium on the skills of logistics and strategy, not unlike playing poker. All of these factors are crucial even before getting to the mechanics and skill of shot making, sweeping, and calling shots. Considerable attention at the elite performance training levels is devoted to the mental aspects of emotion management and intensity. Because the factors that make the social dynamics of a four-member rink are so crucial but delicate in balance, there is considerable interest in understanding successful units and refining aspects of collective strategy.

LOCAL INTEGRITY vs. GLOBAL MARKETING

Estimates place the number of curlers in Canada at 1.3 million. Attendance at the yearly national championships has grown steadily as has the volume of television coverage and the numbers of viewers. These grass-roots participation figures and consumption patterns suggest the continuing popularity of the sport. Certainly as a complement to the international success they suggest Canada's likely continuing dominance in the sport. Maintaining the sport within current circumstances, though, is a matter of considerable concern to curling federations and players. Factors such as increasingly compelling alternatives for children other than curling, growing expenses associated with participation for all curlers, and vastly heightened competition for the consumer dollar of the sports spectator are regularly noted by commentators on curling. To address the current and the expected contexts appears to depend on three interlocked organizational efforts: grass-roots recruitment, professionalization at the elite levels, and aggressive and imaginative competition for national and international television airtime and sponsorships.

The long history of the game in Scotland, Canada, and the northern regions of the U.S. is now encountering choices of growth within a global cultural and economic marketplace. This decision arena provides a fruitful example of the alternative choices posed to organizers in many sports in the U.S. and Canada, as treated elsewhere here. Does a country preserve sports traditions only, resisting prospects for their modification for purposes of export? Does the allegiance to the sport ultimately drive supporters to increase sources of support for development and to compete internationally for spectator and sponsor attention? Then, to add to the difficulty of choice, at what cost does the engagement internationally hold for the integrity of the centuries-old sport?

The following is from a considerably earlier point in curling's global spread, but with some of the same factors to balance as at present:

> It is gratifying to observe the success of the efforts which have been made in this country, during the last few years, to promote and encourage the Game. It is now becoming, and must become, a favorite in Canada. It is admirably adapted to this climate, where the winter is generally cold enough to ensure good ice, and seldom so severe as to render the exercise unpleasant. Being played in the open air, during a season when few out-of-door recreations can be enjoyed, it is well calculated to counteract the enfeebling influence of confinement to our close and heated winter houses. Many objections which may be brought against other sports, are not applicable to this. It calls up none of the low and degrading passions of our nature. Notwithstanding the intense interest which Curlers may feel in a well contested match, no betting ever takes place among them; the excitement arising from gambling, therefore, is altogether removed from the rink. Intoxication on the ice is also unknown among good players. The nice equilibrium of body and the firmness of nerve, essential to scientific curling, would disappear on the first symptom of such a state. But the Game is sufficiently interesting without any extraneous stimulant.[11]

Grass-roots Development

Sweep is a recent magazine that covers national, provincial, and world news on curling and also provides information to meet general player interest in the form of instructional tips and 'state of the sport' news. Regularly the matter of maintaining player and club memberships in the sport occurs. A major institutionalized recruitment system within the schools includes two instructional protocols called the Premier Sports Program and Getting Started in Curling. These both originated in British Columbia, the first in 1981 by Harry Jerome, the famous sprint champion; the second was produced in association with the Coaching Association of Canada. At the national level for support of club participation The Little Rock Program is available in the form of an instructional kit and club participation for children aged from six to nine. Estimates of participation levels vary, but 50,000 is a conservative one reported in 1999.[12] The concept began in the early 1980s with curling stones weighing half as much as the customary 20 kg stone.

There are an estimated 15,000 curlers in the United States. Aggressive efforts at every level of development are under way there. *United States Curling News*, established in 1945, provides extensive coverage of events and promotional suggestions. The USCA Strategic Plan intends an annual rate of growth of 7 per cent. An important catalyst for growth comes from a general donation program 'Keep the Rocks Roarin'!' campaign. This supports club membership marketing seminars costing $1,200 per club, with two sessions, of which the club pays only $300.

Grass-roots sporting participation occurs in the United States primarily through parent/athlete private financing until early adolescence. Training devices similar to those evident in Canada are used to teach the sport, along with formats that use non-ice venues. Through adolescence considerable sports participation occurs in the public schools. There is a possibility for curling to be adopted in physical education and for competition at the high school level. There have in the past been interscholastic high school programs in Minnesota and Wisconsin, though the numbers of institutions and participants involved have waned in recent years. This area of expansion has potential within development plans. Elite levels of sport in the U.S. commonly draw performers from within athletic programs in the universities. This linking of sports and higher education is unusual by comparison with Canada, the United Kingdom, and elsewhere in Europe. Many factions within universities and outside decry this apparent compromising of educational and research pursuits. But college sports have been inextricably intertwined with college and university education at least since the late nineteenth century. Hence within the U.S. it is seen as prudent to nurture university and college student interest in the sport. This is being done at the United States curling facility and by the executive director of the Illinois State Curling Foundation. There were during the 1999–2000 season three separate state events along with a national tournament, drawing in a total of 33 collegiate teams.

Professionalization

Every sport that becomes part of the summer or the winter Olympics program has gone through a series of professionalization steps. These have included the increasingly refined codification of rules, standardization of playing venues, the generating of capital to sustain events, and eventually the provision of prizes, salaries, and expenses for the elite players. Curling has experienced these relatively recently, and certainly, as has been the case with other sports, not without considerable controversy.

Local and Global Marketing

In Warren Hansen's conclusion to his recent book on curling, he estimates that it is unlikely to grow in Europe. Additionally, though there was an impressive interest in Japan during the Nagano Olympics, there is a fundamental problem of space for participation and eventually expense at the grass-roots level there. The growth prospects, in his view, are to the south.

> Canada's top competitive curlers have a dream of a professional circuit that would resemble golf's PGA Tour. It's an interesting idea but has one serious flaw – it won't fly unless Americans are involved in a big way. It's this simple: Canada's 30-million population cannot produce the television revenue or the sponsorship dollars required to make it work.[13]

Ed Lukowich of Calgary, who is now U.S.A. Curling Athletic Development Director, worked to develop a world curling tour for a number of years. In Canada this involved identifying special cash bonspiels as tournament sites. In 1997 the International Management Group (IMG) took over the tour and provided sponsorship dollars. Cash prices for the bonspiels, which occurred over the early part of the curling season, from October to December, were $10,000 for the winning rink. The IMG-sponsored professional tour was complemented by a women's tour running over the early part of the season as well, but with less sponsorship money available. After two years of sponsorship in Canada, IMG support has come to an end. Hence some of the expansion plans for the world curling tour are on hold. Hansen, a former national curling champion who is centrally involved in the Canadian Curling Association, considers that there are formidable barriers to world development, certainly without access to space, populations with potential players, and revenue. Curling in Europe is an upper-class pursuit with modest openings for broad viewership and widespread participation. Japan's cultural affinity for the sport would allow optimism for the growth of participation and the number of viewers there. However, the enormous cost of space there unavoidably limits the prospects for providing venues. Canadian land area allows 2.9 citizens per sq km and the area of the U.S. allows 30 per sq km. But Japan must fit 334 citizens within that space. Only the U.S. has the requisite space at a reasonable cost, the demographic prospects for growth among new curlers, and the potential revenue from sponsors and television coverage. Similar dilemmas have existed within efforts to expand commercially by the Canadian Football League and the Canadian Professional Golf Tour. Both are limited by the Canadian population, which offers a potential set of spectators and television viewers which is considerably smaller than in the United States. And with the geographic reach of the television coverage of the Professional Golf Association and the National Football League events in the U.S., both Canadian professional products must compete with the heavy existing financing of the PGA events and National Football League games.[14]

CONCLUSION

Sport is physical, rule-governed, intrinsic, and consummative in its intensity and import. From the warm understatement of enthusiasm of the quoted excerpt from the early curling manual to participation today at all levels these ingredients seem present in near purity within curling. Given the demand not only for strength and stamina, but also for patience, resiliency, and perceptual and cognitive precision in making shots, the sport is extraordinarily demanding of body and mind. The elaborate written rules of the game include cherished tacit conventions of respect for rink members and opponents. Much of the rule configuration, as in golf, is self-policed. Demands for the national and the international growth of the sport have required more prize money at bonspiels, money for training, and the prospects for network coverage and a professional tour. But for the most part this will provide only supplemental expenses money for elite athletes who traditionally have spent considerable sums to support themselves at bonspiels and at national and international tournaments. Elite men and women athletes compete outside their customary occupations; curling is an enjoyable and compelling endeavor at all levels, but it will never provide athletes with lucrative employment or the monetary return remotely like that which competitors in the NBA and NFL in the U.S. or NHL in Canada receive.

Does curling participation and winning matter? Is the sport driven by the high emotion remembered by Bill Bradley, that being a U.S. Senator is not at all like being a New York Knick and winning an NBA Championship in Madison Square (*'That* is a thrill!')? W.O. Mitchell, in *The Black Bonspiel of Willie MacCrimmon*, gives a fictional answer. Willie's reputation as a curler has reached the ear of the Devil. The evil one, sensing an easy mark, coaxes Willie and his rink into a Faustian deal. If the Devil will help the rink to win the Brier, Willie will have to skip the Devil's team in hell when Willie dies. Willie improves the bargain, maneuvering on the Devil's own athletic conceits. They finally agree that a victory in a match between the Devil's rink and Willie's in Shelby, Alberta would give the Shelby team the Brier championship and Willie's escape from perdition.

The Shelby match is played and won by Willie and his rink, as is the Brier.

> It is hard to say which match is more important to Scottish-born MacCrimmon. When asked how he felt about his rink's performance in winning the Canadian Brier, MacCrimmon, in an accent that owes more to Auchtermuchty than to Shelby, said, 'Aye. It seems we did curl one devil of a match to win it.'

One of us, a curler for much of his life, can provide a substantial list of Canadian curlers who would make the same deal as did Willie – in an eye-blink.[15]

NOTES

David Garber, Warren Hansen, Chad McMullan, Anne Merklinger, Rick Patzke, Gerry Peckham, and Mike Thompson provided information and advice in the preparation of this essay. Their assistance is gratefully acknowledged.

1. Sandra Schmirler skipped her rink (lead, Marcia Guderit, second, Joan McCusker, and third, Jan Betker) to the first-ever official Olympic championship in the 1998 Nagano Olympics. She died aged 36 on 2 March 2000 after unsuccessful treatment to reduce a cancerous tumor behind her heart. Her funeral was nationally televised in Canada.
2. As befitting a sport with so long and powerful a history as curling within Canada, there is a venerable line of historical scholarship. The standard history of the sport is J. Kerr, *History of Curling: Scotland's Ain Game and Fifty Years of the Royal Caledonian Curling Club* (Edinburgh: David Douglas, 1890). The first publication on curling is *An Account of the Game of Curling*, by a Member of the Duddington Curling Society (Edinburgh, 1811). According to David B. Smith's history, the first Canadian treatment of curling is *The Canadian Curler's Manual* (Toronto, 1840). Smith's own carefully prepared history links these sources to the bases of the modern game until the late 1970s: D. Smith, *Curling: an Illustrated History* (Edinburgh: John Donald, 1981). Corresponding with the recent international exposure of Canadian curling through the Nagano Olympics are books that capture both the broad appeal of the sport in Canada, while providing technical knowledge with the intention both to educate the viewing public and potential and future players. Illustrative of this recent genre are R. Bolton and A. Douglas, *The Complete Idiot's Guide to Curling* (Scarborough, Ontario: Prentice Hall, 1998); and a more traditional historical overview in W. Hansen, *Curling: the History, the Players, the Game* (Toronto: Key Porter Books, 1999). Earlier books that illustrate the range of genres devoted to the sport in Canada include a careful history of its reputed center there, such as M. Mott and J. Allardyce, *Curling Capital: Winnipeg and the Roarin' Game, 1876–1988* (Winnipeg: University of Manitoba Press, 1989); and a popular journalistic history of the Canadian championship established in 1927, B. Weeks, *The Brier: the History of Canada's Most Celebrated Curling Championship* (Toronto: Macmillan, 1995). The mythology of the almost inbred compulsion of curling participation is found in W.O. Mitchell's Faustian account of a curling rink's match with the devil, *The Black Bonspiel of Willie MacCrimmon* (Toronto: McClelland & Stewart, 1993).
3. Correspondence from Mike Thomson, and an internal document: 'A Short History of the Federation' (Perth: World Curling Federation, n.d.).
4. J. Hoberman, *Mortal Engines* (New York, NY: Free Press, 1992).
5. J. Bale and J. Sang, *Kenyan Running* (London: Frank Cass, 1996).
6. S. Wieting, 'The Twilight of the Hero in the Tour de France', *International Review for the Sociology of Sport*, 35 (2000), 369–84.
7. Smith, *Curling*.
8. Weeks, *The Brier*.
9. For example, J. Ryan, *Little Girls in Pretty Boxes: the Making and Breaking of Elite Gymnasts and Figure Skaters* (New York, NY: Warner, 1995); A. Guttmann, *The Erotic in Sports* (New York, NY: Columbia University Press, 1996); B. Fabos, 'Forcing the Fairytale'.
10. H. Sundstron, 'A Team for the Ages', *Sweep* (Oct. 1999), 16–19.
11. In the Preface to *The Canadian Curler's Manual* (Toronto: Office of the British Colonist, for the Toronto Curling Club, 1840). Reprinted in D.B. Smith, *Curling: an Illustrated History*), p.219.
12. D. Lamoureux quoted in G. Cabana-Coldwell, 'Little Rockers – the Future is Now', *Sweep* (Dec. 1999), 17.
13. Hansen, *Curling*, p.158.
14. W. Hansen, interview, 18 Oct. 2000. See also Hansen, *Curling*. (Hansen is Director of Event Management and Media Relations of the Canadian Curling Association.)
15. Mitchell, *The Black Bonspiel*, p.135.

THE NATION IN CELEBRATION IN GLOBAL BROADCASTING

America's National Pastime and Canadian Nationalism

SEAN HAYES

If hockey was easy they'd call it baseball.
part of a Molson's Beer 'I AM CANADIAN' advertising campaign[1]

Only when all of us – all of us – recover our memory, will we be able, we and them, to stop being nationalists.
Rubert de Ventos, *Nacionalismos*[2]

'I could have danced naked in the street and not a soul would have noticed.' This was my grandmother's memory of Canada. On her first and only visit, in September 1972, she had observed that we were 'mad with the ice hockey'. As new immigrants, we wanted to impress her with the wonders of Toronto, Canada's second-largest city at the time and a place at least twice the size of Dublin where we had all once lived. And though she appreciated the drive, the only thing that astonished her was that in the heart of this major city, in the middle of a bright and sunny working day, there was not a car on the street, nor a bus moving, nor a single shop door open; the only people visible were gathered around rows of television sets in a large window, watching a hockey game. Unbeknown to my grandmother, she was witnessing one of the defining moments in Canadian cultural history. She was watching us watching television at a moment now burnt into Canadian consciousness. It was the legendary 1972 Challenge Series[3] between Canada and the Soviet Union. All across the country, as any Canadian can tell you, not only were the streets deserted, but factories became silent, farmers stopped harvesting, television sets appeared on the floor of the Toronto Stock Exchange, children missed school or watched the games in crammed gymnasiums. My grandmother was there at the dramatic climax when the now immortal Paul Henderson, in the eighth and final game of a tied series and with only 34 seconds left on the clock, scored the winning goal for Canada and an entire nation erupted in joy. 'Ah sure it's a lovely place all the same', says my grandmother when ever she is asked to recall her memories of Canada, 'but it's awfully dull with all that ice hockey and all.'

FACTORS IN THE CANADIAN COLLECTIVE MEMORY

'Every collective memory', writes Maurice Halbwachs, 'requires the support of a group delimited in space and time.'[4] Having quickly left Canada, my grandmother avoided a 28-year orgy of newspaper, radio, television, magazine, painting, book, theater, coin, documentary film, song and video-box-set commemorations of the 'shot heard around the world' (*sic*). My grandmother's memory of the event is a personal and somewhat less glorious recollection than the one collectively embraced and nurtured in Canada. Unquestionably, the structures of the nation enable this event to exist as an historic and legendary moment. Indeed, this event is only 'historic' and 'legendary' within the confines of this one nation. Likewise, most other countries can probably point to similar moments of national celebration and supposed immortal glory on the international sporting stage that the rest of the world has quickly forgotten or allowed to fade. The distinct collective remembrance and cherishing of such moments are a part of what constitutes national identity. As unfathomable as it may seem to a Canadian, it is doubtful whether anyone outside of Canada and Russia, apart from a handful of hockey fanatics, remembers that these games even took place. Yet for Canadians it was a crucial, mythic moment of a specific time at a particular national place. Like Americans and the assassination of John F. Kennedy, every Canadian alive at the time, it is claimed, can remember where he was when Henderson scored. Reciprocally, if you can remember where you were on 28 September 1972 you are most likely to be a Canadian – or at least an ageing one.

Twenty-years and one month later, on 24 October 1992, a somewhat similar moment of national importance occurred in Canadian sport, but its legacy is less clear. On that date, Major League Baseball's Toronto Blue Jays defeated the Atlanta Braves in Atlanta and became the first and only non-American team to win the World Series (*sic*). Forty-five thousand joyous fans, watching the game in Toronto's SkyDome stadium, on the world's largest television set, pour on to the downtown streets joining thousands of other exuberant and happy supporters. The swelling crowd cheerfully moves about with no specific destination in mind – just an apparent desire to be a crowd and mark the moment. Thousands of strangers purposefully squeezed up against one another, laughing and yelling and occasionally chanting the insipid team cheer 'Okay! Blue Jays!' Sporadically, the crowd erupts in cheers as someone attempts to scale a lamppost. It is a scene, perhaps, repeated in numerous North American cities after a major sporting victory. However, this crowd is set apart by the hundreds of Canadian flags and by the boisterous and repeated singing of the national anthem *O Canada*. Nationally, although the team is 'Toronto's team', and Toronto is typically a much loathed symbolic entity within the rest of Canada, similar smaller celebrations occur across the breadth of the land, even, surprisingly, in parts of Quebec. Another epic moment of national and, indeed, nationalist celebration, pride and self-congratulation had arrived. 'Not since 1972' is a typical media and social refrain. However, the nationalist elements of this celebration contrast strikingly with the 'globalized', or, more accurately, American, corporate structure in which the team is situated and professional baseball in Canada is played. The result is a set of tensions and contradictions in the way the collective receives, uses, and ultimately will remember this event.

Collective memory is, of course, not a given. It is, rather, a socially-constructed notion. Canadians born after 1972, or newer immigrants, or groups who feel excluded from the representation offered by Team Canada (including, for instance, women, non-white and aboriginal peoples) or, indeed, Canadians who simply hate hockey, would find it difficult to remain unaware, unaffected, and undefined in relation to the cultural impact of this most memorable sporting event. Whether personally cherished or not, Henderson's goal is a part of Canadian collective consciousness. It is now an intricate component of another cherished myth: hockey as Canada's game, 'our common passion', 'the Canadian specific', 'the language that pervades Canada'.[5] The legacy and reverence for the history of hockey in Canada is a part of what Eric Hobsbawm and Terence Ranger call the 'invention of tradition'.[6] It actively nurtures a common and enduring sense of experience, place, and affiliation with what it means to be Canadian. And at the same time, it is important to note, it also washes over conflicts, inequalities, and alternative interpretations of that national culture.[7] Hockey, therefore, is both a product and a constitutive element of a larger 'invention', that of Canadian identity. The supplanting of hockey with baseball as a major motif in Canadian collective memory, even if just slightly, represents a shift in the constructed notion of this Canadian identity. Memory, in this way, is the battleground of imperialism.

The central and most obvious means by which Canadians construct their collective memory is in the recollections and accolades that appear and reappear in the national media. Media are, of course, central to the concept of a nation as a construct. They are the principle element in forming, what Benedict Anderson calls, an 'imagined community'.[8] In the case of hockey and the Canadian media, each passing anniversary, or calendar touchstone, or moment of national self-examination, or sporting victory or crisis, seems to evoke yet another media analysis of the game's importance in imagining Canada as a community. To mark the new millennium, for instance, the sports writers and broadcasters of Canada acknowledged the obvious and proclaimed the 1972 Team Canada players to be 'Canada's team of the century'. The relatively recently victorious Blue Jays ranked fourth behind two more hockey teams. More strikingly, in a similar millennium survey, the Canadian press editors and news broadcasters placed Paul Henderson's winning goal in eighth position in a list of Canada's top *news* stories of the twentieth century. The goal beat such historic events as the raid on Dieppe in August 1942, in which 900 Canadians lost their lives in a single day. As absurd as such a contrast may seem, such popular survey results reveal the selective and constructive nature of remembrance. As Lewis Coser points out, '[C]ollective memory is essentially a reconstruction of the past in light of the present.'[9] Canada's collective memory and recognition of the significance of any event are due to a number of complex variables, including periodic celebrations, rituals, symbolic displays, and various elements of 'selective cultural preservation'.[10] In this light, it is a wonder that Henderson's goal did not finish higher on the list.

The selective criteria for the preservation of collective sporting memories may appear intrinsic to the events themselves, but in fact are set by those whose interests are best served by such remembrances. In the case of professional sports that generally means the interests of team owners, the media industry, a few athletes, and various 'promotional partners'. As Gruneau and Whitson point out, hockey was not 'Canada's game' until communication technology made the collective enjoyment of it possible. In turn, a fledgling hockey league and a modern communication industry expanded and profited from the conjectural and conjunctural needs and associations developed between one another.[11] With advances in communication technology and the increasing continental integration of economies, the Canadian sport/media nexus of today has a different set of conjunctural requirements to satisfy. American media 'spillover' and the prevalence and easy access to American cultural products, though by no means new to Canada, are now augmented by the presence of a few 'Canadian' teams in American-centered sports leagues. The Blue Jays World Series victories (they were champions again in 1993) represent the first major Canadian accomplishment in this new media/sport context. Of central significance to this event, for Canadians, was not simply that it was a victory against an American team in an American game, but that it was witnessed by millions of Americans on American television. For once America was watching 'us' as we have so often been compelled to watch 'them'. The *Toronto Star,* for instance, even carried front-page reports on how 'we' were being covered in the American media.[12] Canada had finally made 'the show' – the 'world' stage. 'Our' presence was, for a moment at least, being acknowledged. However, by entering such a discourse Canada partially relinquishes the validation processes for its own identity, of what it collectively holds to be important, and how and what it collectively remembers, to the machinations of the American media.

The National Hockey League (NHL), of course, has long been an American-dominated sporting organization in which Canadian teams have had success, but as a media product it is nearly inconsequential and largely ignored in the United States. Women's World Cup soccer, for instance, outdrew the 1999 all-American NHL Stanley Cup finals on American television, by a ratio of almost four-to-one.[13] Although the Stanley Cup is consistently one of the most watched television shows on Canadian television, the American ratings for a single game of the 2000 all-American Stanley Cup represent the 'lowest national number ever recorded for that night'.[14] Despite the looming realities of American ownership and control, declining percentages of players in the NHL, and fewer and fewer successes at international tournaments, for most Canadians the game is still 'ours' – and separate from the wider 'cultural invasion' from the south. The myth of hockey as 'our game' persists, in part, because there remain the national media with a vested interest in maintaining that myth. Hockey thrives in Canada not simply in spite of American indifference, but, in part, because of it. It is a means of being collectively different, uniquely un-American. As long as there is a separate national sport–media nexus, with unique popular and regulatory requirements, hockey is likely to remain 'Canada's game', even as the contradictions of such claim gradually mount.

CANADA AND THE CONTINENTAL EXPANSION OF SPORT

The expansion of Major League Baseball and the National Basketball Association, each into two cities in Canada, as well as the constant threat/promise of the National Football League's moving into Toronto, represent a significant shift in the way Canadians engage and identify with sports and sport teams. Continental exchanges and rivalries have replaced intranational exchanges and rivalries. As the Canadian sports and media environment becomes increasingly crowded by and attuned to American sports, the ability to preserve and develop Canadian sport organizations and the accompanying cultural exchanges, rivalries, and understandings diminishes. With them, the shared memories of such exchanges begin to vanish, as more 'globally'-oriented ones take their place. Historical sporting moments remain collectively significant only if they prove useful to the present and satisfy the requirements of the dominant sports/media enterprises; this is becoming a diminishing possibility for indigenous Canadian sports and leagues.

Collective memory, however, is not as technologically determined, nor imposed by an elite, as such a scenario might suggest. As Daniel Dayan and Elihu Katz explain in *Media Events*, profound media happenings such as, for Canada, Henderson's goal or the Blue Jay World Series victories, function as collective rites of communication. These events interrupt normal social and media routines, monopolize social and media discourse, viewers actively attempt to celebrate these moments in the company of others, the living room becomes a festive place, viewing becomes almost obligatory, and, once it is all completed, the moment is uncritically recalled and replayed time and again.[15] As such, these historic moments function as collective historic experiences. Such collective rites, as forms of communication, are necessarily participatory endeavors. They affirm common values, legitimize institutions, and superficially reconcile disparate societal elements. It is not possible under these circumstances to simply impose collective acceptance in some totalitarian fashion. 'Central to the success of these events is the complicity of television viewers who are free, in liberal democracies, to withhold approval or express dissent.'[16] In a cycle of mutual signification and affirmation, the collective is a willing participant in making these events significant, because the collective experiences these events as significant. The link between the audience and the media is 'not simply a linear relationship, but one which is circular and systemic, as much contractual as hegemonic'.[17] As an 'imagined community' Canada not only supports the collective memory of Henderson's goal 'delimited by time and space', but is in fact reciprocally constituted and imagined in, through, and by it. For, in the words of Henderson himself, 'I don't think we were ever more Canadian than that day.'[18]

Baseball, on the other hand, is 'America's national pastime'. It is 'their' invention, 'their' tradition. It is 'their' pastoral myth in which 'they' imagine themselves and in which 'they' are constituted. The presence of baseball in the Canadian, or indeed the Japanese or the Caribbean, cultural landscape carries with it the resonance of this American mythical presence. However, in order for a particular moment in baseball history to be incorporated or (re)constructed into Canadian collective memory, requires not only that the moment occur, but also an appreciation on the part of the Canadian collective that the moment matters. Canadians must willingly affirm the moment's significance. It must speak to them in terms of who they imagine themselves to be. Canada, for instance, has repeatedly won the world squash championship, but few Canadians have seen these victories let alone consider them collectively significant or memorable. In order for a sporting moment to be memorable, it must be seen and it must inform and be informed by the values, ideas, politics, and identities of the collective observers. The 1992 and the 1993 World Series Champions fulfilled both of these requirements.

In C.L.R. James's *Beyond a Boundary* he describes how cricket, and in particular the first West Indies victory over England, awoke the formation of a post-colonial Caribbean society and the development of West Indian nationhood. The West Indies beat the British at their own game and turned cricket 'from being a symbol of cultural imperialism to being a symbol of Creole nationalism'.[19] Although the face of colonialism has changed, there is a remarkable resonance in James's work for those Canadians interested in lingering aspirations for national self-determination. For a Canadian, one can no better describe that memorable day in Atlanta, October 1992, than in the words of C.L.R. James: 'It was as though … Prospero had taught Caliban the use of bat and ball only to find himself comprehensively "out-magicked" by his upstart colonial pupil.'[20] In the context of Canadian colonial experience, the Blue Jays' World Series victories represent a triumph of Canada over its American master. This, most of all, is what the Canadian collective celebrates and remembers. However, such attention and adulation inadvertently strengthen the very elements which are most antagonistic to the structures which support, define, and constitute that collective.

As the American sociologist Seymour Lipset has noted, 'Canadians are the world's oldest and continuing anti-Americans'.[21] This, more than any other element, accounts for the tremendous, Canada-wide, nationalist celebration of the Blue Jays. 'We' beat America at their own game. Sport, like no other cultural formation, mobilizes and heightens feelings of identification and collective belonging. It galvanizes the cultural construct of 'us'. It helps to define who 'we' are by positioning 'us' in contradistinction to 'them'. And for reasons perhaps only other colonials can fully appreciate, in a Canadian cultural context the 'them' most savored, acknowledged, and celebrated, at least when eventually defeated, is America.

Far from being mindless or jingoistic, much of Canadian nationalism is both cosmopolitan and progressive. The penchant towards (quasi) anti-Americanism has had some forward-looking ramifications on Canadian polity. Through an historical symbiotic and dialectical relationship with America and, in particular, American capitalism, Canadian nationalism emerged as a decidedly left-of-centre ideological force. As a part of the general, though non-violent, antagonism towards some things American, Canada attempted to develop as a nation that was – if nothing else – not America. As Blair Fraser puts it, 'of all general definitions of the Canadians, this is the most nearly valid: twenty million people who, for anything up to twenty million reasons, prefer not to be Americans'.[22] In the words of a popular bumper sticker: 'It's un-American to be Canadian'. In political and economic terms, this meant a rejection of America's full embracement of unfettered capitalism and a slight leaning towards a more 'mixed economy'. One must be careful not to overstate the success of the Canadian left; Canadian capitalists exploited most of the statist policies initiated for their own self-serving interests. Moreover, anti-Americanism is now critically and socially passé[23] (replaced by a promising but seemingly less tangible critique on 'globalization'). However, the legacy of difference – of 'progressive anti-Americanism' – of being the Other North America, can still partially be viewed in the remnants of policies supporting Canadian cultural protectionism, foreign investment review, a well-developed social welfare system, gun control, safe cities, quality and accessible education, strong public broadcasting system, and fully socialized medicine. In the often-quoted words (in Canada at least) of Graham Spry, the Canadian predicament offers a single choice: 'the state or the United States'.[24]

BLUE JAY NATIONALISM

Until 1989 and the introduction of the continental integration policies of the Free Trade Agreement (FTA) and 1993 with its expansion into the North American Free Trade Agreement (NAFTA), it seemed, a least partially, that 'the state' might prevail. Without going into detail about the content of these Agreements, like the European Community's Maastricht Treaty, they are essentially transnational, corporate bills-of-rights, but between two (now three) unequal partners. It is important to note here that the Agreements were (and still are to a lesser degree) a focus of a divisive public and political debate in Canada. Although the majority of Canadians voted against the FTA in the 1988 federal election, which was essentially run as a referendum on the deal, the Agreement was still signed. With a three-party (at the time) 'first-past-the post' parliamentary system of elections, the Progressive Conservative party, which was the only party supporting the Agreement, won the election and forced the deal through. Furthermore, many of those who voted for it did so with the repeated, well-financed but vague reassurances that 'culture was not on the table'. In a partial response to this, in the next election the Conservatives were humiliated at the polls and reduced to only two seats. The Liberal party, which formed the next government, ran on a platform that falsely promised to restructure or, in the words of Prime Minister Chretien himself, to 'tear up the Free Trade Agreement'. The Agreement, untouched, is still in effect.

Media events, suggest Dayan and Katz, disrupt existing calendars. 'Media events are interruptions marking breaks in time, sometimes signalling the beginning and ends of an "era".'[25] The events surrounding FTA and NAFTA – the skewed election results, the general sense of betrayal, the strong and well financed elitist support of the deal, the economic decimation that followed – are the social and political context the Blue Jays found themselves in 1992. On top of this, one can easily add the 1988 sale of the Canadian hockey icon Wayne Gretzky, 'the greatest player of all time', from the Edmonton Oilers to the Los Angeles Kings, dealt with in detail in the chapter by Jackson and Ponic. The heroic stature of Gretzky in Canada, 'the Great One', cannot be overstated. He is, without a doubt, one of the most recognized and worshipped celebrities in Canadian history. His 1988 wedding to an American actress Janet Jones is often referred to as 'Canada's Royal wedding'. Many perceived the sale of Gretzky as a devastating blow to not only Canadian hockey but to Canada itself. For critics of the FTA, it foreshadowed larger things to come. While upsetting to Canadians, the NHL considered the sale of Gretzky as good for hockey. It brought hockey's brightest star from the hinterlands of Canada to the media center of the world. This move would sell hockey in America – and that was, Canadians are repeatedly assured, something good. Sure enough, there are now professional hockey teams in such unlikely places as Florida, Georgia, and Arizona, where it is unlikely that a natural ice rink has ever formed. However, both Winnipeg and Quebec City have lost their teams to American cities, and the financially viability of professional hockey in Canada, outside Toronto and Montreal, is now under constant scrutiny.

Another contributing factor informing the cultural and historical context in which 'Blue Jay nationalism' arose, is the drug-related disgrace of track star Ben Johnson at the 1988 summer Olympics, also covered by Jackson and Ponic. After the short-lived triumph and jubilation, the memory of which might have surpassed that of the World Series victories in Canada if it had remained valorous, Johnson's disqualification brought an avalanche of collective soul searching, incrimination, and shame. The awarding of this gold medal to the brash American track star Carl Lewis may be viewed as yet another seeding factor predisposing Canadians' collective and abundant joy of eventually defeating an American team at the ultimate American game. This is particularly so in light of the Dubin Inquiry into drugs and amateur sports, in which it was made clear, for Canadians at least, that what distinguished Johnson from most other top-performing athletes in the world was that he got caught. It is perhaps inappropriate and too simple then to identify the underlying sentiment surrounding the Blue Jays in terms of thoughtless 'anti-Americanism'. Indeed, most Canadians would recoil at the notion that they harbor or harbored such feelings towards their southern neighbors, but in its simplest and most essential form, it is an active element of the social context in question.

It is precisely and paradoxically this anti-American sentiment that corporate capitalism taps into to make its cultural product so palpably appealing to so many Canadians. The Blue Jays as a Canadian national symbol and focus of identification and representation are purely and plainly a fabricated commercial construct, as well as a strongly felt and embraced source of pride, accomplishment, and independence. For Canadians the Blue Jays are both a franchised, urban–American, cultural imposition – the 'MacD-ization' of sport – and the very means by which Canadians can collectively demonstrate resentment and resistance to that cultural juggernaut. A typical privilege of not being American is that a group can selectively distance themselves from the perceived vulgarities of American corporate culture, despite its many pleasures, and conveniently align themselves with some supposed genuine, pre-Americanized way of life. This is compounded here by the appeal of sport itself as having some sort of experiential connection to a mythical past and a more pastoral way of life.[26] As a corporate manifestation, it may be argued, Major League Baseball is no less a valid site for contemporary Canadian fan-based celebrations, representations, and identifications than, let us say, modern-day professional hockey. However, its strong and complex incorporation into the fabric of the Canadian collective memory does represent a continental shift in the historic mapping and structure of Canadian consciousness.

One of the most conspicuous, yet blithely overlooked, paradoxes in Canada's national celebration of the Blue Jays is that, although they are possibly the most iconographically nationalist, the most renowned, the most well-examined, most watched, most talked-about, most written on, and definitely the most well-attended and well-paid sports team in Canadian history, they are an unabashedly American cultural formation with negligible Canadian content. The 1992 and the 1993 World Series champions had no Canadian coaches or Canadian players. In fact, not one member of these distinguished teams remained in Canada for more than a week after the victory parades (taxes and weather are often cited as disincentives to actually living in the country where they are feted). The game the Blue Jays play is unreservedly American in official history, tradition, and iconography. Baseball is America's national pastime. The Blue Jays play all their games against American rivals in American cities, except Toronto itself.[27] The Blue Jays play in, with no apologies to them, the American League. Their home stadium, the mostly publicly financed and now privately-owned and -operated SkyDome, is prominently adorned with not only multiple American flags but also American League emblems: a stylized bald eagle clutching a ribbon of stars and stripes in its talons. All salaries, except those of minor Canadian employees, are paid in American dollars, a fact that is continually used to justify the highest priced tickets in the League.[28] Although Canadians now own the Blue Jays, it is Americans who own and control the game.

Baseball has deep historic roots in Canada, but the game is so heavily inculcated with 'Americana', so richly woven into the American identity, that there is little room to exert an independent Canadian presence or history, or even to recognize fully the Canadian contribution outside the dominant American purview. In fact, there is little official League acknowledgement of the Canadian presence and historical contribution to baseball. It was only in 1988, after a long battle on the part of the Canadian Baseball Hall of Fame, that the Baseball Hall of Fame in Cooperstown, New York, acknowledged that the first recorded evidence of baseball in North America is of a game played in Beachville, Ontario in 1838 – a full year before Abner Doubleday 'invented it'. Cooperstown still holds that Doubleday invented the game, but it now acknowledges that the Canadian game somehow preceded that occurrence.[29] In 1994, with the looming possibility of an all-Canadian, Toronto vs. Montreal, World Series (before the players' strike and the owners' intransigence cancelled the season and the championship), speculation arose as to how such a match might somehow 'damage baseball' (as it would, undoubtedly, be a ratings disaster on American television). It is Americans, as the dominant owners, players, and consumers of baseball, who dictate how, where, and when the game is played and by what rules. As a preliminary illustration of the 'globalization' of American sports, professional baseball is a model of assimilation over acculturation.

Despite promotional and media declarations that the Blue Jays represent Canada, there is little, if any, critical undertaking as to how exactly they are doing that or what such representation means. Only the opposite notion has ever emerged from the players themselves. Joe Carter, one of the most celebrated athletes in Canadian history, spoke the unspoken when he declared to an American newspaper, 'We weren't playing for Canada. We're Americans. We want it for ourselves.' Ed Sprague, the 1992 World Series winning back-catcher, demonstrated his allegiances when he became personally embroiled in a dispute between Canada and the United States about the awarding of an Olympic gold medal. Owing to a scoring error, immediately acknowledged by the offending judge, Sprague's wife, Kristen Babb-Sprague, was awarded a gold medal in the 1992 Olympic synchronized swimming event over the rightful winner, Canada's Sylvie Frechette (the situation was partially rectified a year later when the Olympic committee handed her a second gold medal for the same event). For obvious reasons, during the controversy Sprague made no secret of where his personal and patriotic allegiance lay and angrily denounced Canada (which he was supposedly representing at the time) and stated plainly, 'I don't care what Canadians think.' Although controversial at the time and completely germane to the topic of national representation, none of this managed to diminish, alter or diffuse the glow of 'Blue Jay nationalism'. In particular, the collective memory and general recollection of such contributing factors to the larger event have almost completely disappeared. Though intrinsic to the situation, such awkward and challenging messages are not generally memorialized on posters, or framed newspapers hanging in taverns, in television replays, journalistic accounts, or commemorative videos. Beyond a few critical accounts of the event, such memories slowly wither as the 'official' and 'approved' version is extolled.

BLUE JAY GROWTH AND EFFECTS ON CANADIAN POLITY

Although largely seen as a metaphorical intrusion, the American domination of baseball and the expansion of the major leagues into Canada has had real effects and made real challenges to Canadian polity. Unlike trans-European leagues which necessarily accommodate and seek to function under numerous national regulations and systems of governance, the Blue Jays essentially operate as an American franchise under the auspices of American laws and regulations. They have even followed league commands in so far as they may have broken Canadian laws. Omar Linares, a Cuban third-base Phenom, who apparently wanted to play in the major leagues but remain a Cuban national, was forbidden to do so under regulations concerning the U.S. embargo against Castro's 'socialist paradise'. To circumvent this policy, in a little advertised arrangement, the Blue Jays attempted to sign Linares and have him play only during their home games – thus skirting any legal hindrances. Unfortunately, Major League Baseball refused to sanction this imaginative pact.[30] However, in accordance with Canadian legislation, specifically enacted to deter Canadian companies from following U.S. foreign policy towards Cuba, it is explicitly against the law for Canadians or Canadian companies to adhere to such American-imposed directives. Therefore the Blue Jays, 'Canada's Team', are still, presumably, operating in contravention of Canadian law and undermining the valued principle of an independent Canadian foreign policy. In this way the Blue Jays symbolically and actually represent the diminishing possibilities for nation states to control and effect change in the 'globalized' marketplace. If nothing else, such situations provoke the question: if Canada is not willing to challenge a largely symbolic sporting intrusion into its sovereignty, what will it do when confronted by larger incursions?

Similarly, the players' strike of 1993–94 presented another example of MLB's ignorance and/or insensitivity towards Canadian sovereignty and independent legal practises. It was only after major league management had announced their plans to hire 'replacement workers' for striking players that they became aware that this would contravene Ontario's 'anti-scab' legislation. Nor had they fully considered the fact that, under Canadian law, non-Canadians cannot be employed as scabs. To circumvent this legislation the Blue Jays had to arrange to play their 'home' games in Dunedin, Florida. The Montreal Expos, suffering major losses at the gate already, appealed for an exemption from Canadian federal labor legislation by using the embarrassing admission that the foreign workers in question would not be replacing Canadian workers, but, rather, just other foreign workers. The Canadian government obediently granted the exemption.

Likewise, when baseball's Mark McGwire smashed a 37-year-old record by hitting 70 home runs in 1998, he did so while flouting Canadian drug laws. McGuire openly admits that he used the testosterone precursor androstenedione in his ambition to be the 'home-run-king'. While this substance is 'legal' in baseball and is freely available off-the-shelf in American 'health food' stores, it is a banned substance in Canada. Although Major League Baseball exists and operates in two countries, there is no question as to which laws might prevail – even, as in this case, as one country's laws are being violated. Not even independent policies are considered (should McGwire home runs hit against a Canadian team count?). Particularly in the light of Canadian collective memory of Ben Johnson's Olympics disgrace, the adulation heaped on McGwire and the accompanying dismissal of the issue of performing-enhancing drugs in baseball is galling and hypocritical.

> And if, in this corrupt, doped-up world, athletes seemed to be getting away with it – if not lauded for their chemically-aided accomplishments – then what was Ben Johnson? What does it mean to be a cheater and a liar in that context? Why was he the only truly big star to take a fall?[31]

Was it because he was a mere colonial?

In the wider Canadian sportscape the cultural implications of the success and national celebration of the Blue Jays have had their most pronounced and non-metaphorical impact. For with the Blue Jays has come the growth of baseball in Canada and a transformation of the Canadian sporting terrain. For example, the decline in the attendance at and the popularity of Canadian football correspond directly with the introduction of Major League Baseball in Toronto. In 1977, the year the Blue Jays arrived, the average attendance at a Canadian Football League game in that city was 45,395. A mere ten years later attendance had fallen to 26,969 a game.[32] In 1977 nearly 70,000 people watched the Montreal Allouettes win the Grey Cup at Montreal's Olympic Stadium. Today, typically fewer than 22,000 average a three-down football match in Toronto, Montreal, Hamilton or Vancouver.[33]

Even the cherished game of hockey has indirectly felt the impact of the Blue Jays. As Roy McGregor noted, in that glorious World Series year of 1992,

> Toronto city council voted to close nearly one hundred outdoor natural ice rinks, a breeding ground for hockey greats. The money saved would perhaps find its way to Ontario coffers to pay off some of the massive debt incurred with the new baseball coliseum. The hockey rinks cost only $400,000 to maintain but would die as Toronto set a new attendance record in baseball.[34]

Such cultural shifts are not without historical precedent in Canada. Lacrosse, Canada's official summer game, was once the major summer sport, widely played, watched, and followed. However, 'mesmerised by baseball's big league glamour, and spoon-fed by the [ready-made and inexpensive] American wire services, sports editors and reporters [of the 1920s] gave major coverage to baseball at the expense of lacrosse',[35] with the result that lacrosse is now a marginalized minor sport with pockets of interests confined to southern Ontario and British Columbia. That is, ironically, with the exception of the recent (1999) introduction of the Toronto Rock as the sole Canadian club in the American-based National Lacrosse League. With all Canadian players, in front of sell-out crowds in Maple Leaf Gardens the team won the league championship twice in its first two years of operation (1999 and 2000). As one journalist put it, 'Those Yanks could sell us snow.'[36] What remains unsaid is the degree to which Canadian sporting bodies, even those uniquely associated with Canada, such as lacrosse, have grown almost completely dependent on American capital, marketing, and continental interplay. The presence of other Canadian cities in these games, due chiefly to population and geographic restraints, will necessarily be dependent on American concerns.

In an historic parallel to the early twentieth-century use of the wire service, the rise of baseball, and the decline of lacrosse, the Blue Jays have attained their popularity and stature in no small measure due to constant exposure on Canadian national television. Ironically, both the Blue Jays and the Expos owe much of this coverage to the fact that, under the requirements for Canadian television licenses, they qualify as Canadian content. In fact, baseball is an extremely inexpensive way for Canadian networks to meet necessary cultural quotas. New Canadian programming costs approximately $800,000 per hour to produce; in contrast, the Blue Jays sell for the relative paltry sum of $100,000 per (typically three-hours) game.[37] Because of similar costs savings, the 1992 and the 1993 historic World Series wins did not use Canadian television announcers. The Canadian network simply opted to rebroadcast the original American feed, inserting its own advertising at the appropriate times. Therefore the all-American Jays, playing in an otherwise all-American league with all-American (and a few Caribbean) players, in a supposedly all-American game – meanwhile shunting other and more distinctly Canadian sports and cultural formations to the margins – thrive under the auspices of a policy of cultural protectionism. In this way, 'globalized' cultural formations have been legally transformed into Canadian culture as Canadian culture has been socially and culturally transforming into 'globalized' culture.

Such transformations are presented through dominant media accounts as an example of Toronto's, if not Canada's, 'development' and emergence as a sophisticated 'world–class' city/country (though the definition of world-class is never proffered). To reject an American sports franchise, as appears to be the current situation in Montreal, invites derision and the questioning of a city's cosmopolitan stature. A typical admonishment of Montreal reads, 'If this city cannot support us with 9,000 season-ticket holders, then there are bigger issues on the table – like whether this is a major league city.'[38] The failure for Montreal to support professional lacrosse or soccer was never put in such terms. Major league baseball is a game of supposedly global prestige and importance while Canadian football, lacrosse or curling, and sometimes even hockey, are residual, quaint, parochial, historic footnotes of a regionalized past.

Stuart Hall, for one, calls for a more critical assessment and understanding of the reasons why one set of cultural formations is replaced by another:

> Time and again, what we are really looking at is the active destruction of particular ways of life, and their transformation into something new. 'Cultural change' is a polite euphemism for the process by which some cultural forms and practices are driven out of the centre of popular life, actively marginalized. Rather than simply 'falling into disuse' through the long march to modernisation, things are actively pushed aside, so that something else can take their place.[39]

The expansion of Major League Baseball into Canada, followed by the recent introduction of the NBA (and rumblings of expansion from the NFL), lend the mistaken impression that value is being consistently added while nothing is removed. Although one must be careful not to romanticize the pre-'globalized' era of Canadian professional sport, the success of American sports in Canada does represent a shift in social and economic structures. If nothing else, this transformation all but eliminates the possibility of creating alternatives to the corporate monopolies of major professional sports. The potential of Canada to exist as an 'alternative North America' is increasingly submerged under an array of 'global' systems of social, economic, and cultural interaction and organization. These organizations are systematically dedicated to sustaining and legitimizing capitalist hegemony and naturalizing global formations of American culture as world culture.

One might assume that, under these circumstances, any mention of nationalism or question of country would be downplayed and avoided by the Blue Jays – or that any emphasis would be placed on the city and not the country – but the exact opposite is true. The supposed 'Canadian-ness' of the team is precisely what is most prominently marketed and celebrated. This team is purposely constructed and heralded as 'Canada's team'. From the maple leaf prominently incorporated into the Blue Jay logo to the Royal Canadian Mounted Police as color guards for key ceremonies, this team is presented as a representative of the nation and a source of national pride. In turn, the team's two World Series wins provoked a display of uncustomary and unabashed Canadian jingoism, both official and unofficial. These two wins touched off celebrations across Canada. Moreover, when, for example, the team travels to Seattle the crowds there are consistently larger than normal. In the stands there are numerous maple leaf flags and painted faces. Blue Jay fans from British Columbia make the short drive to see 'their' team in action against the local, but foreign, Seattle Mariners. The Seattle team, which is based geographically thousands of kilometers closer than 'Canada's team' and contains just as many Canadians, does not have the right ontological appeal to attract British Columbian identification. The 1992 victory is recalled not merely as Toronto's triumph but as Canada's.

However, as Joseph Maguire points out, '"Global" sport plays a contradictory role of binding people to habitus [commonsense] memories and "invented traditions", yet also, exposing them to the values, feelings and images of the "other".'[40] Although it is impossible to imagine any other event, team or person contextualized in such an incredibly forceful, Canadian nationalistic framework than the 1992 Blue Jays, it is equally difficult to imagine a more potent symbol of popular Canadian capitulation to American cultural domination. For instance, not even the much celebrated 1972 Team Canada received an audience at the Prime Minister's residence, as did the 1992 Blue Jays. However, this was orchestrated entirely to parrot, for the first time ever in Canada, the U.S. custom of a victorious team's visiting the Head of State. However, the Prime Minister is not, of course, Canada's Head of State and thus that visit represented, yet again, the further Americanization of Canadian protocol and official symbolic expression. Furthermore, the Blue Jays, as true colonial representatives, had their victory validated by also receiving a White House audience with President Bush. This set another precedent for a Canadian team and symbolically confirmed the underlying structures of continentalism. Paradoxically, though not surprisingly, while the Blue Jays are marketed and celebrated in a decidedly patriotic and nationalist context, they also undoubtedly represent the opposite: American continental integration.

Although any representation of a national collective might be seen as restrictive and exclusionary, the Blue Jays are a phenomenally narrow portrait of the Canadian collective. Ironically, part of the Blue Jays' success as a national symbol appears to be that they are unencumbered by the restrictions of the state. As a corporate entity they are unrestrained by the niceties of cultural stewardship generally required on the part of national cultural agencies. The demands of bilingualism, multiculturalism, regionalism, sexual equality, and aboriginal sensitivity, which often necessarily inform official or state-sponsored cultural formations and expressions are unobtrusively absent from the Blue Jays. And unlike the less successful (on the field and off) Montreal Expos, the Blue Jays need not be mindful of potential separatist or anti-Canadian sympathies in their core audience. The private corporate ownership of the Blue Jays allows them to be as free and pan-Canadian, English-speaking, and 'nationalist' as their core, middle-class, white, male, English-speaking audience will allow. Within the cultural parameters set by capitalism, the core affluent centre has the power to define the collective. The Blue Jays are free to make the nation in their own image, and see whether it sells.

CANADIANS' INVOLVEMENT

As far as professional baseball is concerned, Canadians are not unwilling participants in this transformational process towards continentalism. The success of the Blue Jays is not something simply imposed upon the Canadian masses. As a commercial commodity, the Blue Jays are one of an array of popular American products happily integrated into the Canadian mindscape. These commodities remain popular precisely because Canadians can actively generate and circulate their own meanings from them. By adapting and using American mass culture as a found resource, Canadians, like other groups, create their own shared pleasures with them. 'Global media-sport products may be resisted, misunderstood and/or "recycled", and thus be subject to a process of hybridization.'[41] It is in this context that the Blue Jays have become a symbol of pride, success, and, ironically, even resistance. It is precisely because, not in spite of the fact, that the Blue Jays operate within an overbearingly symbolic (and actual) American cultural institution that their World Series wins became such a national cause of pride and celebration. In fact, the absence of Canadian content only reinforces the extent to which the Blue Jays' victory is a triumph of Canadian skill, pluck, and ingenuity. 'We' prevailed over America at their own corporate, *laissez-faire* capitalist, monopolizing, mercenaries-to-the-highest-bidder type game. Canada played America's game by America's rules and won.

The Blue Jays present Canadians not with the opportunity to simply integrate more fully into the American imperium, but, remarkably, the opportunity to disassociate themselves from it. National identification, like team identification, necessarily requires a process of inclusion and exclusion, of perpetually situating 'us' against 'them'. By structuring perceived differences in terms of in-group and out-group loyalties, sport helps to define a sense of self and of the other. The emphasized disparities attributed to the out-group, in turn, suggest similarities between the subjects of the in-group. Flag-waving, the maple leaf face painting, and other expressions of supposed Canadian-ness are a consolidation of Canadian in-group solidarity and opposition – a statement of collective difference and defiance – in the face of perceived American out-group homogeneity. The Blue Jays are not another corporate baseball team – they are a *Canadian* corporate baseball team. Therefore the Blue Jays may be viewed as a part of a progressive, even anti-imperial (but hardly radical), cultural force.

However, this accounts for only one aspect of 'Blue Jay nationalism'. As Hall argues, there is another side to consider: 'in the study of popular culture, we should always start here: with the double-stake in popular culture, the double movement of containment and resistance, which is always inevitably inside it.'[42]

Cultural nationalism's resistive impulse, embodied in the expressions and celebrations of Canadian distinctiveness through the Blue Jays, is ultimately contained by the trappings of acquiescent official nationalism and 'global' capitalism which produced the Blue Jays in the first place.

The Blue Jays offer the imagined Canadian community an opportunity, to quote the front page of the *Toronto Star* at the time, 'to thumb their noses' at their American subjugators. In turn, this helps to consolidate a sense of collective opposition towards that entity. However, this offer is made within a structure that profits and valorizes American capitalist hegemony. By adopting the Blue Jays as a focus for the expression of resistance, Canadians financially, culturally, and spiritually, support the values of corporate sport, continental integration, and monopoly capitalism. The increasing dependency on American sport culture for national expression, identification, and representation promotes the values of international competitiveness and naturalizes the capitalist myth of meritocratic success and, inadvertently, confirms America as the site for Canadian cultural validation. Though Canada beat America at its own game, it has now made that game its own.

What is most readily remembered and collectively embraced in Canada about 1992 is not the genuine historic context which propelled 'Blue Jay fever'. The nationalist defeat in the battle against continental integration, the economic devastation that Free Trade wrought, and the accompanying diminution of the principles of national democratic sovereignty are all overshadowed by Canada's splendid victory on the baseball fields of America. As Dayan and Katz point out, 'media events and their narration are in competition with the writing of history in defining the contents of collective memory'.[43] Moreover, 'the professional recording of history is not synonymous with what is remembered'.[44] The manipulation and management of occurrences directly surrounding the World Series demonstrate the ways in which the 'power-bloc' can excorporate the counter-hegemonic and potentially radical zeal of Canadian cultural nationalism and turn it to its own use. The nationalist excitation that propelled Blue Jay fever is appropriated by official nationalism and harmonized with the needs of corporate 'globalized' culture, thus making it politically benign. What made that moment in October 1992 so collectively rich and memorable for so many Canadians has been sanitized from the official (re)constructions and accounts. Although the process of appropriation is ordinarily a subtle modification of hegemonic containment, occasionally examples of it appear more blatant.

One clear and explicit attempt to associate 'Blue Jay nationalism' with a continental-capitalist agenda occurred during the 1992 World Series victory parade and celebration. During that event the Toronto Blue Jays' president, chief executive officer, and key Conservative Party supporter Paul Beeston, hoisted the World Series trophy and then went to the microphone. In front of the 50,000 on-hand crowd and the more than three million watching on television, he declared, 'There's a lot of controversy about Free Trade. I, for one, love it! If you look over on that table there are three [trophies] Free Trade has brought us!' In that moment Beeston made the politically implicit explicit. Of course, the

Blue Jays' victory had absolutely nothing to do with Free Trade and, of course, it had everything to do with it. However, by linking the national ardour for the Blue Jays and the palatable nationalist fervour of the moment direct to Free Trade, Beeston managed to turn Canadian nationalist sentiment on its head. Within a blinking of an eye, the on-hand crowd was cheering the concept of continental integration and national de-evolution, at the very moment they had gathered to celebrate the triumph of the opposite. The partisan, Beeston, seized the opportunity, as Dayan and Katz explain it, 'to talk over the heads of the middlemen who normally mediate between leaders and their public'.[45] And, indeed, as they further argue, 'television itself flies over the heads of historians in proposing its own version of what should be entered in collective memory'.[46]

Another important example of official containment and use of the nationalist sentiment generated by Blue Jay fever was the federal government's incorporation of a baseball motif into its 'yes' campaign during the 1992 National Referendum on the Charlottetown Accord. (The Charlottetown Accord was a failed attempt by the Conservative federal government to alter the constitution in order to make Quebec a signatory to it.) The use of baseball, the quintessential American sport, as a dominant thematic motif in a federally-financed campaign on national unity would have been unimaginable four years previously. The referendum on this constitutional amendment coincidentally[47] happened to conclude two days after the final game of the World Series. This well-financed, one-sided[48] campaign included, among other things, an abundance of television and radio advertising during the broadcasts of the World Series itself. In one typical advertisement a baseball batter, dressed head-to-toe in (Canadian?) red, stands waiting for the 'right pitch' from an opposing player dressed head-to-toe in (separatist? American?) blue. Accompanying this image is a voice-over extolling the virtues of the Accord as a form of nation building. This campaign attempted to draw upon the already established equation between baseball and the national good, generated by national 'Blue Jay fever', and a deep-seated sentiment that there was something threatening the nation. It was 'us' against a purposely obscure 'them'. The entire campaign attempted to harness the nationalist fervor surrounding the Blue Jays and attach it to a 'yes' vote. This strategy had some limited success. For instance, there was a scattering of signs at the SkyDome and elsewhere that received media attention. Such signs, for example, read:

'SAY YES to the Blue Jays' and 'We're Pulling for Canada! Vote Yes', which indicated, somewhat, the successful melding of the two ideas within the popular consciousness.

The day after the Blue Jays won the World Series and the day before the referendum, the *Toronto Sun* attempted to unite the events together on its front cover. In what the editors knew would be an historic, best-selling edition, they presented a full-page color photograph of the 'Joyful Jays' (to use its description) celebrating their win. A banner headline running across the top of the page accompanied the picture. This, which had no legitimate connection with the victory it seemed to be explaining, read: 'Say Yes to Us!', and in much smaller type, 'editorial on referendum p.4'. This deliberate attempt to link 'us', the Blue Jays, victory, and 'yes' on the front of the newspaper was similar to the strategies employed by the government throughout the campaign. Indeed, a few analysts have suggested that the reason the Ontario vote did swing slightly to 'yes' was directly due to the Blue Jay victory. The use of baseball here demonstrates how 'official nationalism' can co-opt the oppositional passion of resistive, counter-hegemonic, cultural nationalism (which is central to Blue Jay appeal) and apply it towards its own ends of corporate and continental acquiescence.

Although the 'yes' forces clearly attempted to harness the oppositional zeal towards the forces that threatened the country, the Charlottetown Accord had nothing to do with the hegemonic resistance they were attempting to be identified with. The 'yes' forces of the referendum strongly contextualized their arguments in terms of nation building, but the Charlottetown Accord offered nothing to appease the aspirations of 'cultural nationalist' and others genuinely concerned with the real threats confronting the nation. This is a point that Lawrence Martin supports: '[The Charlottetown Accord] ... was a question of making Quebec and the other provinces happy. It wasn't a matter of building something to sustain the country against continentalism, globalization and the other forces that preyed upon it.'[49] The fact that the result was a resounding national rejection of the Accord does not mean that the official nationalist strategy of containment failed. Ultimately, voting 'no' in the Referendum simply allowed the oppositional impulse, which was generally read as a virulent distaste for Prime Minister Mulroney and his continentalist policies, to be discharged within a safe and meaningless arena. The containment, in other words, was successful – the referendum was not.

CANADA'S UPSIDE-DOWN FLAG

The infamous (for Canadians at least) upside-down flag incident, in game two of the 1992 World Series, offers another study of containment on behalf of the 'power-bloc' worth noting. This containment was orchestrated by the combined efforts of an official retort and media-generated consensus (its containment was official and hegemonic – if you will). After the United States Marines paraded the Canadian flag upside-down in the opening ceremonies of the game in Atlanta, there was an immediate and vehement popular response across Canada. The CTV television network broke from the game at one point to deliver what was essentially a news flash. They stated that their 'switch boards were jammed' with calls from angry viewers who saw the upside-down flag and were upset. Major league baseball swiftly issued a 'formal apology to the people of Canada'. The fact that the popular response was so quick and large, as the official reaction confirms, betrays the sensitivities of Canadian subjugation. The general feeling was, as expressed on the front page of the next day's *Toronto Star*, that this was another example of 'American ignorance' of Canada and things Canadian. The oppositional fervor was ignited and very palpable.

The following two days leading up to game three in Toronto, the first World Series game ever played in Canada or outside the United States, demonstrated the productive powers of popular resistance and the corresponding strategies of official and hegemonic containment. By the morning after the second game there were thousands of tee shirts printed with variations on the theme of an upside-down American flag. The incident made the front pages of most newspapers in Canada. It was the topic *du jour* of television and radio news broadcasts and radio phone-in programs across the country. Within that ephemeral area of critical thought, referred to by Raymond Williams as the 'structures of feeling',[50] it was easy to sense that something was in the air.

The containment of the growing popular reaction was well orchestrated and involved. Pleas came from many sources, in the words of an announcement on the sports radio station Fan 1430, not to 'act like hicks'. Suggesting that to display what was obviously being felt, to demonstrate, if nothing else, the frustration with American ignorance or disrespect, would mean the loss of treasured 'world-class' status. It would be unsophisticated to demonstrate anger. True cosmopolitan nations rise above such indignities. Aside from media pleas, for the first time ever SkyDome security examined the signs brought into the stadium. This was to ensure that there were no disparaging remarks about America or Americans on them. The stadium as a site of mass spectacle is, in this way, a spectacle of controlled masses. The final image produced for those inside the stadium and for the millions watching on television was that of a large, happy gathering of Canadians apparently oblivious to or unconcerned about the previous night's incident (something palpably untrue). This generates a scene of consensual understanding when, in fact, order has been imposed. In the same manner, the television audience saw no upside-down American flags, either on tee shirts or in hand – though they were an intrinsic part of the setting. Instead, the cameras repeatedly focused on a handful of spectators gleefully flying both national flags (right way up). The orchestrated message was clearly one of 'No hard feelings here, boys.' Corporate sport is not a permissible arena for unregulated, international antagonism.

With the potential still for an international incident if the Canadian crowd booed the American anthem or did something similar, some sort of symbolic gesture of containment was required. Not everything can be controlled by direct censorship and preselecting images. In an effort to ameliorate the situation the power bloc staged an official apology. Before the national anthems were sung, the Royal Canadian Mounted Police marched into the stadium carrying the American flag (inadvertently and colorfully symbolizing the Americanization of yet another Canadian institution), followed by the U.S. Marines carrying the Canadian flag (right way up). Over the loudspeaker the announcer trumpeted an official apology: 'To correct this unfortunate error and show their true respect for the Canadian people, the Marine Corps has requested the privilege of again carrying the national flag of Canada.' The apology, of course, was enthusiastically accepted by the on-hand crowd, for colonial people must take their victories where they can find them.

CONCLUSION

Economic globalization robs the nation state of its conventional role. Cultural globalization modifies the cultural communities constructed in people's minds and collective memories. Paul Henderson's goal is still important to Canadians because it connects them with a mythical idea of a nation that never really was. The ideal of which, however, still gave promise and impetus to an independent and selectively alternative notion of an 'other North America'. The legacy of the Blue Jays, on the other hand, is more complex and less clear. Though it would be foolish to underestimate the resiliency of capital, the impact of 1992 seems to be waning on the Canadian imagination. As baseball once again flourishes in the United States, setting new attendance records, the opposite appears to be true in Canada. Montreal is all but set to close and Toronto is setting its own records for sparse attendances. The collective memory of the historical World Series wins has been undermined by the legitimizing processes of corporate capital. The resistive ardour of Canadian left-nationalism, which essentially propelled Blue Jay fever beyond the level of franchised, municipal boosterism has all but been eradicated from the official accounts and re-creations of what occurred. The World Series victories have become temporal monuments to the glories of continental integration, and thus now symbolize the very opposite notions that compelled the Canadian collective to seize it as a moment and 'rite of communication'. The game, the highlights, and the statistics still remain, scattered memories of fanatic, post-victory celebrations still endure, but without the underlying conflicts and contradictions which gave the moment life; October 1992 runs the risk of being a mere baseball trivia question and a personal memory for 30 million Canadians.

NOTES

1. This quip is a web-based contribution (www.iam.ca) to a controversial and popular beer advertising campaign running in English Canada. The campaign includes a film and television spot called 'The Rant' in which Joe, a 'typical' white, young, Canadian male, takes a stage and addresses some perceived American misconceptions about Canada and things Canadian: 'I don't live in an Igloo ... A toque is a hat.... A chesterfield is a couch... It's zed not zee ...' The popularity of 'The Rant' has been the subject of many media and some academic analyses. Live performances of it have been performed to enthusiastic crowds at hockey games across Canada. The Minister of Heritage and Culture even took a copy of it with her to trade talks in New York. 'The Rant' concludes with an obligatory nod to hockey, with a boast that Canada 'is the first nation of hockey. And the best part of North America! Thank you.'
2. From M. Castells, *The Power of Identity* (Malden, MA: Blackwell Publishers, 1997), p.27.
3. This series is now most commonly referred to as the Summit Series.
4. M. Halbwachs, *The Collective Memory* (New York, NY: Harper-Colophon Books, 1950), p.84.
5. Dryden and MacGregor, Al Purdy, and Scott Young, respectively. See R. Gruneau and D.Whitson, *Hockey Night in Canada* (Toronto: Garamond Press, 1993), p.3.
6. E. Hobsbawm and T. Ranger, *The Invention of Tradition* (Cambridge: Cambridge University Press, 1983).
7. Gruneau and Whitson, *Hockey Night*, p.251.
8. B. Anderson, *Imagined Communities* (New York, NY: Verso 1983).
9. L. Coser, *On Collective Memory: Maurice Halbwachs* (Chicago, IL: University of Chicago Press, 1992), p.34.

10. See G. Lang and K. Lang, *Etched in Memory: The Building and Survival of Artistic Reputation* (Chapel Hill, NC: University of North Carolina Press, 1990).

11. Gruneau and Whitson, *Hockey Night*, pp.80–6.

12. See 'Canada the Talk of America', *Toronto Star* (16 Oct. 1992), A1.

13. J. Goodman, 'U.S. Women Send Soccer Ratings Soaring', *Toronto Sun* (11 July 1999), S2. Though this event was an exception, soccer and women's sport have long been notoriously poor draws on American television.

14. W. Houston, 'Hockey Ratings Free Fall', *Globe and Mail* (8 June 2000), S5.

15. D. Dayan and E. Katz, *Media Events* (Cambridge, MA: Harvard University Press, 1992).

16. J. Curran and T. Liebes, *Media, Ritual and Identity* (New York and London: Routledge, 1998), p.4.

17. Dayan and Katz, *Media Events*, p.225.

18. As cited in J. Kernagham, 'Henderson Gave Us a Memory to Treasure', *London Free Press* (6 Sept. 1997).

19. G. Jarvie and J. Maguire, *Sport and Leisure in Social Thought* (New York, NY and London: Routledge, 1994), p.102.

20. C.L.R. James, *Beyond the Boundary* (Kingston, Jamaica: Hutchinson, 1963).

21. S. Lipset, *Continental Divide* (New York, NY: Routledge, 1990), p.53.

22. B. Fraser, *The Search for Identity* (Toronto: Doubleday, 1967), p.301.

23. 'And good riddance to it' say many of its critics. See, for instance, J.L. Granastein, *Yankee Go Home?: Canadians and Anti-Americanism* (Toronto: Harper Collins, 1996). p.286.

24. G. Spry (1932), as cited in S. Bashevkin's *True Patriot Love* (Toronto: Oxford University Press, 1991), p.9, and elsewhere.

25. Dayan and Katz, *Media Events*, p.212.

26. See Gruneau and Whitson, *Hockey Night*, p.217.

27. Although, as of 1997, they now play two well-attended interlocking matches with the Montreal Expos, Canada's only other entry in Major League Baseball.

28. See, for instance, G. Baker, 'Still a "Bargain", Jays' GM Insists', *Toronto Star* (10 Feb. 1999), C3.

29. F. Manning, in D.H. Flaherty and F. Manning, *The Beaver Bites Back?* (Montreal-Kingston: McGill-Queen's University Press, 1993), p.14.

30. See M. York, 'Jays Try to Acquire Cuban Third Baseman', *Globe and Mail* (27 Jan. 1993), C7.

31. S. Brunt, 'Unforgiven', *Toronto Life*, 34, 4 (March 2000), 68.

32. See M. Dunnel, 'Sell CFL in the U.S.? How about Canada First?', *Toronto Star* (29 Sept. 1991), G.4.

33. *CFL News*, 'Attendance up 8.2%' can be found at www.cfl.com (Oct. 1999).

34. As cited in M. Lawrence, *Pledge of Allegiance* (Toronto: McClelland & Stewart, 1993), p.175.

35. S.F. Fisher and Douglas Wise, *Canada's Sporting Heroes* (Don Mills, Ontario: General Publishing Co., 1974), p.265.

36. B. Todman, 'Those Yanks Could Sell Us Snow', *The Canuck* (May 1999).

37. See P. Foster, 'The Money Pit', *Toronto Life*, 33, 9 (1999), 94.

38. D. Samson as cited in H. Bloom, 'Telling It Like It Is', *The Daily Dose* (3 April 2000).

39. S. Hall, *People's History and Socialist Theory* (Boston, MA: Routledge & Kegan Paul, 1981), pp.227–8.

40. J. Maguire, *Global Sport: Identities, Societies, Civilizations* (Cambridge and Malden, MA: Polity Press, 1999), p.7.

41. Ibid., p.145.

42. Hall, *People's History*, p.228.

43. Dayan and Katz, *Media Events*, p.213.

44. Ibid.

45. Ibid., p.214.

46. Ibid., p.215.

47. Though there is no direct evidence that the date was purposefully planned to coincide with the World Series, there is enough to suggest that such a ploy was not beyond the Machiavellian scheming of the Prime Minister Brian Mulroney. He was renowned for, in his own words, 'rolling the dice' with the constitution and, by his own admission, plotting policy and electoral

strategies starting with the end date in mind and working backwards. B. Kidd, *The Struggle for Canadian Sport* (Toronto: University of Toronto Press, 1996), states that within minutes of Ben Johnson's winning the gold medal at the Olympic Games in Seoul, the Deputy Minister of Fitness and Amateur Sport gleefully declared to him, 'Now the Prime Minister can call the [free trade] election!' (p.7).

48. The MacKenzie Institute, which studies terrorism, conflict, and propaganda, identified the federal 'yes' campaign as propaganda. See J. Thompson, 'Yes Using Propaganda Techniques to Sway Voters', *Toronto Star* (17 Oct. 1992), A10.

49. L. Martin, *Pledge of Allegiance: The Americanization of Canada in the Mulroney Years* (Toronto: McClelland & Stewart, 1993), p.256.

50. R. Williams, *Marxism and Literature* (New York, NY: Oxford University Press, 1977).

Forcing the Fairytale:
Narrative Strategies in Figure Skating
Competition Coverage

BETTINA FABOS

The top three U.S. television networks, ABC, CBS, and NBC, compete every four years for the rights to broadcast the summer and the Winter Olympics, one of 'television's most prestigious events'.[1] When CBS won the rights to broadcast the 1992 Winter Olympics, the network decided to create an especially memorable program, investing $243 million for the U.S. rights alone and then $100–120 million more in production costs.[2] The overwhelming notion within the industry, however, was that the network was taking on too huge a risk. Predictors nagged that, after a 32-year absence, CBS would not be able to sustain high enough ratings actually to make money out of the enormous, 116-hour television event. Perhaps the network would have to back down from their $250,000, 30-second commercial rate. Perhaps the network would not be able to sell out at all. At the least, many speculated that they would fall far below ABC's solid Olympic ratings four years earlier in Calgary.

While prestigious, the Olympics have not always made money for the sponsoring network. In 1980, when the Winter Olympics were broadcast in real time from Lake Placid, New York, ratings were high. In 1984, when they were held overseas in Sarajevo, seven hours ahead of American time and therefore tape-delayed, the ratings were disastrously low. In 1988, when the Winter Olympics took place in Calgary, Canada, they were again broadcast live and again generated high ratings. But in 1992 the Olympics were being held in Albertville in France, another six hours' time difference from American television audiences and another potential for tape-delay disaster. At the end of the two-weeks broadcast marathon, however, CBS led the February television ratings sweeps so comfortably that, by most accounts, they were assured victory for the entire season.³ One glowing CBS executive said, 'We'd have to go dark for the rest of the season to lose.'⁴

Why were ratings so high? The U.S. hockey team did better than expected, but the rest of the events did not see a tumult of American success stories. As it turned out, the reason had to do with a significant shift in narrative strategy. Until 1992 the story of the Olympic Games had been told through the lens of Cold War antagonism. Narrative tension came from medal counts or from the questionable competitive practises of Eastern Bloc countries. Adulation of specific (American) athletes was not much more than descriptions of their performances and why they were doing well. There was already evidence that this storyline was being abandoned by the 1988 Olympics, as ABC began to build narratives around the athletes' personalities and personal histories. Four years later CBS became determined to continue this trend and turn every competitive situation into a compelling story that effectively competed with all the other dramas, theatricals, and specials showing on other networks and cable stations during those two weeks in February, which everyone thought CBS would fail to do. As the CBS executive Neal Pilson had remarked before coverage began, 'We think the Olympics are the best dramatic entertainment programming we could find for February, and I have a lot of confidence that these Olympics are going to make good television.'⁵

This essay analyzes the CBS coverage of the 1992 Winter Olympics and focuses specifically on the women's figure skating competition. From the American broadcasting perspective, this event has traditionally been the highlight of the Winter Olympics and was easily CBS's most highly rated Olympics event in the two-week broadcast, and, up to that point, in the history of American Olympics broadcasting. As the sportswriter Frank Deford aptly forecast,

> This year the women's skaters are more important than ever. There are no big, bad Communists for athletic jingoists to root against, and that tired lightning-in-a-bottle U.S. hockey miracle of the 1980s games just cannot be dragged out and flogged again.⁶

Described by CBS commentators as 'the hottest ticket in town' with 'every seat in the auditorium filled', the 1992 women's skating competition had all the implications of a Broadway musical sell-out before it even began. While CBS was the leading storyteller of the

Olympics, similar, supplementary narratives of the less immediate print media certainly enhanced the narrative process as well.

Besides creating a plethora of overlapping and underlying stories that dramatized and popularized the sporting event, the melodrama of women's figure skating was told according to the comforting and familiar confines of a western fairytale – in this case, *Cinderella*. Narrative success – translated into ratings success – was thus contingent upon the network's ability to position the 1992 crop of Olympic athletes as characters, not athletes, acting out the predictable plot of an age-old tale.

This essay will illustrate how CBS successfully sustained, for the first time in U.S. Olympics coverage, a full cast and range of characters in a fairytale melodrama, manipulating story structure, space, and time for full dramatic effect. It will also demonstrate how CBS, and as an outgrowth of the network coverage, other mass media storytellers within North America, continually restructured the narrative when the real-life skaters' behavior or actions were incongruous with CBS's narrative plan. In doing so, the network advanced traditional (and comfortable) constructs of femininity and the American female ideal as common sense.

THE NARRATIVE

According to the narrative theories posited by Kozloff and Deming, narratives may be split into two parts: the 'story', meaning 'what happens to whom', and 'the discourse', meaning 'how the story is told'.[7]

The Story

In the case of the women's figure skating competition in Albertville, the story was the course of the event itself: five major competitors, Kristi Yamaguchi, Nancy Kerrigan, Tonya Harding (USA), Midori Ito (Japan), and Surya Bonaly (France) vied for the gold medal, depending on how well they skated according to nine judges who monitored and graded their original programs. The event happened over a two-day period.

The Discourse

If the story is 'what happens to whom', the discourse, then, is the manner in which the story is interpreted and inflected through, in the case of CBS, the medium of television.

CBS sent a production crew of 800 to Albertville for the purpose of negotiating this Olympics discourse. Besides those operating the technical apparatuses – the Sony D-2 VTRs, the Grass Valley Switchers, the video cameras, graphic effects, computer systems, and two-way communication channels – CBS relied on directors, writers, and producers to manipulate the story according to a specified alignment of ideas.[8] They also relied on narrators to tell and interpret the story by establishing it intertextually within a certain historical, sociological, and psychological framework, translating episodes in the story for an implied American audience in terms of American mainstream ideology or common sense.

The narrative process ended only when it reached a real audience who could then reinterpret the story interpretations and construct identities and realities from it. As Joan Didion describes this process, 'We live by the imposition of a narrative line upon disparate images, by "ideas" with which we have learned to freeze the shifting phantasmagoria which is our actual experience.'[9] Richard Campbell further suggests that

> narrative enables us to make sense of our phantasmagoria because, in contrast to that experience, narrative is a familiar, concrete, and objectified structure. Narratives, then, are metaphors, shaping and containing the bodiless flow of experience within familiar boundaries of plot, character, setting, problem, resolution, and synthesis.[10]

If narratives are metaphors, the women's figure skating competition in 1992, a narrative with heroines, villains, character development, and plot all motivated by the elaborate push and pull of cause and effect, was told through the metaphor of a fairytale. Kozloff notes that 'American television is remarkably like Russian fairy tales – that is, that certain motifs, situations and stock characters may have a nearly universal psychological/mythological/sociological appeal and thus appear again and again in popular cultural forms.'[11] The 1992 women's skating coverage, a romantic fairytale about dreams coming true, a determination to succeed against possible odds, and a fight against the villains (skating judges, the pestering media, and each other), using the skills available of grace, luck, courage, and family support, was only too evident as a narrative process filtering through CBS and all the mass media outlets. The opening paragraph of a *Newsweek* Olympics cover story said as much:

Surely there must be a fairytale that fits here – the lost Aesop, the only Grimm that didn't get optioned. It'd be the one about the two stylish, gorgeous creatures – swans or butterflies, take your pick, competing against the stronger, more daring beings for the favor of the gods. And, of course, the stronger, more daring beings are certain to win, because spectacular is always better ever after. Only, the stronger, more daring beings reach for too high a sky, hoist too heavy a load, cross too deep a river, and so the stylish, gorgeous creatures glide to victory – and, probably here comes a handsome prince or two, as well.[12]

The event was about skating, but just as much entailed the physical image and behavior of the competing women who were metaphorically defined within the narrative as princesses. Princesses from every country competed for the 'crown jewel' of the Olympic games. American princesses competed to become the appointed American 'darling'. The narrative, it was further implied, was especially satisfying when the media-appointed darling also won the crown jewel. In 1992 the United States had three skaters who were in the coveted top five rankings and had a chance to bring home gold. That is when a dream – the American Dream – comes true.

THE NARRATIVE'S HISTORICAL BACKGROUND

The princess metaphor evolved out of 80 years of mass media coverage of women Olympic skaters. Sonja Henie, the Norwegian champion who won her first gold as a 14-year-old in 1928 and went on to win two more in 1932 and 1936, was the first figure skater to be idolized beyond her technique by popular culture. Dubbed the 'Kewpie Doll' of the American public,[13] Henie transcended skating to star in Hollywood films and 'trailed only Shirley Temple and Clark Gable in box office draw'.[14] While Henie and her contemporaries were known to use more muscular strokes (and risk 'linebacker leg'),[15] Henie was also marketed as a sex symbol, prized for her dimples and blond hair. As a successful skater she established an image of northern European beauties on ice that would be sustained by popular culture and the skating world.

Although the American skaters Tenley Albright and Carol Heiss won Olympic gold medals in 1956 and 1960, respectively, skating was not televised until 1962 when ABC Sports covered the World

Championships in Prague. Six years later the American Peggy Fleming would skate in the 1968 Olympics, marking the first time American audiences would see their own skater compete for (and win) gold on live, color television. ABC's coverage of Fleming, while idolatrous, was once again descriptive metaphor. Fleming, who was younger than most of her competitors, was characterized as a teenage beauty, a heartthrob, and a girl next door. One ABC commentator described Fleming's 1968 Olympic performance as 'dashing, beautiful, comely ... in short she's Peggy Fleming, coming into your homes live and in color via the satellite.' Taking the cue from ABC, *Time* described Fleming as 'a raven haired Colorado College coed',[16] and *Newsweek* called her 'a trim, 109-pound package that keeps its cool on and off the ice. A shy, Bambi-like teen-ager ... the lithe, 5-foot 4-inch Peggy flows into her movements with the fragile grace of a Fonteyn.'[17] While Fleming was noted for her technical proficiency, she was also applauded for keeping her hair in place ('she buys cans of Sudden Beauty hair spray by the half-dozen')[18] and for signing a $500,000 contract with NBC.[19] Fleming's portrayal was one of innocence, glamor, sexual availability, and upward mobility; but she remained the sole object of adoration and description, not the subject of a full-blown narrative.

Clearly, however, it was thin, unmarried, pretty girls like Fleming who won favor in the skating establishment and the American media. This was all too clear in 1972 when the stocky, modest skater Beatrice Schuba from Austria consistently outperformed her 'pixie' American rival Janet Lynn. Schuba excelled in school figures, which at the time held a higher percentage in the overall skating score, and won the gold medal. As Olympic medalist and veteran skating announcer Dick Button explained it in a skating compilation tape entitled *Magic Memories on the Ice*, 'The skating world, having watched Trixie Schuba win the gold medal, decided it was time for a change. A short program was added. The long program given 50 per cent of the scoring and the school figures just 30 per cent.'[20] With this change, school figures could no longer give stockier skaters a potential advantage, and, because the free skate also allowed for a more showy and provocative television program, figure eights were eliminated altogether in 1988.

Now that the thin, lithe body type was strategically positioned to dominate in skating and the more visually appealing free skate would be the highlighted portion of Olympics figure skating, media producers began to see the potential for creating more complex narrative structures to increase the popularity of the event. The 1976 Olympics saw a rise in television coverage, greater network investment in the winter games, and large periods of airtime to fill. Luckily, the 1976 Olympic skating event featured the American hopeful Dorothy Hamill. In their self-conscious effort to create 'the most riveting spectacle for U.S. viewers',[21] ABC assigned Hamill the starring role and interpreted her skating ambitions for the first time in terms of a fragile princess ascending a throne.

The story involved Hamill's shaky nerves, her dependence on her father, and her gutsy and lyrical skating in the face of adversity. Because of a misunderstanding before she skated her final program, Hamill gave the network (and other media storytellers) a serendipitous piece of drama that most likely set the stage for subsequent network choices and story manipulations. *Time* described the incident in this way:

> The drama began as Dorothy, who battles almost uncontrollable jitters on the brink of each performance, waited at the end of the rink to be introduced for her free-skating program. As the points awarded to the previous skater flashed on a scoreboard, the crowd erupted in an explosion of boos and catcalls, protesting low scores. Dorothy thought they were jeering her, and her already fragile composure collapsed. In tears, she ran off the ice into her father's arms.[22]

Hamill's father quickly became a regular feature (and supporting actor to Hamill's leading role) in the televised broadcast, appearing many times in close up and medium shots. As the ABC commentator Dick Button reported during the live coverage, 'They said she could take a rest period, and she said "Oh no", burst out, away from her father, and now the crowd is cheering for Dorothy Hamill.'[23] After Hamill's victorious skate, Button referred to an extended close up of Mr Hamill, saying, 'There's her father ... if ever there was a proud man.' Hamill's story, largely told through television's manipulations, was such a compelling one that even her haircut became the most prominent fashion throughout the late 1970s. Hamill still represented beauty and commercial success, but now she was also portrayed, however sketchily, as a captivating and complex character acting out her emotions and reaching for her dreams in a modern fairytale. As *Sports Illustrated* later reported, 'Her jumps were high, her landings light, and she crackled with championship poise. She had smoked them all off earlier in the compulsory school figures and her crown was secure.'[24]

After two Olympics without an American champion, ABC was ready by 1988 to begin spinning an even more complex narrative around the American hopeful Debi Thomas and her rival (and Olympics veteran) Katarina Witt. The Olympics were in Calgary, which seemingly benefited the network because they could broadcast the event in real time and ensure larger audiences, and ABC set to work creating an embellished story of American dreams and ascendance to the throne.

There were some problems that had to be overcome, however. Although Thomas was poised to win a gold medal, she did not allow herself to be characterized in a princess role. It is not clear whether ABC was prepared to put her in that role in the first place. First, as the first African-American woman ever to advance so far in figure skating, Thomas's darker skin stood in contrast to the white, northern European ideal of beauty that remained predominant in figure skating. 'In a sport so subjective and judgmental, not to mention whiter than several shades of snow blindness', *Time* admitted, 'a black child might be excused for factoring in racism into indecipherable marks.'[25] 'In a world of lily white princesses', remarked Ian Austen of *Macleans*, 'Debi Thomas stands out'.[26] Secondly, as a self-described tomboy who actually gave momentary consideration to playing hockey before taking up figure skating,[27] Thomas was critical of figure skating and the limiting image the sport promoted.

Indeed, here was an interesting character with guts and brains who could have taken skating culture to a new level of social significance. Instead of working a story around the refreshing novelty of Thomas's persona, however, ABC and other media organizations were more comfortable spinning a narrative featuring Thomas as an outsider and spoiler, and chose the East German skater Katarina Witt as the princess-in-the-making – the feminine, heart-stopping, Iron Curtain seductress who dreamed about (and deserved) the crown jewel. Having already won a gold medal in the 1984 Olympics, Witt was already known to American audiences and, in fact, easily negated any old-fashioned, Cold War storylines by openly embracing capitalism and American values.

To increase the dramatic effect, the stories surrounding Witt and Thomas began to extend beyond the skating event itself, with expository video segments before and after the competition to develop the characters of the two skaters and to contrast them. ABC handily positioned Witt and Thomas as artist vs. athlete, but also nearly as female vs. male, showing Witt languidly dreaming of success while positioning Thomas as one with incredible drive, independence, and willpower (it was rarely mentioned that Witt was similarly driven). Described in terms of 'steely resolve', depicted lifting weights, unballing her fists and muttering to herself, Thomas was the intimidating antagonist to Witt's aesthetically-minded, media-friendly girl next door.

Accordingly, ABC built Witt up as a traditional, but sexually available girl, dwelling on the dependent, mother–child relationship between Witt and her coach, and the fan letters that came from a huge number of obsessed American men. This plot line was made more vivid when a photographer caught Witt during a work-out spin as her skating top loosened, exposing her breasts. Meanwhile, the network positioned Thomas as an isolated, asexual, Stanford pre-med student who was perhaps over her head with ambition and work load. One segment showed Thomas driving solo across America in her Toyota and described her as having an 'out-of-fashion perspective', implying that her independent lifestyle did not make common sense. Thomas was not only deglamorized, she was also cast as so out of touch that she was, in effect, made to be inaccessible and even unlikeable. Interestingly, in the effort to force a Western fairytale narrative, American nationalism was soon abandoned and a woman from a communist country was embraced as the American feminine ideal.

ABC successfully orchestrated a dramatic story by playing the two skaters off against each other and expanding the narrative beyond the context of the event itself. In an unfortunate coincidence (although not for ABC), the story climaxed with the two athletes skating their final programs to the same piece of music, Bizet's *Carmen*. Thomas faltered, and Witt glided to a flourishing victory. With the American media clearly supporting Witt, one wonders whether the negative coverage of Thomas influenced her skating performance, or what ABC would have done with Thomas if she had won. In confining the story to a fairytale narrative where only feminine, northern European ideals were reinforced and legitimated, ABC chased a familiar storyline while sacrificing perhaps better, or more important narratives. Even so, this same strategy was the very one duplicated by CBS's Olympics team four years later in 1992 – only CBS would add more characters, create more tension, and further manipulate the spatial and temporal aspects of the narrative. In short, they would do it better.

CHARACTERS AS DISCOURSE

According to Bordwell and Thompson, 'the conception of narrative depends on the assumption that the action will spring primarily from individual characters'.[28] Although the five major competitors in the women's figure skating competition were real people competing in a real event, they were conditioned and defined through the text to inhabit a narrative framework. Their identities, consequently, were related through camera shots, editing, body language, and costume, and were then interpreted to match a predetermined storyline. Here is how the mass media depicted/cast the top five characters in 1992: Kristi Yamaguchi, Midori Ito, Nancy Kerrigan, Tonya Harding, and Surya Bonaly.

Kristi Yamaguchi (USA)

A definite medal contender who had a near lock on the gold medal before the games began, Yamaguchi was 21 years old, 5 ft tall, 93 lb in weight, and an exceptional skater – perhaps the most refined in the history of the sport. A Japanese-American, Yamaguchi came from Fremont, California where her father was a dentist (her mother's occupation was not disclosed). As CBS built her character up for their purposes, viewers learned that Yamaguchi used to be a pairs dancer, was formerly considered an athletic skater, but suddenly 'developed' a very welcome gush of grace. Her artistry compensated for her inability to hit a triple axle like two other competing women skaters (Ito and Harding). In fact, as CBS's Paula Zahn pointed out, 'Her strength is that she can combine artistry with athleticism.' Striking a non-extremist, non-threatening persona because of her ability to mediate (between art and athleticism, Japan and America), Yamaguchi was also consistently labeled with the word 'focused', a word that was complementary enough but lacked effusiveness in its application. As the CBS sideline commentator and former men's figure skating champion (1984) Scott Hamilton phrased it, 'Her concentration is really incredible, that's the key to her consistency.' Yamaguchi effortlessly and predictably won the gold medal in the competition. While ABC and the other media actually used terms such as 'American darling' to describe Yamaguchi's status in the early stages of the drama, she was quickly dropped from her starring role once Kerrigan began to skate better than had been expected. Yamaguchi, it became clear, did not look enough like the part to belong in the heart of CBS's fairytale.

Midori Ito (Japan)

The Japanese 'hope' and main rival to Yamaguchi, Ito was 22 years old, 4 ft 7 in, 98 lb, and came from Nagoya where she lived with her coach (an adopted mother after her parents were divorced). Known as 'the Jumper' and the first woman ever to hit a triple axle, Ito was short, athletic, and lacked the graceful skating lines of Yamaguchi. As the narrative related, she was actually envious of Yamaguchi's taller, more pliant frame, although it was not a malicious sort of envy. Indeed, if Ito was a threat, she was not an evil one because the skater was, according to CBS, sweet, self-deprecating, and media-friendly. Ito, CBS told viewers, 'won the hearts of the skating world' when she collided with the camera stands during a world championship a year earlier, got back up, and finished her program (this video footage was played numerous times). Her 'courageous' character also had difficulty withstanding pressure, however. 'This morning she was surrounded by cameras and was missing combinations', Scott Hamilton remarked. ' I think it's taking its toll.' Although her athleticism provided just the right amount of narrative tension, Ito's character was that of the clumsy princess and lovable foil to the throne. Ito played her part, as CBS hoped, landing a gutsy triple axle at the last moment, but she still could not gain enough artistic points for the gold. She ended with a silver medal in the competition.

Nancy Kerrigan (USA)

At 22 years old and from Stoneham, Massachusetts, Kerrigan was a relatively new face to the skating world. A tall, thin brunette of Irish descent with a large smile, model-like features, and long legs, Kerrigan was quickly characterized by the media as the 'Peggy Fleming of the 90s' (Fleming won the gold in 1968) – even though she was still shaky on the ice with nowhere near the skating ability of Yamaguchi. While Yamaguchi was characterized as graceful (an adjective attributed to her skating only), Kerrigan was graceful and beautiful in face, figure, and form. Indeed, the level of excitement rose in Olympics commentators' voices every time she took to the ice. 'This original program is mature and sophisticated', Hamilton eagerly stated during Kerrigan's program. 'Look at that spin! Beautiful!' As Kerrigan completed a jump, Lundquist similarly gushed, '... that brings a radiant smile from the lovely lady.'[29]

Idealized because, unlike Yamaguchi, Kerrigan physically resembled the fair-skinned, Western-oriented, princess image the mass media had imposed on the competition, she embodied everything an Olympics skater (and an ideal woman in this common-sense narrative) should be: northern European and Peggy Fleming-elegant, with technical skill and artistry to compensate for a lack of athletic ability. As CBS discovered (and exploited for maximum potential), Kerrigan also had a personal history to match. Approximating a New England Cinderella with a welder father and a legally-blind mother, Kerrigan more than any other skater was shaped as a rags-to-riches beauty who was all too ready for a prince. Luckily for CBS, her entire family – two brothers and her parents – made up a regular cheering squad (and consistent photo opportunity) in the stands and were easily portrayed as protecting her from the evil elements in the skating world. Kerrigan's designer white skating costume sealed her princess image: the virgin next door with a hint of sexuality.

Kerrigan's character was further glamorized through a tangential story detailing her adolescence in Stoneham. In a mini-documentary during CBS's main coverage, viewers learned that Kerrigan, who grew up playing hockey with her brothers, was nearly 'a tomboy'. The story detailed her thankful feminization into the 'elegant beauty' she had become. CBS and other media coverage could not applaud Kerrigan's princess qualities enough. Indeed, Kerrigan, and not Japanese-American gold medal prospect (and winner) Yamaguchi had in many ways secured the American darling media label and become CBS's dramatic star, a characterization supplemented by notes on the skater's physical appeal. Kerrigan looked the part, had the background for it, and played it, skating better than was originally expected to win a bronze medal. All this, and not the supposedly requisite gold, was enough for CBS and other mass media outlets to vault Kerrigan to the throne. CBS did this so convincingly that some print media reports actually implied that she should have won the gold.

Tonya Harding (USA)

The third American contender (from Portland, Oregon), and in the beginning a definite contender for the gold medal, Harding, 21, was not given the status of a main character in CBS and print coverage of the competition. For necessary narrative variation, Harding was cast early on as a reckless, shattered, and thoughtless princess: the ne'er-do-well stepsister. Coverage more or less blamed Harding for arriving in France only two days before the competition and for consequently suffering from jetlag. In one CBS update viewers learned that Harding's late arrival was due to her weakness for being 'a homebody', hardly a characteristic of a princess. *Newsweek* echoed the disparagement of the skater, noting that, because Harding was not even punctual for practise and missed part of her music session, she was 'a victim more to her own careless and desultory ways … it was hardly any surprise, then, that she missed her triple axles on both Wednesday and Friday. She was lucky to sneak into fourth place.'[30] Blond, ponytailed, and athletic, with – like Ito – the foreboding triple axle in her repertoire, Harding was consistently portrayed by CBS as tainted, a characterization that was even maintained through unsympathetic reports of her 'problem marriage' that hinted of a physically-abusive husband. To be a true princess, and thus the mass media feminine ideal, it was clear that skaters not only had to look the part, but had to exhibit sexual availability and uprightness; marriage, like athleticism, spoiled the path to the kingdom in the sky. Without an imaginary prince in the shadows (for instance, one of the players on the U.S. hockey team), there was no story.

Surya Bonaly (France)

At 18, Bonaly was the youngest and most intriguing figure to round up the narrative. Another athlete (she preceded her skating career with gymnastics), Bonaly was said to come originally from Réunion in the Indian Ocean but had been adopted by two white parents, who gave her an Indian first name (meaning sun). Oozing multinationality, Bonaly was too far from white, Western, American-darling status to be easily interpreted by the media as genuine princess material. She was therefore cast as the anti-princess, an event spoiler with poor judgement, like Harding, but with the added dose of pernicious intent. More than any other character she was presented in many ways as a villain and was carefully distanced, like Harding, from 'the fairest of them all'.

Back flips are not allowed as legitimate jumps in the Olympics, but during a morning warm-up Bonaly performed a flip – supposedly part of her usual warm-up routine – while Ito practised to her music. The crowd applauded, Ito lost her concentration, and the media narrative turned into a lambasting of Bonaly for her calculating role in destabilizing Ito. Grace, poise, and above all, modesty, were all implied to be beyond Bonaly; her ability even to dress appropriately became a factor in her character's anti-princess configuration. Outfitted in lavish sequins by the fashion designer Christian Lacroix, Bonaly's costumes were subtly translated into being some kind of joke. 'That's a brand new outfit she's skating in', Lundquist slyly said as he introduced each skater, 'she'll be skating to a Spanish song in a rendition of a matador and a bull tonight ...'

Other media storytellers fueled the characterization with sexual commentary. A *Newsweek* article compared Bonaly's matador costume to 'outfits that appeared to come from a garage sale at Hugh Hefner's mansion', a portrayal that denounced Bonaly's style and sexuality at the same time. Even if Bonaly got high skating marks, she was nevertheless characterized as a resolute, conniving, jumping jack who 'stalked the ice rather than addressed it'.[31] Critical attention was even given to Bonaly's mother who visibly argued with Bonaly's coach. Bonaly's own 'bad manners', the narrative suggested, originated from her belligerent and tactless mother. The mother could be easily contrasted with Kerrigan's mother, the one cheering from the sidelines and responsible for pushing Kerrigan towards the 'right direction'.

Looking the Part

Besides figure skating, gymnastics is the only other women's sport that factors in artistry, music, and scoring subjectivity. Unlike the 1992 Olympics women's figure skating event, gymnastics has long been dominated by 14-year-old girls, who are not quite in the realm of sexual desirability.[32] 'What appeals to the sports audience', Deford said of women's figure skating, 'is whatsoever is most beautiful, whatsoever is most lovely, whatsoever is most sexy.'[33] Women's figure skating is so easily welcomed into the sports world – and the real world – as a premier jewel in Olympic sporting events because the beauty contest/fairytale metaphor through which CBS could explain it remains non-threatening to the largely uncontested notions of beauty and sexual roles in our society. Because the more athletic (code masculine, aberrant) skaters are also not as elegant, and because artistry continues to carry more weight in the judging process, CBS conveniently used elegance and artistry as a narrative ploy to judge a skater's moral character.

The sport has also, at least until recently, attracted only women from northern European countries, making the practise of highlighting the Euro-American skaters and casting them as princesses seem normative. Indeed, character similarities and differences within the skating narrative helped to outline an array of narrative judgements that motivated the narrative structure. The top five skaters may all have had a shot at the gold medal, but only one, according to CBS and common-sense notions of feminine beauty and achievement, could be a star.

Playing the Part

Behaving dreamy, nervous, and courageous, as Dorothy Hamill proved in 1972, has been an important factor in the discourse on women's figure skating coverage, as well as in advancing princess and feminine ideals. Whether or not the skaters had dreams or nightmares about their Olympics performances, viewers were told that the skaters, especially the gold medal hopefuls, fell into frequent reveries about their prospects for success. 'I asked her this week if she had dreamt about going to the Olympics', a CBS interviewer said before the broadcast turned to the taped interview of Yamaguchi, 'I haven't had a dream about podiums or medals, but I have dreamed about the performance', Yamaguchi obliged. 'How does the dream come out?' Yamaguchi said that she did not know. Phil Hersh of the *Chicago Tribune* also quoted Yamaguchi as saying 'I dreamed of [going to the Olympics] since I was a little girl and I first put on skates. That it is true is still sinking in.'[34] Yamaguchi was not only dreamy, she was, according to Hersh, the 'embodiment of a million little girls' dreams',[35] and for the entire nation an embodiment of the American dream. This concept of dreaming for success, a passive undertaking, absolved these women (as ideal women) from ambition and drive, characteristics the mass media traditionally award to men. Indeed, the women skaters' male counterparts were characterized as being driven by ambition, with their success a matter of pure intelligence on the ice.

As the discourse continuously highlighted feminine passivity and positioned the women as little girls, CBS also continued the historical tradition of referring to the women's figure skating competition as a 'ladies' event' to couch the competition more comfortably in terms of princess ideals. The word 'lady', implying high breeding, social grace, and femininity, implies a throwback to traditional attitudes regarding women's roles. When CBS's 1992 Olympics host and commentator Tim MacCarver remarked, 'Tonight the stage is set for the crown jewel of figure skating, the ladies' competition', he was not suggesting a competition but a beauty pageant; attention was drawn to costumes and designer labels, 'lovely' smiles and stylish allure. The notion of 'Ladies'

Night' in general also suggests a night at a bar, traditionally a male domain, when women are invited in to be the center of attention and receive drinks for free. The sexual connotations of 'Ladies' Night' in this discourse is unmistakable: As ladies on Ladies' Night, the skaters are not only the center of attention but the subject of male desire. Their desirability is therefore contingent on their availability, and a thematic element in the story of their success.

The characters in the 1992 women's figure skating narrative were also cast as frilly vessels who tragically fell on their bottoms rather than missed competitive jumps. In one pre-edited introduction montage, CBS insinuated how terrifying skating is (for women) by following a skater's feet (in skates) as she walked through the cold, intimidating, underground hallways of the stadium to the sound of a beating heart and entered the arena. Over the audio of a beating heart, a male voice says 'A lifetime of hard work. An Olympic dream begins tonight. Two-and-a-half minutes on the ice, ALONE ... as the world looks on.' Yamaguchi's impressive precision, professionalism, and lack of many visible nervous cues did not leave much room for this thematic device. CBS initially tried to juxtapose her 'focused' face with her mother's nervous expressions in a televised interplay of concern and doting. Backstage, as Yamaguchi waited with her coach, a close-up revealed that they were holding hands. And even though CBS frequently commented on Ito's nervousness as a way to make her personable and accessible, Kerrigan, along with her throbbing, hoping, teeth-clenching family, played up the nervousness best. The newcomer consequently looked the most fragile in the arena, and, when she skated without falling, CBS gushed with relief.

Close ties with family and strong family values were also, as illustrated by CBS and derivative print narratives, a factor in representing the princess ideal. Along with a preoccupation with firm family bonds came an emphasis on the skaters' level of dependency; somehow being childlike and under continuing maternal influence was contingent with maintaining a feminine, princess-like identity. While the other skaters' parents (except Harding's) were present, it was Kerrigan, viewers learned, who had the closest relationship with her mother and her family. During her practises and performances, legally-blind Brenda Kerrigan was constantly shown pressed up against a rinkside television set (gallantly supplied by CBS), watching the outline of her daughter's every move, and hugging her husband Dan when she sensed her daughter doing well. CBS carefully documented this 'special' bond, reiterating a few times how it was her mother who steered her away from becoming a permanent tomboy and pushed her towards figure skating, where, her mother was quoted as saying, 'girls belong'. CBS also glamorized the entire Kerrigan family as a healthy, American, nuclear family (the network's subtle testament to its success) by consistently identifying the skater's parents and two brothers in the stands and showing them frequently embracing each other on close-ups – love pouring all around. The success of American individualism was also sneaking into the narrative; here a working-class family, Massachusetts dialects and all, could work hard, sacrifice, and turn their daughter into a princess.

With attention being given to five distinct character portrayals and the challenge to adapt them to a familiar storyline, the competition as a sports event was forgotten. The real competition as interpreted by CBS was one of artistry, high cheekbones, whiteness, the public exhibition of nervousness, a cohesive family, and a scriptable personal story featuring dreamy goals amid stretches of adversity. On this level, Kerrigan satisfied traditional ideas of femininity and television storytelling, and, with only mediocre skating, easily won the gold.

SPACE AS DISCOURSE

Thorburn refers to the use of space in melodrama as the place wherein most of us act out our deepest needs and feelings.[36] The space in which CBS orchestrated the women's figure skating championship narrative was the ice rink, or Halle de Glace in Albertville, and was melodramatically significant on three levels.

First, the ice rink was a 'battleground' on which the women skaters competed for the 'crown jewel'. Even though skating is not a contact sport, individual desires, looks, technique, fashion, personalities, and the emotional endurance to withstand public pressure were all factors determining victory within the spatial construct of the arena. Secondly, the rink became the site of a theoretical battle over whether the sport should be defined more by artistry or athleticism. Commentators argued for or against the addition of the triple axle to determine which direction the sport was – and should be – going. And thirdly, the rink played out nationalistic battles embodying 'the hopes of a nation'. While one top contender, Surya Bonaly was the nationalistic hope for the host country

France, a more prominent battle featured Kristi Yamaguchi and Midori Ito, a Japanese-American vs. a Japanese. With regard to the political climate surrounding the 1992 Winter Olympics, the ice rink symbolized the battleground for two countries who were falling out of each other's favor at the time.

Contrasting with the battleground motif, the ice rink also represented a 'stage' in the context of the women's figure skating narrative. It was a place for enjoyment, a coveted realm to which one was supposed to feel privileged to have access. After the camera zoomed in on a close-up of a women's figure skating event ticket, CBS's Verne Lundquist (wearing a tuxedo and reporting from the rink alongside Scott Hamilton) revealed that 'in all of Albertville there's no more desirable ticket than the one you just saw'. The emphasis on the event's glamour, theatrics, music, and regalia worked in this narrative to dramatize the feminine qualities imposed on the sport. In another pre-edited montage introduction on the second night of programming, each of the five stars swirled comfortably on the ice to the song 'Wonderful Tonight', sung by Eric Clapton. As one image smoothly dissolved into the next, the song's accompanying words went: 'It's late in the evening/She's wondering what clothes to wear/She'll put on her makeup/And brushes her long blond hair' [Tonya Harding, who happened to be blond, was inserted here] 'And then she'll ask me/Do I look all right?/And I'll say, yes, you look wonderful tonight/Oh my darling you look wonderful tonight.' Unlike a battleground, the stage was set for alluring performances by the world's (insecure and nervous) top artists. As was evidenced by the Clapton song and CBS's frequent shots of little boys peering through stadium fences and supposedly gazing at the skaters, CBS interpreted these skating performances through a male perspective (despite the fact that women make up the majority of the viewers). The interpretation, however, fits the fairytale narrative, where the princesses are skating in hopes of male approval and ultimately, of finding a prince. To quote from Laura Mulvey,

> In a world ordered by sexual imbalance, pleasure in looking has been split between active/male and passive/female. The determining male gaze projects its fantasy onto the female figure which is styled accordingly. In their traditional exhibitionist role women are simultaneously looked at and displayed, with their appearance coded for strong visual and erotic impact so that they can be said to connote to-be-looked-at-ness.[37]

In the space of the rink, the female skater's attractiveness is measured, consequently, by her erotic appeal to men.

Finally, viewers learned that the competitors could also enjoy the ice rink as a kind of home base. Parents sat in the stands urging their daughters on, friends and coaches offered their support. CBS even showed some instances in which competitors befriended each other, or took viewers behind the scenes and underneath the stands to show where competitors stored their gear and picked up their mail. Vast yet familiarized, the rink was a common ground for viewers to interpret who these women were, analyse their similarities and differences, and compare their experience to their own realities.

TIME AS DISCOURSE

Even though CBS was combating the insecurity of tape-delayed programming in 1992, the network used tape delay as an advantage instead of a disadvantage for the first time in the history of Olympics broadcasting. CBS had two important strategies in pulling it off. First, the network organized the women's figure skating competition so that it appeared to be live. Secondly, CBS used the six-hours lag time to edit extra footage and add other pre-edited mini documentaries to create a more compelling program. Indeed, the network created a fully scripted melodrama.

Deming remarks on television's capacity to project liveness and on its ability to emphasize 'the present tense and irreversible flow of time'.[38] CBS accordingly thrust its programming in the modes of anticipation and 'continuous update' by imposing frequent live narration between the tape-delayed broadcast in order to maintain and dramatize the present. 'There's going to be some tough competition out there on the ice tonight, some great jumpers, some great artists', Paula Zahn announced, who was live but commented on dated material. Zahn then handed over commentary from her comfortable living room studio (where she co-hosted the Olympics coverage with Tim MacCarver) to Verne Lundquist and Scott Hamilton, the CBS announcers in the Halle de Glace, who had taped their material hours earlier. 'There are empty seats in the stadium right now because it's early in the competition', Lundquist said.

As the competition progressed, each skater performed her routine while anticipation and speculation were rife. 'Well, Kristi Yamaguchi,

Tonya Harding, and Midori Ito have been in the spotlight, but when considering the ladies' competition here, don't dismiss the medal capabilities of Nancy Kerrigan, the elegant young skater from New England.' These kinds of announcements, notes Deming, 'remind the audience that the fiction is part of television's segmented flow, the flow that continues whether the set is on or not and whether the viewer watches or not.'[39]

Besides projecting the present, CBS also used the six-hours tape delay to expand on the event's dramatic moments and to finesse the coverage. With each skater's routine lasting only 2½ min for the first night and 4½ for the second night, CBS filled the inevitable lag time by manipulating the event's temporal order and imposing prerecorded, pre-edited flashbacks in the form of documentary pastiches that detailed moments in the skaters' earlier careers. Instead of watching Kristi Yamaguchi skate around the rink during her allotted 6½ min of warm-up, viewers were taken back six months earlier to relive the moment when the skater selected the music for her original routine and met a seamstress who fitted her for a costume. In another lull between 2½ min routines (and of course, commercials), viewers were taken to Massachusetts for a flashback visit with Nancy Kerrigan's mother, who admitted that 'it was such a relief that Nancy stopped playing hockey with her brothers … you're a girl … let the boys play hockey and you can do girl things!'

Kozloff discusses how the use of proliferating storylines is a means by which television narratives compensate for their lack of suspense. Such storylines, she writes, 'diffuse the viewer's interest in any one line of action and spread the interest over a large field.'[40] Time to fill made the proliferation of story lines necessary during the women's competition, but also worked to expand the narrative's spatial orientation, stimulate sympathy and recognition for the narrative's characters, and, in this case, continually orient them in terms of their princessy characteristics.

STRUCTURE AS DISCOURSE

While action in a narrative is motivated by individual characters and while these actions and characters somehow connect with the flux of fairytale myth, that shifting flux needed to be organized within a narrative framework, a categorization of human experience. According to the structuralist Claude Lévi-Strauss, we explain experiences by casting them in terms of binary oppositions: male/female, sacred/profane, pure/impure, in/out, kin/other, and nature/culture.[41] By defining data and experience in two-dimensional, dualistic categories[42] we create a dramatic tension that subsequently calls for a resolution. The narrative construction for the 1992 women's figure skating competition followed the same pattern: a structure was first imposed through a series of binary oppositions and then a way was offered for those oppositions, or narrative tensions, to be resolved.

Until 1988, when the typical cold war binary in all Olympics coverage was quickly breaking down, television found in figure skating an event that straddled many more disparate (and potentially exciting) binary configurations: sport vs. musical theater, athlete vs. artist, strength vs. grace, match vs. show, and jump vs. dance. While the women skaters all demonstrated many different levels of technical and aesthetic ability, CBS neatly packaged and paired them in separate, polarized camps: Yamaguchi, artist vs. Ito, athlete; Kerrigan, artist vs. Harding, athlete, with Bonaly remaining the token 'wild card' athlete. Even though Yamaguchi and Kerrigan were legitimate athletes as well – Yamaguchi ironically had been labeled 'athlete' in past events – their artistry and Harding's, Ito's, and Bonaly's athleticism were reconfigured so that the dualistic tension and narrative pattern were more or less intact. And while it was made clear at the beginning of the event that 'artist' and 'athlete' had equal chances for the gold medal (Ito and Harding had both worked up impressive 3½ rotation axle jumps), a failure to complete the terrifically difficult jump successfully throughout the course of the narrative put the 'artists' at an advantage. Narrative tension between athlete and artist was subsequently resolved then, with the artists – the more 'feminine' skaters – coming out on top. At the end of the first night of competition, Lundquist pointed to such a resolution:

> Favoring the artistic over the athletic, we saw Tonya Harding and Midori Ito lose an edge. But it was really a night to admire the artistic ... the beauty of Nancy Kerrigan, the joy of her Mom and Dad, and the exquisite style and grace of Yamaguchi.

The competition's final resolution again confirmed the preference for artistry, but warned that athleticism would be back again in four years. Ironically, it was television that shaped the tension between art and athleticism in the first place with the abandonment of compulsory school figures. The sport's only direction for growth was in jumping.

Another binary opposition in the narrative which was initially encouraged and then subtly dropped was the U.S. vs. Japan dichotomy. The 1992 Winter Olympics were broadcast at a point when U.S. car manufacturing was at a low point and activities such as Toyota sledge-hammering were popular American news events. The binary opposition proved too delicate to maintain, however, due to Yamaguchi's American-Japanese background and what may be considered the touchy subject of American guilt over Japanese internment camps in which Yamaguchi's family were detained. This opposition slid comfortably into the secure non-political realm of artist vs. athlete and lean vs. stout. Had Ito triple-axled her way to the gold instead of Yamaguchi, perhaps there would have been more narrative opposition between the two skaters, and certainly a more problematic message to sift through.

CONCLUSION

CBS was overwhelmingly successful in its broadcast of the 1992 Olympics because the network couched women's figure skating into the already familiar narrative of a *Cinderella*-like fairytale. The skaters, then, did not have to be previously famous to make the event entertaining, but they had to fit into a pre-established storyline. CBS first designated star skaters as ideal princesses fulfilling their dreams. But rather than celebrate the event winner according to the competition's outcome, CBS chose to highlight the bronze medalist (Kerrigan) in 1992 because she more closely fitted into the familiar melodramatic plot line the network was striving to impose and maintain. As an established star after these Olympics, Kerrigan was featured in high-profile television commercials and specials and was chosen to appear in *People* magazine's 'most beautiful people of 1992' issue. Yamaguchi later resurfaced in the pro circuit.

CBS's investment in its characterization of Kerrigan as a real-life Cinderella would reach its full potential two years later when Kerrigan, Harding, and Bonaly competed again in the 1994 Olympics.[43] By 1994 Kerrigan was a more seasoned skater, a gold medal favorite, and a familiar face to American audiences. She was also dramatically assaulted by associates of her skating rival Tonya Harding six weeks before the Olympics at the U.S. national competition. Rather than posing a problem to the narrative, the attack actually allowed CBS to expand Kerrigan's princess-like characterization. The former Cinderella suddenly became Snow White versus Harding's evil queen, and the captivating story allowed CBS weeks of build up to the showdown between the 'pure and innocent' Kerrigan and the 'conniving and baneful' Harding. Luckily for CBS, the Olympics melodrama would garner one of the largest audiences in television history.

Unluckily for Kerrigan, she, like all the skaters, had become a media pawn in CBS's fairytale, and could not withstand the enormous pressure to fulfill the narrative as precisely as the network had planned. With Kerrigan fumbling on the ice and in person, CBS embraced the story of another skater who could be implanted into a more dramatic fairytale story line. The Ukranian figure skater Oksana Baiul (a virtually unknown entity, as Kerrigan had been in 1992) outshone Kerrigan with a brilliant performance and beat her artistic score by a tiny fraction. Kerrigan, who was captured complaining about the scores, was immediately cast as spiteful and spoiled, and became quickly marginalized as CBS heralded Baiul.

Fortunately for CBS, Baiul seemed to have an even better Cinderella story. Orphaned when she was 13 and skating on inferior rinks in the harsh environment of the Ukraine, she was Bambi and Cinderella combined. An artistic skater with a tiny body and a ballet-like skating style, she valiantly sailed through her programs on an injured leg (through an accidental on-ice collision during warm-up), but had only one day of recovery time compared with Kerrigan's three weeks. With Baiul's repeated references to her mother in heaven looking down at her magnificent skating, the Ukrainian fitted the mold of a rags-to-riches princess far more precisely than Kerrigan, who was reconfigured as a cold-as-ice and jealous rival. Kerrigan's media persona would hit rock bottom when she was later caught on videotape in Disney World (one of her corporate sponsors) shortly after the Olympics, disparaging the fairytale kingdom, and later married her (much older) agent. In two short years Bauil's princess image would also self-destruct with an inappropriate article and photo spread in *Esquire* magazine, a drunk driving charge, and weight gain.

By creating such a simple – yet ultimately successful drama for television audiences, CBS also brought many more people into the skating fold, and, in so doing, potentially changed the dynamics of the fairytale narrative altogether. First, the successful ratings of 1994 launched a plethora of televised pro and amateur skating specials and competitions, which sustained interest in the sport and made figure skating the most popular televised athletic event in the U.S. after American football. Unlike the audiences watching the Olympics, these avid skating viewers were knowledgeable enough about individuals and the inherent drama of any given competition that the adding of fairytale storylines would appear overly forced. These televised professional exhibitions also lacked the prestige of an Olympics event – not every top skater competed every time – and without a continuous stable of 'new' characters, the same narrative could not be sustained.

Secondly, the early 1990s saw a rise in other competitive U.S. women's sports leagues such as basketball and soccer, giving viewing audiences athletic alternatives to figure skating that celebrated competition for competition's sake, and would make the configurations of Ladies' Night and the princess narrative seem outdated and almost ridiculous. 'What's going on here?', Mariah Burton Nelson wrote in *Newsweek*:

> How come sports fans' fascination with female athletes has shifted from skirted skaters (Dorothy Hamill, Michelle Kwan) and tiny teenage tumblers (Mary Lou Retton, Keri Strug) to rough, muscular women in their 20s and 30s who grunt, grimace and heave each other aside with their hips? Are we simply wild over their athletic brilliance? Or does the popularity of women's team sports tell us something deeper about how female athletes and fans are redefining themselves, what they really want and who they might become?[44]

According to Nelson, there are plenty of rich stories to tell about female athletes that extend beyond the confining feminine ideal of passivity, artistry and public poise.

Thirdly, a new type of skater threatened to destabilize the narrative. The ironic outcome of skating's move towards jumps is that the best jumpers are not athletes with muscular bodies, but the skaters with the smallest bodies and the ability to spin quickly in the air. That the sport was becoming too muscular was a recurrent fear in the popular discourse of 1992 and 1994. These muscular skaters, who relied on a singular triple axle (the most difficult jump in the female repertoire) and could rarely depend on a clean jump, had a distinct disadvantage, especially when the scores inevitably tipped in the artist's favor. In comparison, the new crop of young skaters, while certainly lacking in artistry, could more predictably handle their increasingly ambitious triple-toe combination jumps – many jumps in a row, and an impossible feat for larger-bodied women. These 13- to 15-year-old girls, with tiny frames and a sort of impish fearlessness, were suddenly favored in the medal count. The skating establishment, with concerns about maintaining the sport's legitimacy, barely embraced the sudden 'girlification' of figure skating. This development also posed potential problems for the fairytale narrative, however. These girls were not old enough for 'their life work' and 'their dreams coming true' to make any sense. They had short (that is, boring) personal histories of stuffed animal collections and trips to the mall, which did not hold up well in terms of proliferating storylines. They were not bundles of 'feminine' nervousness since they had not experienced enough loss and pressure to understand the true weight of Olympic competition. And most importantly, piling a fairytale narrative on such young skaters – which would essentially redefine them as objects of male desire – would create uncomfortable overtones of paedophilia. As it happened, however, CBS would once again force a fairytale on a select skater among the leading 1998 Winter Olympics contestants, modifying the template (as the U.S. networks have done all along) according to who was deemed 'the fairest of them all'.

The 1998 Olympics offered another opportunity to highlight three U.S. skaters, stirring up the promise, once again, of an American gold medal winner and ice princess, and intensifying the exciting prospect of a 1–2–3 U.S. sweep. It soon became clear, however, that the real drama would be limited to two skaters – the 'mature', 17-year-old artist Michelle Kwan, vs. the ambitious, 15-year-old upstart Tara Lipinski. During the four years leading up to the event Kwan had become the favored skater. She had been a stringy 13-year-old at the last Olympics, impressing judges with her upright jumps and girlish giggles. By 1998, however, Kwan was not necessarily a fresh face – she was a fresh figure. 'In the past two years', Starr wrote in 1997, 'Kwan has sprouted from a tiny stick-figure kid into a young woman.'[45]

The network, the skating establishment, and the public's embrace of Kwan – an Asian-American – certainly signaled a refreshing shift away from the northern European model of a feminine ideal. Kwan's story, as CBS would carefully shape it, was about her new womanliness (that is, sexuality), her diligent training with a not-as-talented older sister, strong family ties, and tremendous personal dignity. Once believed to have the

1998 gold locked up even before she skated (like Kerrigan in 1994), Kwan came into the Olympics competition, surprisingly, as an underdog. During the previous year Lipinski had stolen the show, winning the national and then the world title, and proving that her consistent jumps and unparalleled triple-loop, triple loop combination were fierce competition to Kwan's on-ice elegance. Even if Lipinski was disadvantaged in terms of artistry and youth, her team of handlers had her strategically skate to the film score of Disney's *The Lion King* – in effect, pre-empting the network's narrative by assigning her the role of princess during her routine – and wearing lipstick to make her appear older. 'Now if you look and perform like a mature young woman – no matter what your age – you'll get good results,' her coach was quoted as saying.[46]

Because it was comparatively easy for her 75-lb frame, Lipinski was able to complete an awesome number of jump rotations and ended with a gold medal, beating Kwan by a tiny percentage. The young skater's 'good results' did not translate into positive media coverage, however. After the dust from Lipinski's 'crowd-pleaser' win had settled,[47] the young skater was cast as obsessively competitive, as was her mother, who had fired a coach and then moved with her daughter to the best training site possible (while Lipinski's oil executive father remained in Houston). Lipinski's team was described as 'beating an unhappy, at times angry, retreat from the public eye',[48] suggesting that Lipinski's accessible, effervescent smile was a front for conniving operators. And her own personality was examined: commenting on the skater's 'picture-perfect moment' at the 1998 Olympics, a *Maclean's* magazine writer jabbed at the young skater's persona:

> Watching the marks come up from the kiss-and-cry section at the rinkside, the girl from Sugar Land, Tex., elicited perhaps the loudest, most ear-piercing series of screams ever heard in an Olympic venue. It hurt just being in the same building.[49]

Clearly, Lipinski did not 'belong' in the ice rink. With composure a key ingredient to the assigned role of ice princess, Kwan had it – Lipinski did not.

Indeed, the big story of 1998 was not Lipinski's win, but the graciousness of Kwan's acceptance of defeat. After the event, both Kwan and Lipinski were the featured skaters in competing ice tours, but it was Kwan, not Lipinski, 'who landed a coveted array of Disney deals for TV specials, books, and, likely, a film version of her autobiography, *Heart of a Champion*.[50] As Starr put it, Kwan's popularity and marketability had not diminished, and perhaps had even grown. As with Kerrigan in 1992, Kwan was even included in *People* magazine's year 2000 list of the 50 most beautiful people in the world.

Despite the numerous pro and amateur skating specials, other competing women's sports, and new ways of redefining the sport, the fairytale narrative clearly lives on in the context of U.S. network Olympics broadcasts. As we have seen with the earlier U.S. Olympics skating competition coverage, all the variable ingredients in the drama – skating proficiency, sexual desirability, a good personal story, and poise – are part of the narrative mix, but winning the gold medal is not necessarily the key to becoming an anointed media fairytale star.

NOTES

1. T. Tyrer, 'CBS Banking on Olympic Games Payoff', *Electronic Media* (3 Feb. 1992), 18.
2. 'Paying for the Olympics', ibid., 12.
3. CBS would successfully bid for the next two Winter Olympics in 1994 (Lillehammer) and 1998 (Nagano).
4. T. Tyrer, 'Olympics Put CBS Ahead of Sweeps in Race', *Electronic Media* (24 Feb. 1992), 2.
5. Tyrer, 'CBS Banking', 18.
6. F. Deford, 'The Jewel of the Games', *Newsweek* (10 Feb. 1992), 46–53.
7. See S.R. Kozloff, 'Narrative Theory and Television', in R.C. Allen (ed.), *Channels of Discourse* (Chapel Hill, NC and London: University of North Carolina Press, 1987), pp.67–100. Also see C.J. Deming, '*Hill Street Blues* as Narrative', in R. Avery and D. Eason (eds), *Critical Perspectives on Media and Society* (New York, NY and London: Guilford Press, 1991), pp.240–64.
8. Tyrer, 'CBS Banking', 18.
9. J. Didion, *The White Album* (New York, NY: Simon & Schuster, 1979), p.11.
10. R. Campbell, 'Securing the Middle Ground: Reporter Formulas in "60 Minutes"', in R. Avery and D. Eason (eds), *Critical Perspectives on Media and Society* (New York, NY and London: Guilford Press, 1991), pp.265–93.
11. Kozloff, 'Narrative Theory', p.49.
12. F. Deford and M. Starr, 'American Beauty', *Newsweek* (2 March 1992), 50–2.
13. 'Sweet Life of an Olympic Doll', *Sports Illustrated* (11 Nov. 1968), 26.
14. Deford, 'The Jewel', 50.
15. 'Peggy Fleming: A Golden Grace', *Newsweek* (5 Feb. 1968), 48–9.
16. 'The Olympics', *Time* (16 Feb. 1968), 57.
17. 'Peggy Fleming'.
18. Ibid.
19. 'Sweet Life'.
20. '*Magic Memories on Ice: Three Decades of Great Moments in Figure Skating*', CBS/Fox Video Sports, produced by ABC Sports in association with Jack Nicklaus Productions (New York, NY: 1990).
21. 'An Arcane Discipline', *Time* (2 Feb. 1976), 61–3.
22. Ibid., 61.
23. '*Magic Memories*'.
24. J. Bruce, 'When You're No. 7 You Try Harder', *Sports Illustrated* (19 Jan. 1976), 24–5.

25. T. Callahan, 'The Word She Uses Is "Invincible"', *Time* (15 Feb. 1988), 44–57.

26. I. Austen, 'Chasing a Crown', *Macleans* (Feb. 1988), 30.

27. Callahan, 'The Word', 46.

28. D. Bordwell and K. Thompson, *Film Art: An Introduction* (New York, NY: McGraw-Hill, 1990), p.70.

29. Lundquist's parallel comment for Yamaguchi after a flawless set of jumps was 'And look at the smile.'

30. Deford and Starr, 'American Beauty', 52.

31. Ibid.

32. Since Nadia Comenici won gold as a spry 14-year-old in 1976, Olympic gymnastic competitors have all been young teenagers. Figure skating is also moving in this direction as the sport grows to demand more difficult jumps. A small size allows for easier completion.

33. Deford, 'The Jewel', 50.

34. J. Powers, 'U.S.' Yamaguchi 1st; Kerrigan Gets Bronze', *Boston Globe* (22 Feb. 1992), 1, 35, 41.

35. P. Hersh, 'U.S. Skater on Top of the World', *Chicago Tribune* (22 Feb. 1992), 1.

36. Deming, '*Hill Street Blues*', p.251.

37. L. Mulvey, *Visual Pleasure and Narrative Cinema* (Basingstoke: Macmillan, 1989), p.62.

38. Deming, '*Hill Street Blues*', p.249.

39. Ibid.

40. Kozloff, 'Narrative Theory', pp.51–2.

41. C. Mukerji and M. Schudson, *Rethinking Popular Culture* (Berkeley, CA: University of California Press, 1991), p.19.

42. Campbell, 'Securing the Middle Ground', pp.265–93.

43. Both the winter and the summer Olympics are scheduled to occur every four years. The International Olympic Committee began alternating summer and Winter Olympics after 1992. The next Winter Olympics were thus rescheduled for 1994, making this the first (and only) time athletes would wait only two years between competitions. CBS won the rights to broadcast the 1994 Winter Olympics, as well as the 1998 winter games in Nagano.

44. M.B. Nelson, 'Learning What "Team" Really Means', *Newsweek* (19 July 1999), 55.

45. M. Starr, 'Dueling on the Ice', ibid. (17 March 1997), 64.

46. Ibid.

47. M. Starr, 'Beautiful Dreamer', *Newsweek* (9 Feb. 1998), 62.

48. Ibid.

49. J.D., 'A Pixie-Perfect Moment', *Macleans* (2 March 1998), 42.

50. M. Starr, 'The Long, Winding Road to Gold', *Newsweek* (29 March 1999), 66.

The Whole World Isn't Watching
(But We Thought They Were):
The Super Bowl and U.S. Solipsism

CHRISTOPHER R. MARTIN and
JIMMIE L. REEVES

A little more than a decade ago, as the symbolic Berlin Wall was coming down, political leaders in the United States assured their citizens that a New World Order had come to fruition. This new, international, political arrangement would bring peace, of course, but more important was that it was implicitly an orderly peace – one which would be administered and maintained by the United States, to the advantage of the United States. In other words, to the winner go the spoils.

Almost as quickly, the New World Order got disorderly. A Gulf War quelled, but did not dislodge Saddam Hussein's regime in Iraq; hundred of thousands died in Rwanda as warring factions engaged in genocide; Pakistan and India rattled sabers with nuclear tests; and the worst act of terrorism visited U.S. soil, performed by a U.S. citizen. Daily NATO bombings of Serbia (including a few that were unfortunately aimed at the Chinese Embassy in Belgrade) failed to quickly halt ethnic cleansings in Kosovo, nor end the rule of the Serbian leader Slobodan Milosevic. And at a mostly white, upper-middle-class high school in Littleton, Colorado, two students turned guns and assorted weaponry on their peers and then themselves, ultimately killing 14 people and seriously injuring many more.

In countless ways U.S. political hegemony has been deflated in this New World Order. Although the U.S. side of the global economy mostly hums along, the problems of ungovernable international leaders, ineffective military interventions, and chronic internal violence make the U.S.'s favorite chant of 'We're Number One' ring a little hollow in the post-cold war era.

Into this tableau enters the Super Bowl. Each year, this supremely nationalistic event – the United States' most-watched television program – is marketed to people in the U.S. by the National Football League (NFL) and the mainstream national news media as an international affair. World-wide audiences of nearly one billion are routinely announced in the pre-game hyperbole, and actively promoted during the broadcast. Many reports proclaim, as a public relations official for the NFL told us, that the Super Bowl 'is the greatest one-day sporting event around'.

But, is the Super Bowl the most super and most watched of sporting events in the world? What is the cultural significance of laying claim to being the sporting event with the most television viewers world-wide, especially in the historical conditions of this New World Order?

In a paper related to material in this chapter ('Rewriting the Super Bowl: From Cold War Spectacle to Postmodern Carnival'), we documented and examined transformations in the Super Bowl experience since the 1970s.[1] Over the course of more than 30 years the centrality of the Super Bowl's championship game spectacle has been undermined by a decentralized Super Bowl carnival with multiple narratives. The chief aspects of the post-modern rewriting of the Super Bowl experience include the foregrounding of commercial discourse, the conspicuous display of promotional discourse, and the hyper-hyping of half-time discourse. These three companion narratives come together with the football championship narrative to form something of a metanarrative – one that captures compelling mutations in the Super Bowl experience, and that accounts for its enormous U.S. television audience and its significant place in U.S. culture.

Another paper ('Re-Reading the Super Bowl'), updated Michael R. Real's influential and widely-read interpretation of football's championship game event as 'mythic spectacle'.[2] Whereas Real's structuralist reading of the 1974 Super Bowl focused on outlining the central features of the NFL's utopian vision of winning at all costs, our post-structuralist re-reading of the 1994 Super Bowl emphasized the struggle to uphold this embattled vision in the increasing fragmentation and declining expectations of post-Fordist television and society.

Our analysis in this paper begins with Real's interpretation of the 1974 Super Bowl. His 'The Super Bowl: Mythic Spectacle' concludes with a summation of the football's structural values: 'American football is an aggressive, strictly regulated team game fought between males who use both violence and technology to win monopoly control of property for the economic gain of individuals within a nationalistic, entertainment context'.³ Ultimately, Real makes a relatively convincing argument that the 1974 Super Bowl is best understood as a vehicle for displaying what he terms 'the sexual, racial, and organizational priorities' of U.S. cold war culture.

Of course, the Super Bowl is still a major cultural event that, like the Balinese cockfight, renders 'ordinary, everyday experience comprehensible'.⁴ But what happens when a ritual originating in one regime of experience is applied to a very different set of historical conditions? In our re-reading of the Super Bowl we do not set out to negate any of Real's insights. Instead, we use them as a point of departure to explore how the Super Bowl ritual has been transformed by the changing economic, technological, and political realities of deindustrialized, post-modern, Nafta-esque America – a United States in which the cold war values of Vince Lombardi and Richard Nixon have given way to the New World disorder of Monica Lewinsky, war in the Balkans, and the Columbine High School massacre.

This chapter first reviews the origins of the Super Bowl, especially how the event has evolved from a cold war, mythic spectacle to a televised carnival, with multiple – but still U.S.-centric – narratives. Secondly, we analyse the meaning of the Super Bowl as an international phenomenon. Our arguments on its relevance to the rest of the world will be supported with data from the CNN World News Archives and from a close textual reading of an introductory package from the 1995 broadcast of Super Bowl XXIX. Finally, we discuss why the United States' favorite professional sporting event is unlikely to become the favorite sporting event of the rest of the world.

FROM A MYTHIC COLD WAR BATTLE TO THE POST-COLD WAR CARNIVAL

As the subheading suggests, we characterize these transformations as a shift from the mythic to the carnivalesque. We argue that the ritual competition of the actual championship game has steadily declined in cultural relevance – especially in relation to the increasing public fascination with both the advertising discourse and half-time entertainment. In fact, our analysis suggests that the tracing of transformations in the meanings and pleasures generated by the Super Bowl is one way of mapping the cultural deterritorializations and reterri-

torializations of a fundamental change in the U.S. television experience
– the shift from TV I to TV II.⁵

A shorthand term for the broadcasting system that emerged in the
U.S. in the 1950s, triumphed in the 1960s, and was slowly displaced in
the 1970s, the term 'TV I' refers to what has also been studied as
'network era television'. A period dominated by a three-network
oligopoly, TV I played a central, ideological role in promoting the ethic
of consumption, naturalizing the nuclear family ideal, selling
suburbanization, and sustaining cold war paranoia. Put another way, TV
I was one of the chief products and producers of Fordism – a 'rigid'
economic order named after Henry Ford that drove the general
prosperity of the post-war boom through an expansive manufacturing
economy of assembly-line production and mass consumption.⁶ And, as
an expression of Fordism, television popularity during the 1950s and the
1960s is most properly studied as mass culture oriented toward
attracting the largest possible audience. The Super Bowl is, of course, a
relic of the 1960s. And, like TV I, after emerging from the Fordist order
it then contributed, actively, to the reproduction of Fordism.

As such, televised professional football is an almost pure expression of
values associated with Fordism. Like the Fordist assembly line, football,
more than any other popular sport, is marked by a highly differentiated
division of labor, with each position on both the offense and the defense
carrying with it highly specific responsibilities. It also exhibits Fordist
hierarchies of control that reach from the quarterback (often called a 'field
general'), through specialty coaches and co-ordinators, through the head
coach, through the managerial elite, to ownership. Furthermore, as an
expression of the utopian visions of the Fordist economic order, football is
infatuated with discipline, conformity, and winning. After all, under
Fordism, the world of work was supremely a masculine domain devoted to
the ethic of competition. And the Super Bowl is the ultimate
manifestation of this ethic. This competitive ethic was perhaps most
clearly stated by the legendary Vince Lombardi (who coached the Green
Bay Packers to victory in the first Super Bowl) when he said, 'Winning
isn't everything, it's the only thing.' Standing in stark contrast to an older
sports ethic ('It doesn't matter if you win or lose, it's how you play the
game'), Lombardi's words have been echoed over and over again by people
such as the Oakland Raiders owner Al Davis ('Just win, Baby').⁷

Indeed, Real's analysis presents a compelling 'reading' – grounded in
the political concerns and interpretive trends of the period – of how the

Super Bowl performed as a mechanism of ideological reproduction. But what Real was not able to discern at the time, and what his structuralism was simply not designed to address, is how this same sports ritual can, at one and the same time, operate as a conservative celebration of Fordism's aggressive masculinity while also performing as an instrument of change, a mechanism of ideological transformation that now exhibits all the attributes of a new order of popularity associated with 'post-Fordism' and TV II.

What we refer to as TV II (or 'post-Fordist TV') emerged in the 1970s, triumphed in the 1980s and in the 1990s was being marketed under the alias of the 'information superhighway'. Although TV I's broadcasting distribution system is still an integral part of this new communication order, TV II also incorporates satellite, cable, VCR, and personal computer technologies. To say that these new forces in the marketplace have undermined the dominance of TV I's three-network oligopoly would be an understatement: where once ABC, NBC, and CBS commanded over 90 per cent of the prime-time audience, today the major network audience, even with the addition of a fourth national broadcast network, has decreased to less than 60 per cent. In this transformation, older notions of popularity would be rewritten as television's mass audience was systematically fragmented into lifestyle sectors and niche markets – and the rigidities of Fordist TV would give way to more flexible programming and scheduling strategies devoted to generating 'quality demographics'.

This rewriting of popularity signaled a shift from mass culture and its unifying influences to something that might best be described as 'cult culture', a divisive system of taste distinctions that has figured prominently in supporting and masking the radical inequalities of our times by segmenting the audience into 'insiders' and 'outsiders'. This re-visioning of the American television experience is most clearly manifested in cult shows of the past dozen years such as 'Twin Peaks', 'Mystery Science Theatre 3000', 'The X-Files', and 'South Park'. Even some of the latest programming trends in U.S. television, which seek to re-establish mass audiences for the major broadcast networks, do so with a post-Fordist twist. The biggest and most copied hit of the 1999–2000 television season, ABC's 'Who Wants to be a Millionaire?', is reminiscent of America's love affair with prime-time game shows during the TV I era of the 1950s, but breaks the traditional proscenium of the glass screen. The show invites home viewers to be contestants by dialing a toll–free telephone number, and collects data on the fans who visit the show's web site to play an on–line version of the game or who complete a marketing survey for ABC in an attempt to win prizes. Other programs, including CBS's 'Survivor' and 'Big Brother', inspired by similar television programs in Europe and 24–hour webcam Internet sites, turn to an unprecedented voyeurism regarding ordinary people's daily lives to attract mass audiences to television and to companion web sites offering live video streaming and free subscription newsletters. Although CBS hopes to gain huge audiences with these programs, the Internet elements of the programming allow the network to distill mass audiences into niche markets and even targeted individuals. The viewers watch programs of surveillance and are themselves tracked by the network during their visits to program Internet sites.[8]

Thus the shift in the culture of U.S. television is apparent in the segmentation of mass audiences via cult television and the Internet, and also through other programming strategies: the hybridization of the police show, the yuppification of the family drama, the tabloidization of the news, and, more to the point of this analysis, the carnivalization of the Super Bowl. Drawing on terms that David Harvey uses to describe the difference between the cold war era of modernity and post–cold war era of postmodernity,[9] we argue that – in the ascendancy of TV II – the authority, permanence, and centrality of the Super Bowl's championship spectacle has been undermined by an eclectic, ephemeral, and decentralized Super Bowl circus with multiple side-shows.

Although our 'Re-writing' paper also considers promotional discourse and half-time entertainment, here we limit the discussion to the most flagrant aspect of the post-modern mutation of the Super Bowl experience: that is, the hyper-hyping of commercial discourse. In fact, we have informally observed that many viewers are now more attuned to the advertising extravaganza than to the actual game. At many Super Bowl gatherings partiers will converse during game time, ignoring the contest in favor of good company, but then will be hushed during the commercial breaks. One can only imagine how Vince Lombardi would respond to such callous indifference to his beloved competition.

At least since Super Bowl III,[10] advertising space on the annual event has attracted widespread attention simply because it is one of the most expensive commercial slots of the broadcast year. A 30–sec commercial for what is now remembered as the first Super Bowl in 1967 would have cost between $37,500 and $42,500. By 1985, 30 sec of Super Bowl time cost an average of $500,000; the price jumped to $1 million by 1995.[11] Because of the continuous decline of audience size for regular network television programs since the early 1980s, the Super Bowl now has no peers in its per-minute advertising price. Thus it is unlikely that we shall ever again see a situation where another special program can command more money than the Super Bowl, as the last episode of 'M*A*S*H' did in February 1984. In that special 2½-hour final episode, CBS charged an average of $450,000 for a 30-sec slot, $50,000 more than NBC charged during Super Bowl 18 months earlier.[12] By 1995 the Super Bowl's $1 million-for-30-sec advertising price was far above the other high rated programs of the same period: a 30-sec slot cost an average $643,500 on the Academy Awards show, $305,000 on the number-one rated 'Home Improvement', and $214,000 on the well-hyped NCAA men's basketball finals. The Super Bowl advertising price continues to increase: the average cost for 30 sec of time in 1999 hit $1.6 million[13] and $2.2 million in 2000.[14]

Through the 1970s, mass media (and public) fascination with Super Bowl advertisements was limited to the issue of their relatively exorbitant cost, and the demand to buy them as a sort of indicator of the health and confidence of American business. The content of Super Bowl commercials was not a popular topic of discussion. However, on 22 January 1984 a single 60-sec Super Bowl XVIII advertisement revolutionized the way advertisers would approach the game. The Super Bowl would no longer be a means to reach a large audience, with the same old truck or motor oil commercial, but a way to make a stunning, dramatic, entertaining commercial statement. In the third quarter of the Los Angeles Raiders' blow-out of the Washington Redskins, viewers were confronted with a visually compelling 60-sec advertisement directed by the British filmmaker Ridley Scott (*Blade Runner* and *Alien*) and costing nearly $400,000 to produce – four times the cost of a typical 30-sec advertisement at the time.[15] It ended with the tag line, 'On January 24th, Apple Computer will introduce Macintosh. And you'll see why 1984 won't be like *1984*'. For those who missed the message, the Apple chairman Steve Jobs suggested two days later that the real 'Big Brother' was the computer industry leader IBM. The Macintosh advertisement has attained 'classic' status, and is now part of the advertising industry's Clio Awards Hall of Fame.

But, whereas the Macintosh advertisement is now famous for making the Super Bowl a showcase for innovative advertising and a time for strategic product introductions, a largely forgotten Burger King campaign two years later initiated the practise of advance publicity for Super Bowl advertisements – in other words, advertisements to watch advertisements. The $40 million Burger King promotion began in November 1985 with the search for 'Herb the Nerd', a man who was purportedly the only person in America who had not eaten at a Burger King restaurant. The advertisement-induced excitement over the identity of Herb reached its peak in January 1986, when Burger King promised to reveal his identity to the more than 100 million people watching the Super Bowl. The rather anticlimactic Super Bowl commercials unveiled Herb – an actor adorned in horn-rimmed glasses, ill-fitting clothes, and white socks. Shortly after the Super Bowl appearance, the *Chicago Tribune* columnist Bob Greene wrote that, with all of the media exposure, 'Herb is currently one of the most famous men in America'.[16] Herb toured America for the next few weeks, stopping at Burger Kings in each state for surprise Herb-sightings, but the campaign flopped after the Super Bowl advertisements broke the mystery. The Herb promotion had little impact on hamburger sales, but was innovative in its use of the Super Bowl.[17] The commercial narrative began to catch on; CBS ran the first-ever network news story about Super Bowl commercials on 21 January 1987.

The most successful advance promotion of Super Bowl advertisements is the recurring 'Bud Bowl' campaign. The Anheuser-Busch promotion began with the 1989 Super Bowl, and fully embraced its spirit of transforming mundane, inconsequential events into larger-than-life-drama. The Bud Bowls are certainly inconsequential: animated, long-necked beer bottles – Budweiser and Bud Light – play a mock football game in a series of commercials during the Super Bowl. Real sports announcers, such as NBC's Bob Costas, ABC's Keith Jackson, the former ABC Monday Night Football personality Don Meredith, and ESPN's Chris Berman, provide the authentic-sounding drama to pun-filled voice-overs (such as 'This looks like a real brew-haha').

Nevertheless, the first Bud Bowl campaign was elevated into a significant event, if only because of its 'super' status. Consider this lead from a *St. Louis Post-Dispatch* article: 'The world's largest brewer will be the world's largest spender at the world's largest single sporting event.'[18] In all, the brewing giant spent $5 million on the first Bud Bowl campaign: about $1 million to make the commercials, $4 million for the Super Bowl advertising time, and another $1 million for store displays and other promotions. For that money Anheuser-Busch gained exclusive beer advertising rights to the 1989 Super Bowl and experienced a jump in January beer sales of 17 per cent that year. One report noted that sales during the cold, post-holiday month of January were once weak, but Super Bowl promotions such as the Bud Bowl had lifted the month to be one of the best-selling beer months of the year.[19] The Bud Bowls have continued in various forms each Super Bowl since 1989, adding Roman numerals to the Bud Bowl name to achieve Super Bowl-style nomenclature. Following the success of the Bud Bowls, many Super Bowl advertisers now run teaser advertisements to build audience anticipation for their brief-but-glorious moments.

Perhaps the most important development in making the Super Bowl commercials a significant cultural story was the advent of the *USA Today* Super Bowl Ad Meter, also in 1989. The Ad Meter moved stories that had previously appeared only in trade journals, such as *Advertising Age*, and made them part of the news media's Super Bowl metanarrative. By social science standards, the Ad Meters are simplistic and sloppy. But the Ad Meter still managed to generate the infinitely valuable stuff that most sports stories are made of: statistics. With these questionable data, *USA Today* could authoritatively determine winners and losers and create a new 'battle' for Super Bowl Sunday. On the debut of the Ad Meter, *USA Today* proclaimed that: 'The real competition at the Super Bowl wasn't on the field. It happened during the commercial breaks. Advertisers spent millions of dollars for commercial ad time in a dazzling and dizzying pitch to the giant Super Bowl audience.'[20] Other news outlets were quick to catch on to this narrative, either by reporting the Ad Meter results, reporting the results of other advertising survey agencies, or at the very least assigning a reporter to review the Super Bowl advertisements.[21]

Like the Bud Bowl, the Ad Meter has deemed itself a Super Bowl tradition, and now counts each yearly appearance with Roman numerals. The surest sign that devices such as the Ad Meter will continue to feed the Super Bowl metanarrative is that blockbuster Super Bowl advertisements themselves have been formally enshrined in a museum. The Museum of Broadcasting in New York presented an hour-long collection of Super Bowl advertisements in a 1995 show, appropriately entitled 'The Super Bowl: Super Showcase for Commercials'.[22]

Of course, a large number of Americans still tune in to this perennial mega-event to watch the spectacle of the football game, and, obviously, some things about the Super Bowl have not changed since its origins.

For example, as a cold war spectacle not unlike the Soviet Union's May Day parade, the Super Bowl operated as a primary site for the display of military nationalism. A *New York Times* account of Super Bowl VI in 1972 noted that the game

> got under way with a patriotic-military display. While a giant U.S. flag, surrounded by smaller U.S. flags, was carried on to the field, Phantom jets roared over the crowd and viewers were requested to say a prayer for those servicemen missing in action or captured in Southeast Asia.[23]

Although the Cold War had ended by 1991, this Vietnam-era symbolic language was recovered in Super Bowl XXV's ritual response to American involvement in the Gulf War. As flags waved (small U.S. flags were provided to each of the 72,500 fans, who had been checked at the gates with a metal detector because of heightened fears of an Arab terrorist attack) and Whitney Houston performed the National Anthem in Tampa Stadium, a jet fly-over added emphasis to the lines 'and the home of the brave'.[24] The fly-over tradition continued in 1999, as the 93rd Fighter Squadron zoomed in the skies above Joe Robbie Stadium in Miami while Cher completed the final notes of the National Anthem.

Yet, as we hope to demonstrate, such continuities are not as decisive as the changes in the Super Bowl experience. Although residual values associated with Fordism and cold war culture are still imprinted in the Super Bowl competition (that is, in the game itself), these values are now the subject of a great deal of controversy and discussion. In fact, the presentation of the game itself has had to acknowledge and accommodate contradictions in the NFL's utopian vision of winning at all costs, as it has expanded into a carnival of multiple narratives. As we have noted elsewhere, Vince Lombardi's professional football credo that 'winning isn't everything, it's the only thing', now competes with a more recent, unofficial doctrine for the way the NFL and the Super Bowl operate: '*Image* isn't everything; it's the only thing'.

The Super Bowl (and its administrators – the NFL and its broadcast partners) has been immensely successful in this difficult cultural balancing act of competing values. The enormous popularity of the Super Bowl – nine of the ten most-watched television programs in American history are Super Bowls (the other is one of the evening skating competitions from the 1994 winter Olympics featuring the dueling of Tonya Harding and Nancy Kerrigan, as described in the essay by Bettina Fabos) – is a testament to how deeply engrained the Super Bowl is in American culture. In 2000 the game drew 130.7 million viewers in the U.S., easily the highest rated program of the year, and the fifth highest program ever (behind four other Super Bowls).[25] But, for the United States to consider the Super Bowl as the most popular *international* sporting event requires both an excessive amount of hype (which the Super Bowl supplies perhaps better than any other event) and an equal amount of solipsism.

THE GLOBALIZATION OF THE SUPER BOWL

With the overwhelming dominance of U.S. entertainment content – especially films, television, and music – around the globe, it is no surprise that the National Football League has worked to build a world-wide audience for American football and its premier television event. From the NFL's perspective, it is expanding the market for its product. Don Garber, then senior Vice President of NFL International, explained in 1999: 'We invest in a long-term plan to help the sport grow around the world. The vision is to be a leading global sport. We need to create awareness and encourage involvement.'[26]

But the desire for global dominance of American football extends beyond just the NFL's profit-oriented interests. As an American cultural ritual, it is increasingly relevant (and increasingly common) that the Super Bowl is represented as the greatest and most watched sporting event on the planet. The enormous, *estimated* Super Bowl audience of between 800 million and a billion represents at least two competing ideals. On one hand, the Super Bowl's portrayal in mainstream U.S. news media as the leading international sporting event seems to combat post-cold war fragmentation by emphasizing increasing global unity, via a world-wide, shared Super Bowl experience. On the other, it is significant that this international unity is a unity not focused around World Cup soccer (which is *football* to the majority of the planet), but around *American football*, a U.S.-controlled export. Herein lies the great solipsism of the Super Bowl. To a large extent, Americans (and their mass media) cannot imagine – or do not wish to – the Super Bowl as being anything less than the biggest, 'baddest', and best sporting event in the world.

To imagine the Super Bowl as being this top sporting event is to ignore the counter-evidence of several other major sporting events:

- The estimated audience for the soccer World Cup (held every four years) is more than two billion viewers world-wide for the single-day championship match. In 1998 an estimated cumulative audience of 37 billion people watched some of the 64 games over the month-long event.[27]

- The Cricket World Cup, held every four years (most recently in England in 1999) and involving mostly the countries of the former British Empire, has an estimated two billion viewers world-wide, but receives scant attention in the United States.[28]

- Even the Rugby World Cup, also held every four years (most recently in Wales in 1999), claimed 2.5 billion viewers for its 1995 broadcast from South Africa.[29]

- Canada, perhaps the country outside the U.S. most likely to adopt the Super Bowl as its own favorite sporting event – given Canada's geographic proximity, limited language barriers, and familiarity with the NFL, favors its own sports championship. The Grey Cup, the title game of the Canadian Football League, regularly draws three million viewers, more than the annual broadcasts of the Super Bowl and hockey's Stanley Cup final. Only the Academy Awards generate a larger Canadian television audience each year.[30]

For more empirical evidence of the relative global insignificance of American football in general and of the Super Bowl in particular we turn to another manifestation of the post-modern spirit that has transformed the Super Bowl into a carnival of consumption: the CNN World Report (CNNWR). According to corporate legend, CNNWR is Ted Turner's maverick attempt to correct the distortions of American television news coverage of the global scene. Launched on 25 October 1987, CNNWR was designed to provide an alternative vision of global journalism, a vision that transcends the nationalistic framing that contaminates conventional international reporting by the U.S. broadcasting networks. As the program's founding executive producer, Stuart Looring, describes it, Turner's 'Big Idea' for CNNWR was deceptively simple: 'Our basic role is to be a huge bulletin board in space on which the world's news organizations can tack up their notices, unedited and uncensored.'[31] But while CNN does not edit nor censor the content of the stories submitted to CNNWR, a few ground rules still apply:

- The report must be in English;

- The report can be no longer than 2½ min;
- It must be understandable.

According to Ralph M. Wenge, current executive producer of CNNWR, 'the only time we ever work with any of those reports is if somebody has such a strong accent that we can't understand it; then we retrack it in Atlanta.'[32] Furthermore, in providing this unique 'horizontal news channel', CNN still reserves the right to 'arrange the individual contributor segment packages into the most appealing sequences for maximum viewer interest.'[33]

Our own sampling of World Report programs suggests that the CNNWR has remained just as ungovernable and diversified and refreshingly deviant as when it was launched.[34] A collection of conventional hard news stories, thinly-veiled propaganda, unpaid advertising for tourist industries, funny animal videos, environmental activism, and insightful cultural features, the metaphor that seem most able to capture the meaning and significance of CNNWR is not a carnival, but a circus. With wild animals, clowns, ring masters, and death-defying heroics, the CNNWR is an example of post-modern culture in which all truth is a matter of point-of-view – and the distinctions between high and low, strong and weak, professional and amateur, information and entertainment, First World and Third World, friend and foe, no longer matter.

Using the several key-word searches of the CNNWR Archive, we determined that, if coverage in this post-modern, transnational, news venue is any indication, the Super Bowl is a relatively minor blip on the global sports scene. Here are the results:

- The key words 'Super' and 'Bowl' produced only one result. Airing on 22 January 1989, the story was prepared by CNN's own staff and reported on riots that broke out in predominantly black sections of Miami as the city hosted the Super Bowl.

- The key word 'football' produced 37 results. However, only eight of those stories made any reference to American football. The others were about soccer.

Of the eight American football stories:

- Three were from CNN (the Miami riot story, a story on Thanksgiving football games, and a story on the O.J. Simpson murder scandal).

- Two were from Canada (one about financing stadium construction and one on O.J. Simpson).

- One was from France (about entertaining U.S. servicemen during Operation DESERT SHIELD).

- One was from the Netherlands and one from Finland (both about attempts to introduce American football to the two countries).

By way of comparison, consider the preceding results in relation to key-word searches linked to other sports and sporting events:

- The key words 'World' and 'Cup' and 'soccer' produced 18 results from 12 different countries.

- 'Hockey' produced 15 results (but 'Stanley' and 'Cup' produced zero results).

- 'Baseball' produced 30 results (and six were related to the World Series).

- 'Tennis' produced 16 results.

- 'Basketball' produced 18 results.

- 'Olympic' produced 164 results from 56 countries.

Clearly, American football occupies a marginal position in the world of sports reported by CNNWR – a position that puts it in roughly the same place on the hierarchy of world sports as cricket (which produced 11 results in the key-word search of the CNNWR Archive).[35]

IMAGINING THAT THE U.S. IS THE CENTER OF ATTENTION

Although the Super Bowl holds second-level status among world sporting events, the National Football League and other organizations have actively promoted American football to an international audience at least since the early 1980s. In England in 1982 the then-new Channel 4 joined with the NFL and the U.S. brewing giant Anheuser-Busch to show a weekly edited highlight program of American football. This program (edited versions of a featured game's highlights with flashy graphics and rock and roll music) offered novel programming for Channel 4 and strategic marketing opportunities to develop a British taste for American football and Budweiser beer. (Anheuser-Busch later even established the Budweiser League that organized a competition of local, American-style, football clubs.) Although the size of the television audience for American football in the United Kingdom grew between 1982 and 1990, its popularity peaked in the mid 1980s and leveled off to a little over two millions for the average game audience by 1990, leading the British sport researcher Joe Maguire to conclude that, 'while American football may be an emergent sport in English society, it certainly has not achieved dominance.'[36]

The first instance of an international audience for the Super Bowl mentioned in the *NFL Record and Fact Book* on-line is for the year 1985.[37] That Super Bowl, notable for President Reagan doing the game's coin toss shortly after he took his second term oath of office, attracted nearly 116 million viewers in the U.S. The *Record and Fact Book* also notes that, in addition, 'six million people watched the Super Bowl in the United Kingdom and a similar number in Italy.' In that same year the NFL adopted a resolution to begin its series of preseason, international, exhibition games, which would field NFL teams in foreign countries to build interest in American football.

In 1986 the *Record and Fact Book* noted, 'Super Bowl XX was televised to 59 foreign countries and beamed via satellite to the *QE II*. An estimated 300 million Chinese viewed a tape delay of the game in March' (more than a month later). The international broadcast remained at about 60 countries for the next several years; but by the end of the cold war the NFL greatly expanded the Super Bowl's reach. In 1993, according to the *Record and Fact Book*, the game was shown live or taped in 101 countries. However, the data for the numbers of countries and viewers are often wildly reported. For the same 1993 Super Bowl (this one was notable for Michael Jackson's 'Heal the World' halftime performance), the *Los Angeles Times* reported that the NFL estimated 'an audience of more than one billion people in the United States and 86 other countries', *USA Weekend* noted 'an estimated one billion viewers in more than 70 countries', and *Amusement Business* (an industry journal concerned with the halftime program) explained the 'television audience is estimated at 1.3 billion in 86 countries, which is one reason Jackson agreed to participate.'[38]

By 1999 the estimates of audience size were smaller, but the scope of the international coverage had expanded to include more nations and more languages. The NFL reported that:

Nearly 800 million NFL fans around the world are expected to tune in to watch. International broadcasters will televise the game to at least 180 countries and territories in 24 different languages from Pro Player Stadium: Chinese (Mandarin), Danish, Catalan, Dutch, Norwegian, English, French, German, Italian, Japanese, Russian, and Spanish.

In addition, the game will be broadcast in Arabic, Bulgarian, Cantonese, Flemish, Greek, Hebrew, Hindi, Icelandic, Korean, Portuguese, Romanian, Slovak, Thai, and Turkish. Approximately 90 per cent of the international coverage will be through live telecast of Super Bowl XXXIII.

ERA in Taiwan, RDS (Canada), SAT 1 (Austria, Germany, and Switzerland), Sky (United Kingdom), TV-2 (Norway), and TV-2 (Denmark) will be broadcasting on-site for the first time.[39]

On Sunday, 30 January 2000 the *Los Angeles Times* noted that 'the game will be broadcast on 225 television stations, 450 radio stations, and in 180 countries. The cliché about a billion people in China not caring is no longer applicable.'[40] Yet the notion that the entire world pauses to pay homage to the Super Bowl is national mythology, continuously constructed via the NFL and the U.S. mass media. As we shall argue below, it is likely that more than a billion people in China do not even have the opportunity to care about the Super Bowl.

The most interesting element of the international audience claims is that the trend (with the exception of 1993 – perhaps a top talent like Michael Jackson was expected to draw a larger audience and thus generate record audience estimates) is always upward. This climbing trajectory, of course, is the trend expected of everything connected to the Super Bowl. Yet the growing number of countries receiving the broadcast and the enormous numbers of the *estimated* or *potential* audience seem to us to be more of a technical achievement than an indication of popularity. In fact, the record of the NFL's appeal beyond the borders of the United States is mixed. The League's exhibition games overseas have often gone well. For example, the first of the so-called 'American Bowls' on 3 August 1986 at Wembley Stadium in London (and co-sponsored by the American football booster, Budweiser beer) drew a sell-out crowd of 82,699. The NFL did not take any chances, and scheduled the Super Bowl champions, the Chicago Bears, to play the high-profile Dallas Cowboys in the game (which the Bears won). In August 1994 a record crowd of 112,376 attended an American Bowl game in Mexico City between Dallas and Houston. By 2000, 34 American Bowls had been played in 11 cities outside the U.S., with an average attendance of 58,474.[41]

Although the one-day American Bowl events do well in local attendance, as the fans watch the very best NFL talent, the NFL's attempts to establish international American football leagues have been mediocre at best. In 1991 the NFL created the World League of American Football, which would be the first sports league to operate with teams in North America and Europe, playing on a weekly basis. In 1995, after a two-year hiatus, the WLAF (an acronym with potentially annoying puns for a struggling league) returned to action with just six teams in Europe. On 23 June of that same year the Frankfurt Galaxy defeated the Amsterdam Admirals 26–22, and won the 1995 World Bowl before a crowd of 23,847 in Amsterdam's Olympic Stadium. There were plenty of empty seats there, and the NFL made no claims to a huge world audience for the World Bowl. By the 1998 season the WLAF was renamed the NFL Europe League, which continues to play with six teams. The NFL's international division – formerly founded as NFL International in 1996 – continues its efforts to build grass-roots interest in American football through activities such as sponsored flag football leagues in every NFL Europe city and in Japan, Canada, and Mexico.[42] By 2000 NFL International boasted that more than one million children around the world played NFL Flag Football,[43] and counted Canada, Mexico, Australia, and Japan among its 'priority markets'.[44]

SUPER BOWL SUNDAY EVERYWHERE

That reports of the Super Bowl's international appeal are always estimated figures is disconcerting. While it is impossible to get an exact count of the viewers – the United States might have the most technically advanced television ratings systems, yet methodological deficiencies are commonly noted – the number of 800 million viewers is never documented in any way by the NFL nor the news media.

We were curious about this and approached the NFL's public relations department. According to one of the NFL's officials, the figure for the 800 million global audience for the Super Bowl is estimated, based on ratings-company figures from the U.S. (Nielsen) and from similar companies in each of the 180 other nations and territories that carried the game.[45] Yet the estimates of the audience always are announced during the pre-game hype, and are never – to the best of our knowledge and research – verified after the game (except for the U.S. numbers). Who could possibly check out these statistics, particularly if the NFL is not forthcoming? (Our NFL source seemed initially surprised that anyone would question the global audience figures, then just recited the same data.) The NFL official did acknowledge that the 800 million means that that number of people tuned in to watch at least a portion of the broadcast, not necessarily the entire one. This, of course, is similar to the American viewing experience; as ratings data indicate, many viewers tune out halfway through the game, particularly if the competition is lopsided.

Although the hyped international audience figures suggest that the whole planet is sharing the same American Super Bowl cultural experience, the time differential (particularly if 90 per cent of the international coverage is via a live feed, as the NFL claims) makes the viewing experience quite different. First of all, Super Bowl Sunday in the United States is Super Bowl Monday for the bulk of the world's population. With a kick-off time at approximately 6 p.m., Eastern Time in the U.S. (the time zone shifts, depending on the annual location of the game) on Sunday evening, game time for European viewers ranges from 12 midnight to 2 a.m., Monday morning. Kick-off is 7 a.m. Monday morning in Beijing, 8 a.m. in Seoul, and 9 a.m. in Brisbane. Thus the Sunday evening weekend party atmosphere that typifies the U.S. experience is awkwardly transplanted to an all-night ordeal in Europe or a Monday morning working day in east Asia and Australia. The Super Bowl's Sunday evening time slot – the evening with the heaviest television viewing in the U.S. each week contributes to the Super Bowl's big viewership. But the Super Bowl's broadcast time in Europe, Asia, and Australia is clearly out of the realm of prime time and is one when few can afford to watch television.

Moreover, while the Super Bowl has free broadcast delivery in the United States, bringing the game to the more than 99 per cent of American households that have a television set, in other global markets the program's live distribution often comes only via paid cable or direct broadcast satellite television, both of which have a limited number of subscribers. The global audience is further limited by the fact that significant portions of the world's population are not even served by the cable or satellite signals that carry live feeds of the Super Bowl. For example, ESPN Star Sports, a joint venture between ESPN, Inc. (owned by Disney) and Star TV (owned by the News Corp., Ltd), was the sole carrier of the January 2000 Super Bowl XXXIV game to most Asian nations.[46] In fact, with China, India, Indonesia, Pakistan, Bangladesh, Vietnam, and South Korea among the markets exclusively served by ESPN Star Sports for the Super Bowl broadcast, the company was the provider of the event to a geographic area representing more than three billion people, over half of the world's population. Yet, as of November 1999, ESPN and Star Sports combined to serve fewer than 93 million households in all of its Asian national markets.[47]

The problem of access, however, does little to halt programming that suggests that the whole world stops for the Super Bowl. A 1½-min, prerecorded television package broadcast in the pre-game program for Super Bowl XXIX in 1995 is the most stunning example to date of U.S. solipsism with regard to the Super Bowl broadcast. The segment begins with a introduction by the ABC television network announcer Brent Musburger [voiced over live video of the shot from an airship of Miami's Joe Robbie Stadium at dusk, which later cuts to a shot of the field, with a pre-game show of balloons, music, and line-kicking women]:

> So there we are. A game that has grown so much over the last 29 years. Remember back in Super Bowl I? There were empty seats in the Los Angeles Coliseum. Seats were priced at $25 a piece. Now we're getting ready in Joe Robbie and the cheapest ticket is $200. The world awaits Super Bowl XXIX. A 174 countries will take the feed. And we estimate the audience for this Super Bowl will be in excess of 750 million. We hope everyone enjoys Super Bowl XXIX!

[The program then cuts to the prerecorded package, which begins with a spinning, animated globe and upbeat, suspenseful music. Then Musberger's voice-over resumes over an international montage of seven locations]:

> In Maine, they come in from the shore to watch the Super Bowl. [*Video*: screen text that says 'Cape Elizabeth, Maine' over a shot of a lighthouse on a rocky beach] The DMZ in Korea. Our young soldiers are ready. [*Video*: screen text that says 'The DMZ, Korea' over a shot of an American military check point in South Korea at the demilitarized zone border with North Korea] In San Diego, the Charger fans are euphoric. [*Video*: screen text that says 'San Diego, California' over a shot of whooping partiers on a yacht] Down under, they're ready. [*Video*: screen text that says 'Queensland,

Australia' over a shot of a rugged Crocodile Dundee lookalike walking toward the camera] Greybull, Wyoming, where the cowboys come in to watch the game. [*Video*: screen text that says 'Greybull, Wyoming' over several men dismounting from their horses and walking into a barn] And in Antarctica, they're bellying up. [*Video*: screen text that says 'McMurdo Station, Antarctica' over shot where two people dressed in parkas are watching a television outside while a lone penguin in the background falls and slides on his belly] In San Francisco, can the 49ers win it for a fifth time? [*Video*: screen text that says 'San Francisco, California' over a black (we note this because all other subjects shown except for a U.S. serviceman are white) man who puts a 49ers baseball cap on a black boy who is in a hospital bed; the man then turns on the television set; implicitly, they are father and son.]

Musberger then says, 'The stage is set.' The package then builds with a fast montage of each place just visited, as the music modulates to ever-higher keys:

- a night-time shot of Joe Robbie stadium (to give the illusion that this is live)

- a shot of cowboys in a Wyoming barn, crowded around the television set, with the same shot of the stadium on the screen

- the father and son in the hospital, with the same shot of the stadium on the screen

- the Australian takes a seat in his living room, explaining to his wife that this is 'American Footy – the Super Bowl'

- U.S. soldiers in a cafeteria line in Korea

- the mostly male partiers on the San Diego yacht

- the two researchers watching outside in Antarctica, high-fiving each other, and inexplicably drinking what looks like canned beer

- a middle-aged man with a golden retriever dog at his side, in front of a television set, with a warm mug of drink and a roaring fireplace in the background; man, dog, television set; no woman.

Finally, the music shifts to a tympani-heavy crescendo. Close-up shots are edited to the beat, and suggest a world-wide climax in anticipation of this great event:

- a cowboy close-up
- a smiling boy in hospital in a 49ers cap
- a smiling, pretty, young woman in a Chargers cap (the only woman emphasized in this entire package)
- an interested Australian watching the television set
- a captivated Antarctica viewer
- a close-up of the golden retriever's head, being patted by his master.

The montage dissolves to a live aerial shot of the stadium, Musburger says 'Super Bowl XXIX is coming up', and screen text appears that reads, 'SUPER BOWL SUNDAY EVERYWHERE'.[48]

The US-centric thrust of this presumably international Super Bowl promotion is clear. The piece is mired in the old rituals of the Super Bowl: an emphasis on men, on white men, on white men in English-speaking countries and/or U.S. outposts, on U.S. military readiness, on rugged, masculine places like a rocky Maine coast, Wyoming ranches, the Australian outback, the icepack of Antarctica, and the dangerous DMZ. Women appear as the silent wife (Mrs Aussie) and as a cute, young thing (woman in Chargers cap). It is not surprising that a man's loyal hunting dog gets more screen time than a woman.

CONCLUSION

In a New World Order and an era of globalization that the U.S. seeks to master, imagining the Super Bowl as the premiere international television sporting event is a way to control 'our' American (U.S.) sport and 'our' superiority. But, in the solipsistic vision of the 1995 ABC television pre-game package, the imagined global audience looks largely like the imagined U.S. audience: people who either are Americans located at various points of the world, or people who look like white, middle-class Americans (the Australian couple), experiencing the telecast from the sofa in the living room, in the appropriate American style. This global vision contradicts the carnivalesque richness of the actual U.S. broadcast of the Super Bowl and the diversity (racial, ethnic, sexual, etc.) in the U.S. and the global population.

The sports historian Allen Guttmann has noted that 'a nation that exercises political and/or economic power usually exercises cultural power as well'.[49] In a way, the symbolic nature of the Super Bowl works in reverse: the Super Bowl's high international stature is constantly reaffirmed in American culture as a self-comforting indication of the United States' political and economic power. Yet the vision of the Super Bowl's global status – particularly with its heavy reliance on symbols of masculinity, whiteness, and U.S. military might – is more Old World Order than New.

The fact that the Super Bowl is not the number one television sporting event may speak volumes about America's overestimation of its global might. It is not surprising, then, that soccer (the world's genuine top televised sporting event) remains a sport to ridicule for many people in the U.S. The *Los Angeles Times* in 2000 wryly stated that:

> the NFL estimates that more than 800 million people will watch the Super Bowl. An estimated 1.3 billion people watched the 1998 World Cup soccer final between Brazil and France. Can you remember the final score? Hint: one of the teams probably had 0.[50]

The comment, a typical joke about soccer's low scoring, which presumably makes it boring for the sporting fan, allows American football fans to dismiss soccer as a sport that does not matter. Meanwhile, soccer continues to diffuse into U.S. culture much more quickly than the American football game extends globally.

Ironically, the hope for extending interest in professional American football in global markets requires the sport itself to be flexible – more malleable than the franchise managed closely by the NFL bureaucracy. But the game is likely to become less American and more internationalized if it should succeed in diffusing widely into other cultures, which is the case with the three leading world team sports – soccer, basketball, and volleyball.[51] Thus the traditional mythic elements of NFL football that are so distinctly American are the same elements that prevent the Super Bowl from becoming the most-watched sporting event in the world.

NOTES

1. J.L. Reeves and C.R. Martin, 'ReWriting the Super Bowl: From Cold War Spectacle to Postmodern Carnival', presented at: 'A Comparative Approach to Sport', Texas Tech University's 29th Comparative Literature Symposium, Lubbock, TX, Jan. 1996.
2. R. Martin and J.L. Reeves, 'Re-Reading the Super Bowl', presented at the meeting of the Association for Education in Journalism and Mass Communication, Qualitative Studies Division, Anaheim, CA, August 1996.
3. R. Real, 'The Super Bowl: Mythic Spectacle', in H. Newcomb (ed.), *Television: The Critical View* (New York, NY: Oxford University Press, 2nd edn, 1979), pp.170–203.
4. C. Geertz, 'Person, Time, and Conduct in Bali', in Geertz, *The Interpretation of Cultures: Selected Essays* (New York, NY: Basic Books, 1973), pp.443–4.

5. See S. Behrens, 'Technological Convergence: Toward a United State of Media', in *Channels of Communication 1986 Field Guide* (New York: C.C. Publishing, 1986), pp.8–10; J. Miller, 'International Roundup: The Global Picture', ibid., pp.16–18.

6. For a discussion of Fordism, and post-Fordism, see J.L. Reeves and R. Campbell, *Cracked Coverage* (Durham, NC: Duke University Press, 1994), pp.84–90; also A. Amin (ed.), *Post-Fordism: A Reader* (Oxford,: Blackwell, 1994).

7. See G.B. Leonard, 'Winning Isn't Everything. It's Nothing', *Intellectual Digest* (Oct. 1973); reprinted in D.F. Sabo and R. Runfola (eds), *Jock: Sports and Male Identity* (Englewood Cliffs, NJ: Prentice-Hall, 1980), pp.265–6.

8. See M. Sella, 'The Electronic Fishbowl', *New York Times Magazine* (21 May 2000), 50–7, 68, 70, 72, 102, 106.

9. D. Harvey, *The Condition of Postmodernity* (Cambridge, MA: Blackwell, 1989), pp.340–1.

10. Super Bowls are traditionally marked with Roman numerals, which add to the event's sense of pomp.

11. See D. Lieberman, 'The Big-Bucks Ad Battles over TV's Most Expensive Minutes', *TV Guide* (26 Jan. 1991), 11–14; D. Enrico, 'Ad Game Was a Blowout, Too', *USA Today* (30 Jan. 1995), 5B.

12. R. Corliss, 'M*A*S*H, You Were a Smash; After 11 Years of Daring Good Humor, TV's Finest Half-Hour Signs Off', *Time* (28 Feb. 1983), 64ff.

13. S. Elliott, 'Trying to Score Big in "Ad Bowl"', *New York Times on the Web* (28 Jan. 1999), http://www.nytimes.com

14. S. Springer, 'Sure, There's a Football Game Being Played Today, but Don't Forget about the Other Stuff', *Los Angeles Times* (30 Jan. 2000), S6.

15. D. Burnham, 'The Computer, the Consumer and Privacy', *New York Times* (4 March 1984), Sectn 4, 8. See also 'The New TV Ads Trying to Wake Up Viewers', *Business Week* (19 March 1984), 46ff.

16. B. Greene, *Chicago Tribune* (2 March 1986), C1.

17. B. Moran, 'Herb Helped BK Visibility, but Little Else', *Advertising Age* (24 March 1986), 1; also see S. Elliott, 'Super Triumphs and Super Flops', *New York Times* (30 Jan. 1994), Sectn 3, 5.

18. J. VandeWater, 'Anheuser-Busch: Super Advertiser', *St. Louis Post-Dispatch TV Magazine* (9 Jan. 1989), 5. St. Louis is Anheuser-Busch's hometown.

19. Lieberman, 'The Big-Bucks', 14.

20. 'The Super Battle Behind Super Bowl XXIII', *USA Today* (23 Jan. 1989), 4B.

21. Also see M.P. McAllister, 'Super Bowl Advertising as Commercial Celebration', *The Communication Review*, 3 (1999), 403–28.

22. 'Remembering the Advertising of the Super Bowls', *New York Times* 8 Jan. 1995, Sectn 13, 9. The Museum of Broadcasting has held subsequent exhibitions of Super Bowl advertisements.

23. J.J. O'Connor, 'TV: Watching Thomas to Astaire to Hope to Bunker', *New York Times* (19 Jan. 1972), 75.

24. See S.C. Jansen, 'Sport/War: the Gender Order, the Persian Gulf War and the New World Order', presented at the International Communication Association Annual Meeting, Miami, FL, May 1992; and C. Scodari, 'Operation Desert Storm as "Wargames": Sport, War, and Media Intertextuality', *Journal of American Culture*, 16 (1993), 1–5.

25. R. Huff, 'Tight Contest Pulls Super Ratings', *New York Daily News* (1 Feb. 2000), 82. It is worth noting that the U.S. audience of 130.7 millions represents the total number of people who saw at least part of the game. During the average minute about 88.4 million viewers were tuned in to the game.

26. J. Buckley, 'Football Is Booming around the World' (28 Jan. 1999), http://www.nfl.com/international/990128future.html

27. 'More than Super Bowl; World Cup Worldwide TV Audience', *Financial Post* [Toronto] (1 June 1994), 82. Also see B. Giussani, 'World Cup Sites Target Ticketless Fans', *New York Times on the Web* (12 May 1998), http://www.nytimes.com; see H. Dauncey and G. Hare (eds), *France the 1998 World Cup: the National Impact of a World Sporting Event* (London and Portland, OR: Frank Cass, 1999) for a book-length treatment of the impact of the World Cup.

28. T. Melville, 'A World in Love with Cricket (Except in US)', *Christian Science Monitor* (14 May 1999), 18.

29. International Rugby Board, 'Off the Field', 16 May 1999, http://www.rwc99.com/OffField/OffField.html

30. 'Game Still an Easy Sell for the CBC', *Toronto Star* (21 Nov. 1998).

31. J.E. Fryman and B. Bates, 'Bypassing the Gateways: International News on CNN CNNWR', *Communication Research Reports* (1993), 3.

32. R.M. Wenge, 'Global Perspectives in Communication: the 1996 Robinson Speech' (Peoria, IL: Department of Communication, Bradley University, 1996), p.3.

33. Fryman and Bates, 'Bypassing the Gateways', 3.

34. J.L. Reeves, 'Ten Years of Achievement on the CNN World Report: A Critical Analysis of an Exemplary Text', in J. Oskam and K. Ward (eds), Proceedings of the International Mass Communications Conference (Lubbock, TX: Texas Tech University, forthcoming).

35. We conducted our search of the Archives in 1999.

36. J. Maguire, 'More than a Sporting Touchdown: The Making of American Football in England 1982–1990', *Sociology of Sport Journal*, 7 (1990), 213–37.

37. See *NFL Record and Fact Book*, 'Chronology: 1981–1990', www.nfl.com/randf/chron90.html

38. See R. Rauzi, 'It's so L.A.: Super Bowl Goes Show Biz', *Los Angeles Times* (26 Jan. 1993), F1; T. McNichol, 'Will Michael Finally Touch Down?', *USA Weekend* (31 Jan. 1993), 20; Linda Deckard, 'Halftime Show to Blend High-Tech and Traditional Entities', *Amusement Business* (25 Jan. 1993), 15.

39. 'Super Bowl XXXIII Expected to Be Broadcast in 180 Countries in 24 Languages' (22 Jan. 1999), http://www.nfl.com/tvradio/990122sbskedintl.html

40. Springer, 'Sure, There's a Football Game', 6.

41. 'NFL Returns to Canada' (27 Jan. 2000), http://www.nfl.com/international/000127.html

42. See Buckley, 'Football Is Booming'.

43. 'NFL International is a Success' (27 Jan. 2000), http://www.nfl.com/international/000125 international.html

44. 'Quinn Named Senior VP of NFL International' (7 Oct. 1999), http://www.nfl.com/international/991007quinn.html

45. Interview with Greg Solomon, NFL Public Relations Office, 14 May 1999.

46. '1999 Country Table: List of Countries where the NFL Can Be Seen' http://www.nfl.com/international/990512countries.html (2001).

47. ESPN Star Sports, 'Corporate Information', (2001); the company broadcast the NFL to China, India, Indonesia, Pakistan, Bangladesh, Vietnam, South Korea, Myanmar, Nepal, Malaysia, Sri Lanka, Cambodia, Hong Kong, Laos, Papua New Guinea, Singapore, Mongolia, Bhutan, Macau, Brunei, the Maldives, and Guam exclusively, and competed with other NFL broadcasters in the Philippines, Taiwan, and Thailand.

48. The authors thank Prof. Murray Sperber, of Indiana University, for additional videotape of this program.

49. See A. Guttmann, 'Sports Diffusion: A Response to Maguire and the Americanization Commentaries', *Sociology of Sport Journal*, 8 (1991), 185–90. Also see B. Kidd, 'How Do We Find Our Own Voices in the "New World Order"? A Commentary on Americanization', ibid., 8 (1991), 178–84; E.A. Wagner, 'Sport in Asia and Africa: Americanization or Mundialization', ibid., 7 (1990), 337–402; J. McKay and T. Miller, 'From Old Boys to Men and Women of the Corporation: The Americanization and Commodification of Australian Sport', ibid., 8 (1991), 86–94.

50. T.J. Simers, 'The Super Bowl Will Have a Global Audience of about 800 Million, Many of Whom Are Passionate, Some of Whom are Curious; the Others Just Need a Reason to Party', *Los Angeles Times* (30 Jan. 2000), D1. For U.S. soccer fans, the victory of the U.S. team in the 1999 Women's World Cup was an enormous event, yet the championship did not have the same cultural impact (nor the television ratings) as the Super Bowl.

51. See Wagner, 'Sport in Asia and Africa', 399.

Epilogue: The Future of Exchange between Local Culture and Global Trends

STEPHEN G. WIETING and JUDY POLUMBAUM

The contributors to this volume have re-emphasized, we believe, the great potential of sports scholarship for capturing variations among human societies and contributing to a more richly textured picture of the globalization process. We wish to conclude here by drawing together findings from the growing body of literature on global sport with themes from the preceding essays to suggest fruitful directions for continued research.

In our prologue we noted that the decade or so of concerted scholarly attention to globalization processes in sport delineates a general picture of colonization of smaller cultures by larger ones, but carefully shaded to reveal the simultaneous persistence, preservation, and re-invention of national cultures. Joseph Maguire's influential article seeking to clarify associations among concepts of modernization, Americanization, colonization, and globalization did much to set the discursive stage for extensive treatment of these tensions.[1] Ensuing commentary and debate have recognized considerable variability among countries in the processes of sporting production, consumption, and representation even in transnational transactions that increasingly are subject to ostensibly homogenizing influences.

That variation, including prior variety that endures as well as great variety in novel manifestations, owes much to the centrality of sport for collective memory and its close association with public culture. Societies and individuals rely on some stability in visions of the past construed for the purposes of present tasks, and sport has been seen as an important technical and metaphorical container for such cultural ballast. Memorializing entails strategic selection, meaning not simply the evocation of past events but also the restriction of recall in opportunistic ways as part of the adaptation to changing current circumstances. In sport as in other fields, global imbalances of power and resources coming to bear differentially on local cultures accentuate relationships of dominance and subordination, and sporting activities, like phenomena in other realms, become marked by compromise and hybridity, and in some cases engulfment and surrender. However, even extreme adaptation arising from local confrontation with global duress will never entirely dispense with valued representations of the past which culturally distinguish the present; indeed, under some circumstances exaggerated retrieval from the past may become an especially potent adaptive device.

Examining configurations of local – global interactions through sport, we can identify four prototypical patterns of exchange between the local and the global that are likely to remain fruitful sites for further investigation. We describe these arrangements below in terms of limited dependency, strategic accommodation, opportunistic variability, and selective concealment. Each has as a critical component the strategic use of memory in mediating between global forces and local identity.

LIMITED DEPENDENCY

Bruce Kidd's work on Canadian sport lays the basis for understanding outcomes and implications of a country's importing of sport dollars and products – in the Canadian and most other cases, of course, the dollars being American. The 1920s and the 1930s were when Canada experienced 'the triumph of capitalist cultural production over the more avocational or associational forms of cultural activity pursued by the middle and working classes', Kidd writes. 'Purchased identity replaced the loyalties of roots and self-realization. The public-spirited attempt to develop a pan-Canadian system of sport with organic links to communities across the country was subordinated to the profits of metropolitan and continental interests.'[2]

Kidd is describing hockey in particular, but his observations are apt as well in tracing the spread of the transnational capitalist model through baseball, as we have learned in the case of the Toronto Blue Jays and as occurred earlier with the Montreal Expos. This history also includes the more recent addition of the National Basketball Association's Toronto Raptors and Vancouver Grizzlies.

Montreal was the first non-US Major League Baseball (MLB) franchise permitted, as of 1969. As part of Canada's efforts to establish new trading partners after the diminution of the east – west links with Britain, and in line with a quest for economic status and cultural superiority that included the hosting of the 1967 World's Fair, Montreal's politicians and business leaders, with backing from Quebec Province and Ottawa, lobbied aggressively to gain the franchise. The Expos also figured into the subsequent bid to host the 1976 Olympics, for which it was expected that a sensational new stadium would be needed – representing Montreal culture on a world stage, with extended use as a special Canadian site for the baseball team.

Clearly, lucrative pay-offs were anticipated for the satellite operations of U.S. sports. However, in his study of Major League Baseball, Rosentraub finds major differentials in the benefits of MLB affiliation, as well as only a tenuous relationship between baseball success and larger economic and cultural success.[3] Toronto's endeavors to improve its fortunes have pivoted partly on competition with Montreal, and, to date, the limited dependency arrangement has worked more to Toronto's advantage. Athletically and financially, the Blue Jays have done much better than the Expos. Toronto's team plays in a huge entertainment center, the Skydome, with a retractable dome 'that works' – a slap at Montreal, where a retractable roof continues to malfunction. Rosentraub believes that Toronto was on its way to these achievements with or without the Blue Jays, even as the extensions of U.S. sports industries nurtured there have proved mutually reinforcing. He characterizes the Skydome as the most popular venue for sporting events and other forms of entertainment in North America, and indirectly a draw for other businesses, including the Raptors with their nearby stadium.

Sean Hayes's chapter offers a detailed examination of the cultural dynamics of local – global exchange under this model through the example of the Blue Jays, illuminating dependency but also resistance and elaborate efforts to incorporate the foreign element within the national framework. Similarly, Andrews and his colleagues have examined the ways in which NBA basketball is selectively assimilated in New Zealand, Poland, and Britain.[4] Studies of this sort, revealing the elasticity, resourcefulness, and sometimes self-deluding properties of national cultures, also show how the construction and representation of collective memory become key elements of cultural endurance.

STRATEGIC ACCOMMODATION

Balance between local integrity and global expansion becomes an especially important strategic question surrounding small, marginal, or otherwise vulnerable sports. Curling in Canada, and with it Canada's stake in the world development of elite curling, presents such a case. Curling has substantial market draw in Canada, but with the country's population being only one-tenth that of the U.S., audience growth through television coverage is seen as desirable and perhaps essential for further development. As described earlier, curling's inclusion in the 1998 winter Olympics was largely contingent on an increase in the number of member nations of the World Curling Confederation. The effort succeeded, but media response was mixed: Japan, the host country, considered curling to have a television draw for its own market, while the commercial U.S. media broadcast little of it. Canadian as well as American curling officials consider the sport's commercial viability at the 2002 winter games in Salt Lake City a crucial ingredient for its continuation as an Olympic sport beyond 2006.[5]

Similar merchandising concerns occupy all sports originating in national cultures which must be reconciled with new environments to make them competitive in markets outside their places of origin. Thus Michael Silk explains how the 1995 Canada Cup of Soccer had to be framed strategically to widen its commercial appeal to audiences outside Canada.[6] Even sporting sectors with lucrative metropolitan markets reformulate themselves to infiltrate peripheries, since another factor is the relentless appetite of U.S. capital, as exemplified in Friedman's description of the NBA's global push.[7] And as Martin and Reeves show in their essay on the Super Bowl, the logic of international expansion has multiple domestic purposes, symbolic if not material: even if the success of the global dissemination is dubious, the claim of universal popularity is broadcast to the U.S. consumer.

Conditions liable to command special care in packaging a product that originates within a specific culture are suggested by other contributions to this volume. Jackson and Ponic's study discusses the acute problems for Canada when a prized national sports icon, Wayne Gretzky, was 'lost' to the U.S.; whereas in the contrasting case of Ben Johnson, a potential repository of cultural capital, loses value and then must be normalized in some way – absorbed through accommodation, or, as in this instance, rejected with disciplinary regimes drawing boundaries between acceptable and unacceptable behavior. U.S. sports are replete with accommodations to drug use, such as the New York Yankees' endeavors to manage Darryl Strawberry's cocaine habit through regular testing, and Major League Baseball's disregard for home-run slugger Mark McGwire's use of androstenedione. A related thread is the alignment of tobacco and sports in marketing. McQuistan and Squier show how, most markedly in the U.S. context, growing public awareness of tobacco's harm has eroded the plausibility of linking smoking or chewing tobacco with sports participation, along with the economic value of drawing the association. Tobacco as an industry, though, has shifted much of its marketing focus outside the U.S., and in its multinational ventures continues to seek to associate its product with the healthy activities of sport. Government and private interests in developing countries, meanwhile, have found it expedient to accept tobacco advertising and sponsorship to help to build or sustain national sporting programs and/or forays into high-profile global sports.

OPPORTUNISTIC VARIABILITY

The examination of sport in a given country is likely to reveal commonalities with sport elsewhere that are genuinely universal in nature, other historically shared attributes stemming from or accentuated by global exchanges, and unique points of articulation with local culture. For examples of the latter, we point to the idiosyncratic arrangements in U.S. sport that originate with and also perpetuate peculiarities of American history and culture, resonate with and are reinforced by explicit and implicit convictions about the 'American way' of doing things, and in paradoxical ways may act as conservators of conventional norms and practises in the guise of promoting progress and social change.

Commercialized sport in the United States is organized around two basic institutional structures. One centers on the concept of a franchise, or a proprietary right to conduct business in a specific population center. The purchase and the sale of franchises are regulated by other franchise holders, who make up a monopoly of the given business. The system represents a unique form of commerce within U.S. law, entailing exceptions from the Sherman Antitrust Act of 1890, unusual restraints over the free market of employees, special rules regarding the accounting of labor costs, and provisions for subsidies from cities and states in the form of direct pay-outs as well as levies for stadium construction and repair.[8] The National Basketball Association, the National Football League, and Major League Baseball receive additional value, at little or no expense to those professional interests, from colleges and universities, which subsidize development costs to prepare potential players for these leagues. (Of the three 'big' U.S. sports, only baseball provides a nominal payment to colleges enrolling selected players.)

The other institutional arrangement is a national body, the National Collegiate Athletic Association (NCAA), established in 1905, working through educational institutions and now commandeering nearly a thousand member schools. Its budget has been growing precipitously since the early 1980s, reaching $326 million in 2000.[9] While technically amateur, educational, and separate from the professional system, the NCAA has many commercial interests stemming from event and broadcast revenues, and many interests which dovetail rather than compete with the professional sector. As a conduit for professional players in basketball and football, and somewhat less so in baseball, the NCAA sustains a Professional Sports Liaison Committee. With its chief loyalties purportedly to member institutions and the educational prospects of participating athletes, this committee has not made the obvious move of seeking compensation from the leagues for player development. In this and other respects, the NCAA displays a relatively deferential stance toward sports industries.

Considerable contention regarding the balance of costs and benefits for athletes surrounds and sometimes enters and disrupts these structures. One prominent fissure cutting quite directly through the NCAA structure and indirectly entering the professional structure is legal – Title IX, the sexual-equity legislation, as dealt with by Sarah Fields. Title IX is one in a sequence of Education Amendments to the Civil Rights Law passed by the Congress in 1972, and its express purpose is to stipulate the illegality of any inequality within education – although, as Fields shows, its implications for male and female involvement with U.S. sport have been especially salient. The preamble reads: 'No person in the United States shall, on the basis of sex, be excluded from participation in, be denied the benefits of, or be subject to discrimination under any educational programs receiving federal financial assistance.'

A Department of Education summary of developments 25 years after the law's passage discerned a variety of changes for females, including changed expectations, a lowered school drop-out rate, increased opportunities in mathematics and science, greater proportions receiving advanced degrees (25 per cent of doctorates earned in 1977 growing to 44 per cent by 1994), and increased professional opportunities (for instance, 8 per cent of gynecological-obstetrics specialists in 1970 rising to 39 per cent in 1995).[10]

Turning to the discussion of Title IX surrounding the athletic participation of females, we find both marked improvement and continued dispute. The dramatic expansion of sports opportunities for girls in secondary schools has raised the proportion of females taking part in high school sports from 8 per cent in 1971 to 68 per cent in 1997 – 98.[11] Since virtually all colleges and universities receive federal funds, they have been obliged to establish equity for males and females in athletics programs by demonstrating compliance with at least one of three criteria: participation rates in sports corresponding substantially with the sex proportions in enrollment, achievements as well as on-going efforts in expanding sports programs for women, and attempts to accommodate the athletic interests and abilities of women students. Much debate continues over the measurement of compliance – with the one measure that lends itself most readily to documentation, participation, clearly lagging. A mandate in 1992 by the presidents of the 'Big Ten' universities (including the University of Iowa) to achieve 40 per cent female participation in athletics by 1996, compared with a women's enrollment generally of about 50 per cent, was not met by any institution. The average was 33 per cent, with Michigan State displaying the highest at 37 per cent.[12]

Although the NCAA has formally embraced Title IX, history reveals a general attitude of resistance. Efforts to prevent the law's passage were succeeded by efforts to constrain its application. The NCAA sought to supplant the separate organization for women's sports, successfully absorbing it in 1983. Gradually, many women's athletic departments came to be headed by male directors. We also find a complex pattern of accounting methods whereby the NCAA, with impetus from many larger schools in the top tier of its athletic programs, contests the equity principle with the claim that certain male sports, foremost football, raise revenues that contribute to the general educational resources of the schools.[13]

Title IX and its evolution extend two traditions of legal reasoning in the U.S.[14] One, the historical presumption, grounds the interpretation of cases in the interest of assuring consistency with the established values and traditions of the republic. This view is often associated with the opinion written by the Supreme Court Justice Byron White in *Bowers* v. *Hardwick*, upholding the state of Georgia's anti-sodomy laws, partially to conform to the principle of the rights of individual states assured in the Tenth Amendment, but based furthermore on the assertion that homosexuality departed from American historical norms of conduct. The other mode, in line with legal principle, hinges on concepts of inclusion within express guarantees in the Constitution, foremost among them the due process and equal opportunity provisions of the Fourteenth Amendment. This was the approach used in the 1973 *Roe* v. *Wade* decision, which essentially legalized abortion in the U.S., and more recently in several cases involving special protection for gays and lesbians, as well as in cases involving assisted deaths.[15] Roe ultimately hinged on Justice Harry Blackmun's contention of an implied privacy right within the due process and equal protection clauses, with contesting views premised on historical precedent proving unsuccessful.[16]

The weight of constitutional guarantees rather than the inertia of historical interpretation prevailed in the early 1970s, when both Roe and Title IX were argued and passed. Yet the two currents remain in constant tension, and the weight of historical argument has proved to be a drag on the realization of Title IX much as at times it has threatened to roll back the declaration of Roe. The fact that the 1964 Civil Rights Act had to be repeatedly repaired, including also the amendment of Title IX, and that resistance to sexual parity in sports persisted even after Title IX, is entirely consistent with the historical presumption. Although on balance, constitutional protections have weighed more powerfully from the mid 1970s on, relentless forces of traditionalism persist in the NCAA as in U.S. society broadly.

Nevertheless, Title IX's uncertain influence on sports parity has exerted a certain influence on many life chances for women. Over time, the economic interests of participants and consumers have made the commercial advantages of supporting female participation in sport and producing sports programming for women and girls glaringly obvious. In no way can U.S. institutions be said to have shed their long non-egalitarian traditions. Yet it can be said that aspects of this institutional history – for our purposes, equal protection and due process on the one hand, and a penchant for mercantile profit on the other – are relatively sex-neutral at their face value. In our view, the research on sport shows no appreciable institutional change, but rather the selective use of laws and cultural priorities, by interest groups and then commercial vendors, resulting in some important outcomes for women over the last two decades.

Thus, while claims about the U.S. women's soccer team 'changing the world' in its build-up to and victory in the 1999 World Cup are clearly excessive, they are partially correct.[17] The event's commercial success did indeed benefit women players in the U.S. with a league, higher salaries, and, for some, commercial contracts. Similarly, advertising campaigns by

Nike or Adidas capitalizing on assertions about improvements for women in sports contain a modicum of truth. What we should heed is the mixed character of the apparently positive developments. Increased female participation has gone hand in hand with marketing opportunities, chances enhanced and celebrated always with an eye to revenue production, but still with reluctance by commercial interests, and even with recalcitrance by bodies such as the NCAA.

In sum, the gains in women's sports participation as well as in educational attainment and other areas have been substantial, but remain far below the legal mandates, are won only in spite of entrenched institutional resistance, and are propelled not by principle so much as by commerce. Furthermore, the marks of progress for women in sport and other fields have not eroded other invidious distinctions within U.S. society. Increasingly, for instance, African-American achievement in sport is regally depicted in journalism and opportunistically used in merchandising, but acknowledgments and representations of blacks in athletics, men and women alike, not only fail to erase racism and what some scholars term 'racialism', but in some respects exacerbate them. Studies of the coverage of women's sports in a variety of contexts, including Fabos's chapter on the presentation of skating stories, reveal that the assertion of positive changes in some dimensions also incorporates enduring patterns of discrimination and stereotyping in others.[18]

Evolving scholarly trajectories related to sex and sport supply instructive approaches in the study of opportunistic variability. Attendance to bodily portrayals in the media, valuable for making analytical comparisons across time and cultures, is not by itself sufficient to unravel how the acting body incorporates experience and identity. The emergence of conceptual literature with potential explanations takes us somewhat further;[19] ethnographic retrievals, seeking to illuminate the experiential level through observation and interviewing, further yet.[20] Recent work from non-American cultures displays considerable complexity in the identities and meanings experienced by female athletes relative to the dominant cultural conceptions.[21] Another productive line of research, elaborating experiences of sporting activity in additional ways, entails compiling and examining the varieties of literature written about and by women.[22]

Information on images of athletes may present consistent or diverse pictures, depending on where the information comes from and how it is mined. Whereas a focus on mass media portrayals consistently shows a disproportionate interest in males over females as well as a consistent pattern of support for heterosexuality, efforts to consider the experiential level of sports reveal considerable diversity. The variability of experiences within country and sport, as well as by country and sport, suggest that the theme of the homogenization of idealized images is not accurate at either the national or the global level. Indeed, at the frontier of this recognition are the most sophisticated strategists of multinational marketing, who increasingly apply concepts of 'glocalization' to tailor advertising and promotions to consumers in diverse cultural settings. The expectation is that as performers and audiences of sport vary, national consumers become more diversified, and media marketing strategies will reflect this. Thus sports depictions, which always incorporate appeals to collective memory, are unremittingly predictable not in their specifics, but rather in their pragmatic responsiveness to the competition for viewers, readers, and revenues. When expressions of new (over time) or different (across contexts) modes of experience and preferences are seen by commercial interests to be worthy of altered images, the market will provide them.

SELECTIVE CONCEALMENT

Collective memory displays, but also excludes and distorts. In contrast to the correlation of gains in sports for women with general gains in sexual parity in the U.S., which are found to have genuine substance even if they must be qualified, the picture is very different for minorities. In this book, McMahon's chapter on the historical treatment of black athletes in U.S. higher education, and ultimately in professional sports, shows how uneasiness within schools, professional teams, and consuming publics about black participation has led to historical ambiguity and amnesia. Black males display favorable rates of participation in athletics at every level in three major sports, yet this apparent success belies the endurance of racial stratification in U.S. society. The emphasis of black sporting success in the media, as well as by promoters, researchers, and educators, represents a crucial concealment of persistent inequality.[23]

The relatively recent rise to visibility of the golf prodigy Tiger Woods, technically Asian-American as well as African-American, is germane to this point. Woods tends to be 'counted' as black, and, despite the fact that he is unique on the Professional Golf Association tour, his prominence and epic level of performance on that circuit are held up by journalists and certainly by advertisers as evidence that any black can succeed in sports and within the U.S. economy. The extraordinary presence within a few days of Tiger Woods on the covers of both *Time*, the best known general news magazine in the country, and *The New Yorker*, a venerable medium of art and aesthetics for the U.S. upper middle class, suggests a pervasive satisfaction, cutting across socio-economic strata, about purported improvements in racial opportunities.[24] The achievements of the African-American sisters Venus and Serena Williams in tennis offer similar reassurance in another markedly homogeneous sport, constituting the exception that somehow by its marginality proves the sport to be ultimately permeable by minorities.

For several decades the rosters of the three biggest U.S. professional sports leagues have exhibited moderate to extreme over-representation of African-Americans compared with their proportion in the general population of 13 per cent. At the last accounting, 77 per cent of players in the National Basketball Association, 65 per cent of National Football League players, and 15 per cent in Major League Baseball were black (with another 25 per cent of MLB players classified as Latino).[25] Yet such figures do not reflect fundamental racial discrepancies persisting in society at large. The proportions in ownership, managerial, and coaching positions are more reflective of prevailing social indicators: minorities do not have a majority ownership in any league, with just a handful of minority general managers and head coaches.

An extensive scholarly literature documents the continuation of a racial caste system in America whose fundamentals have changed little from the situation described by Gunnar Myrdal over a half-century ago.[26] Virtually every effort seeking to demonstrate a durable narrowing of critical black – white differentials has not found it. Discrepancies are particularly glaring in matters of health and basic life chances, and also in crime statistics. Despite laws and affirmative action programs implemented since the civil rights activism of the 1960s, the lower life expectancy of male blacks relative to white males has not changed – it was 0.89 in 1975 and 0.88 in 1995. Nor has the comparison improved for black women, although there is more equality, with the ratio of 0.93 in 1975 unchanged in 1995. The risks of neonatal death and infant mortality for black children, both male and female, have actually increased relative to whites. Blacks are seven times more likely than whites to contract tuberculosis, more than six times more likely to be murder victims, more than three times as likely to suffer from HIV or

AIDS, meningitis, or anemia. Blacks have higher levels of kidney, liver, and heart disease, as well as of diabetes and cancer. Unemployment rates for blacks have remained more than double those for whites for 30 years. Blacks are far more likely to remain below the official U.S. poverty level than whites, and although the overall differential has decreased slightly over three decades, the percentage of black children below the poverty line is still more than double that of whites – 36.8 versus 15.4.[27]

Commentators striving to explain the stamina of racism in supposedly enlightened America seldom do so, arriving instead at a position of dismay and deep perplexity. There are many such moments in a remarkable *New York Times* series published in the summer of 2000, examining the complexities of race in America in areas ranging from religion, the military, and industrial labor to adolescent friendship. A recurring expression of bafflement appears in a caveat running with each of the major articles:

> Two generations after the end of legal discrimination, race still ignites political debates – over Civil War flags, for example, or police profiling. But the wider public discussion of race relations seems muted by a full-employment economy and by a sense, particularly among whites, that the time of large social remedies is past. Race relations are being defined less by political action than by daily experience, in schools, in sports arenas, in pop culture, and at worship, and especially in the workplace. These encounters – race relations in the most literal sense – make up this series of reports, the outcome of a yearlong examination by a team of *Times* reporters.[28]

This contention that, at the experiential level, broad generalizations are vapid is echoed in recent popular writings on race and sports, notably David Shields's ruminations on Seattle Supersonics basketball, and in a very different way, John Entine's book reviving genetic arguments about African and African-American athletic performance.[29] Perhaps more importantly, the *New York Times* series and these books also help to construct and document a race code that whites and blacks alike reify. Blacks and whites both know they must dampen differences, ideally in the civil domain, certainly in the conduct of occupational and commercial activity. By prevailing social standards, this conviction is intellectually indisputable. But members of both races also discern a gap that cannot be bridged – a difference defined not by race in traditional senses but by patterns of consumption, demeanor, and style. This is embodied, experiential, lived and learned knowledge. One is either black or white; one cannot be both. Ultimately, while acquiescing in reciprocal tolerance and undertaking concerted efforts to co-operate in public, black and white retain distinctly separate spheres of private affiliations and affections.

Using the ambiguities of professional basketball to address the quandaries of black – white relationships in the U.S., Shields observes:

> What John Edgar Wideman calls 'our county's love/hate affair with the black body' can be seen nowhere more clearly than in the National Basketball Association, which is a photo negative of American race relations: strong young black men have some of the power, much of the money, and all of the fun. The NBA is a place where, without ever acknowledging it – and because it is never acknowledged, it's that much more potent and telling – white fans and black players enact and quietly explode virtually every racial issue and tension in the culture at large. Race, the league's taboo topic, is the league's true subject.[30]

Entine might seem to be following in the steps of John Hoberman's earlier attempt to broach the incongruity of black athletic success and black stagnation within the class structure of the United States.[31] Unlike Hoberman, however, who hopes to understand a studied silence in U.S. scholarship as well as in the black community itself – and unlike Shields, who probes the same silence among white fans and turns up primarily self-loathing – Entine further obscures understanding by purporting to offer biological truths, insisting that science gives credence to genetic theories of African athletic superiority as well as diversity among elite sports participants from different African nations.

Our position is that the deep memory of institutionalized inequality, carried into the present of continued structural racism, is the source of the reticence of scholars, journalists, fans, athletes, and Americans generally, to discuss race. The explanation is known; the reasons refuse to go away. Biological definitions of race in fact are irrelevant. The most credible modern science has distanced itself from more than a half-century of egregious claims about race-related deficits; but in any case, genetic arguments about sports performance explain nothing about the persistence of racial inequality.

Popular culture generally frames itself as cutting-edge and even revolutionary. The commercial face of sport does its utmost to exploit this posture. But the essays here suggest the more powerful currents are conventional and conservative, with sport serving more to reinforce and transmit constitutive norms and values of cultures. In American life, this occurs in pronounced and intransigent manner on the dimension of race.

Wilson examines one manifestation in the media's tendency to characterize as 'good' black athletes who display apt use of opportunities for mobility in the U.S., often against great odds; and as 'bad' those who are surly and temperamental or break the law.[32] The former as exception and the latter as rule accord with public mythologies about America's allowances for individual advancement and with media and public stereotypes of blacks. Journalists and audiences alike know the historical basis of the frame, which continues to provide reassurance and rationale, and thus endures.

Sport that travels cannot entirely disentangle itself from originating frames: Even when the NBA establishes outposts in Canada in the form of two franchises, the Toronto Raptors and the Vancouver Grizzlies, commercial media are constrained by ambivalence over black skills and deportment. Yet much else will transpire in the process of encounter and exchange. To talk about the exporting of a sport or the assimilation of one requires an informed sense of history, for sport going and coming distills and disseminates recaptured and reconfigured versions of history in different ways for its different participants and publics. It is not sufficient to speak of Americanization, which posits the transfer of monolithic products. The character of the product is always related powerfully to the deep institutional histories of both the exporting culture and the potential new markets.

Nations have their durable sports traditions that seem predictable from both inside and outside the culture – the enthusiasm surrounding baseball's World Series each fall, for instance, or the start of the hockey season. But within a culture's seemingly normal course of events come other occurrences that may seem surprising, remarkable, absurd, or even insane to cultural outsiders. In the United States and Canada the inventory in any given season will run a gamut of criminal, civil, and moral transgressions. Just in the fall of 2000 we have had the conviction of Marty McSorley of the National Hockey League for assault with a deadly weapon and for inflicting a serious head injury on another player with a hockey stick in the previous season – and McSorley's trying to exculpate himself by saying that he took the blame for the league, because they know that it happens all the time. Alan Iverson of the Philadelphia Seventy-Sixers, who led the NBA in scoring in the

1999/2000 season, releases a rap video deemed anti-gay, anti-women, and overly violent by critics, and faces likely censure by the league commissioner David Stern. Heather Mercer, a woman who was cut as a place-kicker for the Duke University (men's) football team, is awarded $2 million dollars in damages from the school in her lawsuit alleging violation of civil rights. These items require a patient untangling from within Canadian and U.S. cultural histories.

THE STAKES IN INDIVIDUAL AND COLLECTIVE MEMORY

The conception of memory has proved pivotal in the field of psychology for the development of a modern, secularized view of humans.[33] Similar attention to the ways collectivities memorialize defining moments emerged prominently among early sociologists. Emile Durkheim, elaborating how social arrangements generated and retained a society's cultural storehouse, saw intentional rituals as essential vehicles for preserving the culture's images and thereby energizing the collective. Obligatory commemoration of the abdication of aristocrats to the French Revolution, marking the destruction of the remnants of feudalism, is his emblematic example:

> It suffices to think of the night of August 4th [1789] where an assemblage was suddenly transported to an act of sacrifice and abnegation to which its members had refused the day before and surprised the day following. It is for this reason that all parties, political, economic, confessional bear the need to engage periodically reunions of their members in order to revivify their common faith by manifesting it in common.[34]

Durkheim's student and eventual colleague Maurice Halbwachs also foreshadowed current analyses of collective memory with the suggestion that personal and social are inextricably linked.[35]

The key insight is that prospects for the accumulation of memory, the substance of memory, and the various forms memory takes are tied to the social arrangements of individual actors' lives. As we noted in the prologue, three common vehicles by which society assures memory have been: written and oral texts, inscriptions on bodies, and public rituals.[36] Our specific interest has been the highly durable and serviceable images of sport for encryption, retention, enactment, and re-enactment of collective memory.

What is at stake in memory? Does memory matter? Crucially, memory provides connective tissue for the individual to his or her own biography as well as to the social environment and the collective past. Memory enlivens the distinct features of the individual even as it links him or her to small and large social arrangements. The loss of memory eviscerates self as well as cutting the nurturing ties to others.

This, at any rate, is the lesson of classic clinical studies in which dramatic events have damaged portions of the brain, disrupting thought, memory, and essential person-hood. A.R. Luria tells us of Zazetzky, who suffered a bullet wound to the brain in World War II shortly after joining the defense of the western Russian front against the German invasion. The wound left him with an ostensibly intact present but without a memory, and taunted with a recognition that a learned past existed in some locked mental compartment. In his notebooks, he inscribed:

> Again and again I tell people I've become a totally different person since my injury, that I was killed 2 March 1943, but because of some vital power of my organism, I miraculously remained alive. Still, even though I seem to be alive, the burden of this head wound gives me no peace. I always feel as if I'm living out a dream – a hideous, fiendish nightmare – that I'm not a man but a shadow, some creature that's fit for nothing …'[37]

And the Iowa neurologist Antonio Damasio reminds us of the earlier case of Phineas Gage, a railroad worker whose skull was pierced by a rod he was using to tamp a powder charge. The rocketing projectile severely damaged his frontal brain before exiting. The result was a physically intact person with no connection to the being he had been before.[38]

These are singular cases; but what about the manipulation, mutilation, or ruination of collective memory? Novelists recognize that this may spell modification to an unrecognizable degree, and the eventual extinction of the group. George Orwell's *1984* envisions mechanisms and outcomes of this pernicious washing and revising of a society's past.[40] Ivo Andric's *The Bridge on the Drina*, recounting Bosnia's tragedies through the history of a bridge on the Serbian border from its construction through the events that led to its destruction during World War I, illustrates how successive political regimes recast the past they supplant when they refashion their realm.[41] In the twentieth century such fictional horrors have been realized as national regimes attempt to reconstitute themselves through the selective destruction and rewriting of memory. And external invaders now know that effective annihilation must go beyond killing physical bodies and destroying ecology; in addition, it requires the demolition of the victims' history and culture as constructed and retained through memory. Memory, it seems, is a necessary condition for collective as well as individual survival.

NOTES

1. J. Maguire, 'More than a Sporting Touchdown: the Making of American Football in England, 1982-1990', *Sociology of Sport Journal*, 7 (1990), 213–37.
2. B. Kidd, *The Struggle for Canadian Sport* (Toronto: University of Toronto Press, 1996).
3. M.S. Rosentraub, *Major League Losers: the Real Cost of Sports and Who's Paying for It* (New York, NY: Basic Books, 1997), p.358.
4. D.L. Andrews, B. Carrington, S.J. Jackson, and Z. Mazur, 'Jordanscapes: a Preliminary Analysis of the Global Popular', *Sociology of Sport Journal*, 13 (1996), 428–57; S.J. Jackson and D.L. Andrews, 'Between and Beyond the Global and the Local: American Popular Sporting Culture in New Zealand', *International Review for the Sociology of Sport*, 34 (1999), 31–42.
5. W. Hanson, *Curling: the History, the Players, the Game* (Toronto: Key Porter Books, 1999).
6. M. Silk, 'Local / Global Flows and Altered Production Practices: Narrative Constructions at the 1995 Canada Cup of Soccer', *International Review for the Sociology of Sport*, 34 (1999), 113–23.
7. T. Friedman, *The Lexus and the Olive Tree* (New York, NY: Farar, Straus and Giroux, 1999).
8. Rosentraub, *Major League Losers*.
9. 'NCAA Approves Budget Increase', Associated Press, 11 Aug. 2000.
10. 'Title IX: 25 Years of Progress', US Department of Education (1997), at http://www.ed.gov/pubs/TitleIX.
11. *Statistical Abstract of the United States* (Washington, DC: U.S. Census Bureau, 119th edn, 1999).
12. A. Zimbalist, *Unpaid Professionals: Commercialism and Conflict in Big-time Sports* (Princeton, NJ: Princeton University Press, 1999).
13. Ibid.
14. R. Dworkin, 'Sex, Death, and the Courts', *New York Review of Books*, 43 (8 Aug. 1996), 44ff.
15. *Roe* v. *Wade*, U.S. Supreme Court, 1973; *Bowers* vs. *Hardwick*, U.S. Supreme Court, 1986; *Compassion in Dying* v. *State of Washington*, U.S. Court of Appeals, Ninth Circuit, 1996; *Quill* v. *Vacco*, U.S. Court of Appeals, Second Circuit, 1996.
16. J.T. Noonan, 'An Almost Absolute Value in History', in J.T. Noonan (ed.), *The Morality of Abortion: Legal and Historical Perspectives* (Cambridge, MA: Harvard University Press, 1970), pp.1–59.
17. J. Longman, *The Girls of Summer: The US Women's Soccer Team and How It Changed the World* (New York, NY: Times Books, 1999).
18. See, for instance, M.G. McDonald, 'The Marketing of the Women's National Basketball Association and the Making of Postfeminism', *International Review for the Sociology of Sport*, 35 (2000), 35–47; A. Chisholm, 'Defending the Nation: National Bodies, U.S. Borders, and the 1996 U.S. Olympic Women's Gymnastics Team', *Journal of Sport and Social Issues*, 23 (1999), 126–39; G. Daddario, 'Gendered Sports Programming: 1992 Summer Olympic Coverage and the Feminine Narrative Form', *Sociology of Sport Journal*, 14 (1997), 103–20. More broadly, sport studies have greatly increased our understanding of sex through heightened interest in the social definition and experience of the acting body in sport performances and mediated representations. The literature in this area is becoming voluminous. Most analyses of media representations of female athletes have been in explicit or implied contrast with male depictions. Analyses of male depictions, which are far fewer, tend to stress the exceptional or address problematic images, for instance, in association with illness, drugs, or homosexuality. These media images coincide with U.S. and other Western societies' deference to males in sport along with phobia toward non-traditional sexual orientations.
19. M.C. Duncan, 'The Politics of Women's Body Images and Practices: Foucault, the Panopticon, and Shape Magazine', *Journal of Sport and Social Issues*, 18 (1994), 48–65.
20. P. Markula, 'Firm but Shapely, Fit but Sexy, Strong but Thin: the Postmodern Aerobicizing Female Bodies', *Sociology of Sport Journal*, 12 (1995), 424–53; E. Sironen, 'On Memory-work in the Theory of Body Culture', *International Review for the Sociology of Sport*, 29,(1994), 5–12;

J. Maguire and L. Mansfield, 'No-body's Perfect: Women, Aerobics, and the Body Beautiful', *Sociology of Sport Journal*, 15 (1998), 109–37.

21. Examples include B. Cox and S. Thompson, 'Multiple Bodies: Sportswomen, Soccer and Sexuality', *International Review for the Sociology of Sport*, 35 (2000), 5–20; and C. Mennesson, 'Hard Women and Soft Women: the Social Construction of Identities among Female Boxers', ibid., 21–2).

22. M. Kane, 'Fictional Denials of Female Empowerment: a Feminist Analysis of Young Adult Sports Fiction', *Sociology of Sport Journal*, 15 (1998), 231–62; J. Sandoz (ed.), *A Whole Other Ball Game: Women's Literature on Women's Sport* (New York, NY: Noonday Press, 1997); J. Sandoz and J. Winans, *Whatever it Takes: Women on Women's Sport* (New York, NY: Farrar, Straus and Giroux, 1999).

23. R.E. Lapchick, '1998 Racial and Gender Report Card', Northeastern University Center for the Study of Sport and Society, at http://www.sportinsociety.org/rgrc98.html; the sociologist Harry Edwards has emphasized this disparity for 30 years; see, for instance, H. Edwards, 'Educating Black Athletes', *The Atlantic*, 252 (August 1983), 31–8.

24. *Time* (14 August 2000); *New Yorker* (21, 28 August 2000).

25. See Lapchick, '1998 Racial and Gender Report Card', p.7.

26. G. Myrdal, *An American Dilemma: the Negro Problem and Modern Democracy* (New York, NY: Harpers, 1944). Recent books on the structural durability of U.S. racism include: A. Hacker, *Two Nations: Black and White, Separate, Hostile, Unequal* (New York, NY: Charles Scribner's Sons, 1992), D. Bell, *Faces at the Bottom of the Well* (New York, NY: Basic Books, 1992), E. Anderson, *Code of the Street: Decency, Violence, and the Moral Life of the Inner City* (New York, NY: Norton, 1999), D. Cole, *No Equal Justice* (New York, NY: New Press, 1999) and R. Kennedy, *Race, Crime, and the Law* (New York, NY: Vintage, 1997). The last two are provocatively juxtaposed in E. Press, 'The Color Test', *Lingua Franca*, 10 (2000), 46ff.

27. *Statistical Abstract*.

28. The *New York Times* series ran intermittently from 4 June to 16 July 2000, concluding with a special issue of the *New York Times Magazine*.

29. D. Shields, *Black Planet: Facing Race during an NBA Season* (New York, NY: Crown, 1999); J. Entine, *Taboo: Why Black Athletes Dominate Sports and Why We're Afraid to Talk about It* (New York, NY: Public Affairs, 2000).

30. Shields, *Black Planet*, p.xiii.

31. J. Hoberman, *Darwin's Athletes: How Sport Has Damaged Black America and Preserved the Myth of Race* (with a new preface) (New York, NY: Houghton Mifflin, 1997).

32. B. Wilson, '"Good Blacks" and "Bad Blacks": Media Construction of African-American Athletes in Canadian Basketball', *International Review for the Sociology of Sport*, 32 (1997), 177–289.

33. I. Hacking, *Rewriting the Soul: Multiple Personality and the Sciences of Memory* (Princeton, NJ: Princeton University Press, 1995).

34. E. Durkheim, *Les formes éleméntaires de la vie religieuse* (Paris: Presses Universitaires de France, 1913 and 1969).

35. M. Halbwachs, *Les cadres sociaux de la memoire* (Paris: Alcan, 1925; republished by Presses Universitaires de France, 1950) ; edited English version, *On Collective Memory* (Chicago, IL: University of Chicago Press, 1992); M. Halbwachs, *La Memoire collective* (Paris: Presses Universitaires de France, 1950), English version, *The Collective Memory* (New York, NY: Harper & Row, 1980).

36. P. Connerton, *How Societies Remember* (Cambridge: Cambridge University Press, 1989); A. Kleinman and J. Kleinman, 'How Bodies Remember: Social Memory and Bodily Experience of Criticism, Resistance, and Delegitimation Following China's Cultural Revolution', *New Literary History*, 25 (1994), 707–23.

37. A.R. Luria, *The Man with a Shattered World: The History of a Brain Wound*, trans. Lynn Solotaroff (Cambridge, MA: Harvard University Press, 1972).

38. Recounted in Antonio R. Damasio, *Descartes' Error: Emotion, Reason, and the Human Brain* (New York, NY: Putnam, 1994). See also A. Damasio, *The Feeling of What Happens: Body and Emotion in the Making of Consciousness* (New York, NY: Harcourt Brace, 1999).

39. Ibid., p.12

40. G. Orwell, *1984* (New York, NY: New American Library, 1949 and 1983).

41. I. Andric, *The Bridge on the Drina*, trans. L.F. Edwards (Chicago, IL: University of Chicago Press, 1945 and 1977).

Notes on Contributors

Bettina Fabos is a Professor in Communication Studies at the University of Northern Iowa. She has studied media representations of figure skating since 1992. Currently she is analysing the role and implications of Internet technologies in education.

Sarah K. Fields received a BA in psychology from Yale University and a law degree from Washington University, with an emphasis on constitutional law. She has a MA degree in American studies from Washington State University and is completing doctoral work in American Studies at Iowa specializing in sport and constitutional law. Her dissertation is entitled 'Female Gladiators: Contact Sport, Gender and Law in America'.

Sean Hayes is completing his doctorate in communication at Simon Fraser University. In addition to work on 'cultural boundary' disputes over North American sports, he does research generally, on sport, media, and political economy.

Steven J. Jackson is a Senior Lecturer in the School of Physical Education, University of Otago where he teaches courses in sport, media, and culture, and the sociology of sport. His research interests include sport and identity politics, globalization and sport, and sport, culture and advertising. A member of the editorial board for the *Sociology of Sport Journal*, he is currently co-editing (with David Andrews) two volumes: *Sport, Culture and Advertising* (Greenwood) and *Sport Stars: Public Culture and Private Experience* (Routledge).

Michael A. Katovich is a Professor of Sociology and Criminal Justice at Texas Christian University. He teaches courses in sociological theory and media studies. He has done extensive work extending the theoretical ideas of George Herbert Mead.

Danny Lamoureux is Manager of Club Operations for the Canadian Curling Association. He spent 17 years as the manager of a large, private curling club before accepting a position with the national body. His role focuses on helping volunteer-run curling clubs to adopt better business practises and improving membership development.

Christopher R. Martin is an Associate Professor of Communication Studies at the University of Northern Iowa. In addition to his research on the Super Bowl and the Olympics as media events, his writings include publications on the media coverage of labor in the United States and the Internet as an educational technology. He is co-author of the second edition of *Media and Culture: an Introduction to Mass Communication* (Bedford/St. Martin's).

David R. McMahon, a doctoral student in history at the University of Iowa, has published articles on black athletes, including entries in the *Encyclopedia of Ethnic Sports in America*. He is completing work on his dissertation and is preparing a book about Iowa's African-American history.

Michelle McQuistan is a fourth-year dental student at the University of Iowa. She received a BA from the University of Notre Dame with a double major in history and pre-professional health studies.

Judy Polumbaum has taught at the University of Iowa's School of Journalism and Mass Communication for 11 years and does research on mass media in mainland China.

Pam Ponic is a former Teaching Fellow in the School of Physical Education, University of Otago, and is currently a doctoral student at the University of British Columbia. Her research interests include sport, gender, and organizational policy, and the social aspects of health.

Jimmie L. Reeves teaches courses in television and multimedia at Texas Tech University. He is a co-author of *Cracked Coverage*, a book addressing television news coverage of the Reagan-era anti-drugs campaign that includes an analysis of the scandal surrounding the death of the basketball star Len Bias. In other publications he has written about the stardom of Muhammad Ali, the spectacle of professional wrestling, and the significance of sportscasting.

Christopher Squier, Professor and Associate Dean at the University of Iowa College of Dentistry, is an oral pathologist. Educated in Britain, he came to Iowa in 1975. In addition to his research work, he is the editor of several important pathology textbooks. He has a special interest in the health consequences of the international marketing and consumption of tobacco products.

Stephen G. Wieting, of the Department of Sociology, University of Iowa, teaches courses in popular culture, family law, and methods. His research activities include the history of Icelandic domestic law, and collaboration with scholars in Norway, Iceland, Luxembourg, India, Kenya, and North America on sport and the moral order.